CHARLIE CHAPLIN

CHARLIE CHAPLIN

PETER ACKROYD

Chatto & Windus
LONDON

Published by Chatto & Windus 2014

2 4 6 8 10 9 7 5 3 1

Copyright © Peter Ackroyd 2014

Peter Ackroyd has asserted his right under the Copyright, Designs
and Patents Act 1988 to be identified as the author of this work

First published in Great Britain in 2014 by
Chatto & Windus
Random House, 20 Vauxhall Bridge Road,
London SW1V 2SA
www.randomhouse.co.uk

Addresses for companies within The Random House Group Limited can be found at:
www.randomhouse.co.uk/offices.htm

The Random House Group Limited Reg. No. 954009

A CIP catalogue record for this book
is available from the British Library

ISBN 9780701169947

The Random House Group Limited supports the Forest Stewardship Council® (FSC®), the leading
international forest-certification organisation. Our books carrying the FSC label are printed on
FSC®-certified paper. FSC is the only forest-certification scheme supported by the leading
environmental organisations, including Greenpeace. Our paper procurement
policy can be found at www.randomhouse.co.uk/environment

Typeset in Adobe Garamond Pro by Palimpsest Book Production Limited,
Falkirk, Stirlingshire
Printed and bound by
CPI Group (UK) Ltd, Croydon CR0 4YY

CONTENTS

List of Illustrations

1

A London childhood

Welcome to the world of South London in the last decade of the nineteenth century. It was frowsy; it was shabby; the shops were small and generally dirty. It had none of the power or the energy of the more important part of the city on the other side of the Thames. It moved at a slower pace. All the accounts of it, in the late nineteenth and early twentieth centuries, describe it as a distinct and alien place. It was in a sense cut off from the life of the greater London; this may account for the air of exhaustion, and of torpor, which could hit the unwary. It was the site of small and noisome trades such as hat-making and leather-tanning. Factories abounded for the manufacture of biscuits, jam and pickles. Glue factories stood adjacent to timber warehouses and slaughter-houses. The predominant smells were those of vinegar, and of dog dung, and of smoke, and of beer, compounded of course by the stink of poverty. By the end of the nineteenth century Kennington, the earliest home of Charles Chaplin, had all the characteristics of a slum.

The areas south of the river had for centuries also been the place of somewhat suspect pleasures, such as brothels and pleasure gardens. That tradition was continued in the nineteenth century with the public houses, gin palaces and music halls of the area. One of the first music halls, the Winchester, opened in South London in 1840. The Surrey followed eight years later. Two of the great halls, the Canterbury and Gattis-in-the-Road, were in the vicinity along the Westminster Bridge Road; smaller halls were to be found everywhere. The stars of the music hall would congregate on Sunday mornings at the White Horse, the Queen's Head, the Horns or the Tankard, public houses which the young Chaplin knew well. The music-hall booking agents were located in Lambeth.

Since South London was separated from the rest of the capital, it acquired its own communal atmosphere; the houses and tenements were bursting with people, so the women and children spent much of their time on the streets close to their dwellings. They sat outside on chairs, or leaned from the windowsills. As a result the neighbourhood itself, rather than the individual household, was the true family; wives looked out for each other, and the children played together. One of those children was Charles Chaplin. 'They are my people, these cockneys,' he wrote in a magazine article in 1933. 'I am one of them.' South London would remain the source and centre of his inspiration.

The origins of Charles Chaplin are mysterious. No certificate of his birth has ever been found, and no entry in a baptismal register exists. He once travelled to Somerset House in search of his birth certificate, but there was nothing there. He sought himself here, he sought himself there, but he could not find himself anywhere. He might have come out of nowhere. The place of his birth is equally mysterious. He believed that he had been born in 'East Lane', off the Walworth Road; the narrow thoroughfare is called East Street, but it was locally known as a 'Lane' because it boasted a loud and vigorous Sunday morning street market with its costermongers, old-clothes sellers and various hawkers or traders. ('Lane' was the nomenclature generally given to a street market.) He may or may not have first seen the world there. Another difficulty arises. He confided on occasions to his friends that he was not sure of the identity of his biological father; nevertheless he took the name of a successful music-hall artist, Charles Chaplin, who was for a while married to his mother. He once said to an assistant,

Eddie Sutherland, that 'I don't know, actually, who my father was.' He may have been, in the phrase of the period, a love child.

There is less difficulty about the identity of his mother. Hannah Chaplin gave birth to a boy in the middle of April 1889, at eight o'clock in the evening. An announcement was placed in a music-hall paper, *The Magnet*, in the following month. 'On the 15th, the wife of Mr Charles Chaplin (née Miss Lily Harley) of a beautiful boy. Mother and son both doing well. Papers please copy.' *The Magnet* was out by a day: Chaplin was born on April 16.

Hannah came from a somewhat rackety family, the Hills, many of whose members lived in the immediate vicinity of East Street; toil and poverty had left their mark on some of them, compounded by a streak of madness in the female line. Lily Harley was her stage name. She went on the boards as a singer at the beginning of 1884, and her musical career earned some success before entering a decline.

There is no doubt that she met Mr Chaplin when he found lodgings with the Hill family in Brandon Street, Walworth; she was nineteen years old, and already pregnant, but the baby was not Chaplin's. The child, Sydney, was said by Hannah herself to be the result of an elopement to South Africa with a rich book-maker named Sydney Hawkes. Whatever the truth of the matter Charles Chaplin married her in June 1885, and gave the infant his surname. He also gave Hannah's second son his surname. This child bore his first name, too, but he walked out on Hannah a year after the birth. It must be suspected that the fault was her infidelity. He may have guessed, or suspected, that the infant son was not his. Chaplin later confessed that his mother had enjoyed many affairs; it is also more likely than not that, in moments of distress and poverty, she took to the streets. In *My Autobiography* Chaplin states that 'to gauge the morals of our family by common-place standards would be as erroneous as putting a thermometer in boiling water'. In his subsequent films he is preoccupied by the role of the prostitute.

It is a complex and bewildering saga, but perhaps not an unusual one in working-class South London, where husband and wife were often parted and where women drifted in and out of prostitution to save their families. Drink played its part, too, in the dissolution of family ties. Alcohol was, in a sense, the ruin of the Chaplins.

Charles Chaplin senior's first recorded performance took place in 1887. His image, complete with topper and dress coat, is to be found on the cover of a music sheet for a song entitled 'Pals Time Cannot Alter'; he also achieved success with songs such as 'Eh, Boys?', 'As the Church Bells Chime' and 'Oui! Tray Bong!'. He had a pleasant baritone voice and an easy stage presence; he played the 'swell', the man about town, whose debonair attitude is matched by his elegant dress of top hat, cravat and morning suit. Champagne, however, may have been his drink of choice off as well as on the stage; in the manner of so many music-hall artistes, he descended into alcoholism.

It was often surmised that Chaplin possessed Jewish blood; he denied it, saying that 'I have not that good fortune.' Yet on other occasions he hinted, or meditated upon, a possible Jewish identity. Since he did not know who his father was, there was some room for speculation. Yet it seems certain that he had Romany ancestors; he claimed that his maternal grandmother was 'half-gypsy'. In a letter, found after his death, he was informed that he had been born in a gypsy caravan at Smethwick, near Birmingham; since the informant was named Jack Hill, there may be some truth to the story.

Chaplin's adult friends accepted his mother as a gypsy; it is reported that he himself was familiar with the English variant of Romany, and in particular was fluent in the patois among gypsies and street entertainers of London. Chaplin's eldest son Charles Junior wrote, in his memoirs, that 'my father has always been inordinately proud of that wild Romany blood'. Towards the end of his life Sydney Chaplin, Charles Junior's older half-brother, married a Romany woman known as 'Gypsy'.

Hannah and her two small sons did not remain long in East Street. Sydney's school records indicate that they moved from address to address in the same neighbourhood; this pattern would continue throughout Chaplin's childhood. Hannah had embarked on yet another affair when Chaplin was two or three years old; she bestowed her affections on a successful variety star, Leo Dryden, who composed music-hall songs on the theme of queen and country. One of his most successful ballads is the still remembered 'The Miner's Dream of Home'. His prosperity may have marked the moment when mother and children moved from the rowdy and populous neighbourhood of East Street to the relative quiet and salubriety of West Square. It was only half a mile away, but it was a move to another country.

The newly established family now had a housemaid, and Chaplin remembered the Sunday excursions they made down the Kennington Road. He wore a blue velvet suit, and blue gloves to match it. He recalled the elegance of the Westminster Bridge Road, with its fruit shops, restaurants and music halls; he remembered sitting on top of a horse-drawn bus and putting up his little hands to touch the flowers of the lilac trees. He never forgot those moments of pure delight. He also recalled the odour of freshly watered roses, sold by the flower-girls on the corner of Westminster Bridge. In his subsequent films, flowers are often a token of fragile or doomed love.

These are descriptions quite different from the more sordid realities of his South London childhood. Nevertheless they can be considered true memories of the past and, as such, the first stirrings of his imagination. It is clear enough that there was a short period, perhaps of two or three years, in which he and his family were not in poverty; this is perhaps significant since the 'little fellow', as Chaplin often referred to his character on screen, the tramp by the name of Charlie, gives the impression of having come down in the world from a presumed state of greater affluence.

In this happy period Hannah Chaplin had a child by her lover, Leo Dryden; Wheeler Dryden was born at the end of August 1892, and had no discernible place in his half-brother's childhood. Hannah's relationship with Dryden in any case came to an end in the spring of 1893 when he left her, removing his son with him. She was not considered by him to be a fit mother. This was the time when all her troubles started. Her mother, Mary Ann Hill, had been committed to an asylum a few weeks before. The doctors recorded that Mrs Hill 'is incoherent. She says that she sees beetles, rats, mice and other things about the place.'

Hannah, with two sons in her care, was therefore forced to shift for herself as her family could offer her no support. It is not certain how she lived. She may have found another lover or a succession of casual lovers. Chaplin later related a story in *My Autobiography* that she had, at some point in 1894, found a singing engagement at the Canteen in Aldershot. This was a military venue, with a correspondingly rough and vocal audience. Hannah's voice failed during her performance and she was booed off the stage, whereupon the theatrical manager put on the young Chaplin in her place. He sang a popular song of the period, ''E Dunno Where 'E Are'. The public threw coins at the stage whereupon he decided to pick up the money before resuming his performance. This provoked more laughter and the young boy continued a routine of song and impersonation; at one point he imitated the cracked voice that had curtailed Hannah's act. Eventually to much applause she appeared once again before the audience, and carried off her child. Chaplin said that she never regained her voice, although she did in fact manage one last engagement at the Hatcham Liberal Club where she was billed as 'Miss Lily Chaplin, Serio and Dancer'.

It is an interesting story and may indeed be true, although the exhaustive music-hall listings of the trade paper, *The Era*, have no record of the event at the Canteen. In another version of the story he claimed that his 'father' had propelled him on to the stage; in this version, too, his mother was drunk rather than incapacitated by laryngitis. It would be too pedantic to state that he lied about his childhood; let us say that he was inspired to tell different stories about his past as the mood or the moment took him. In the official version he is his mother's protector and saviour, which is also the role the Little Tramp would assume towards young women in Chaplin's later films.

Hannah Chaplin must have still visited the booking agents, and for a while she obtained work as a dancer with the Katti Lanner ballet at the Empire in Leicester Square. Another dancer at the Empire recalled how the young Chaplin 'would stop there in the wings, singing my choruses half a line ahead of me . . . The harder I frowned at him, the wider he grinned.' She added that 'he had a wonderful ear for music even then, and picked up almost everything I sang'. A schoolmistress from the Victory Place Board School in Walworth, which he briefly attended, remembered 'his large eyes, his mass of dark, curly hair, and his beautiful hands . . . very sweet and shy'.

Hannah Chaplin's career, however, was effectively over. She found occasional employment as a mender of old clothes, and then as a seamstress, but it was laborious and underpaid work. In this period she turned to the church for comfort in her distress. In 1895 she became a member of the congregation of Christ Church, on Westminster Bridge Road, where in the record of her enrolment she is described as 'an actress who lives apart from her husband'. She also added to her precarious income by making dresses for some of the congregation, but her health began to suffer from the strain.

She was admitted to Lambeth Infirmary on 29 June 1895, where she remained for a month; she was suffering from severe stress that seems to have taken the form of migraine headaches. Sydney Chaplin was sent to the local workhouse from which after a few days he was transferred to a school for indigent children in West Norwood. Chaplin was taken in by a relative of his grandmother, John George Hodges, who lived in the neighbourhood.

The Chaplin boys were reunited with their mother in the early spring of 1896, but their address is not certain. They moved from cheap rented room to rented room, and in the space of three months they found themselves in six different garrets or basements. Chaplin's memories of this London period are generally unhappy. Sydney had outgrown his only coat, and so Hannah made him one out of an old velvet jacket she owned; Sydney was also forced to wear a pair of his mother's high-heeled shoes cut down to size. The boys pilfered goods from street stalls. The family relied upon parish charity, with relief parcels and visits to the soup kitchens of the mission houses. Chaplin never tasted butter or cream as a child and, as a prosperous adult, he could never get enough of them. The sculptor who in 1981 fashioned his statue in Leicester Square, John Doubleday, has stated that, according to Chaplin's exact measurements, the adult still possessed 'the undeveloped thorax of an underfed child'.

There were happier moments. The young Chaplin earned a few pennies by dancing outside the doors of public houses to the melody of a passing accordion. One day Sydney found a purse of gold coins on a bus while selling newspapers. It may be, however, that he had stolen it. On the proceeds the Chaplins went down to Southend for their first sight of the sea. They swam, when they could afford it, at the Kennington Baths. They attended magic-lantern shows at the Baxter Hall, where admission cost a penny. Hannah, in moments of health and vitality, also managed to entertain them by imitating the expressions and movements of the people in the street below. Her youngest son may have inherited her pantomimic skills.

In an essay for *Photoplay* magazine in 1915 Chaplin wrote that 'it seems to me that my mother was the most splendid woman I ever knew. I can remember how charming and well mannered she was. She spoke four languages fluently and had a good education . . . I have never met a more thoroughly refined woman than my mother.' Yet he may have overestimated her skills and virtues. A neighbour recalled that 'he thought no one who ever lived was like his mother. The lad thought she was the cleverest player in the world, a great lady and his ideal.' Her nickname for her second son was 'the King'. Such love, perhaps, is doomed to be disappointed.

Separation from her was soon to follow. In the spring of 1896 Hannah's sewing machine was repossessed for lack of payment, and there was now no way of continuing her old trade. She succumbed once more to sickness and was taken to the infirmary. There was now no recourse for the Chaplin children but the local workhouse, the place that poor families most feared. 'You'll end up in the work'us!' was a familiar expression. So in May they were despatched to Southwark Workhouse, according to its register, 'owing to the absence of their father and the destitution and illness of their mother'. Their bewilderment may be imagined. Nevertheless in the same article for *Photoplay* Chaplin declared that 'English people have a great horror of the poorhouse; but I don't remember it as a very dreadful place.' His strongest memory was 'of creeping off by myself at the poor-house and pretending I was a very rich and grand person . . . I was of a dreamy, imaginative disposition. I was always pretending I was somebody else . . .'

They remained in this institution for approximately three weeks while the Lambeth Board of Guardians pursued the supposed father, Charles Chaplin senior. He was eventually found and brought before the board; he agreed to take in Charles but not Sydney, on the grounds that the older child was clearly illegitimate. But the board believed it best that the boys should stay together, and Chaplin agreed to pay the sum of fifteen shillings a week to maintain them at Hanwell Schools, an institution twelve miles out of London. He never kept his promise of regular payment.

In the middle of June the two boys were taken in a horse-drawn baker's wagon to Hanwell Schools for Orphans and Destitute Children. Here they were separated, Sydney at the age of eleven being taken to the upper division of the boys' school while Charles at the age of seven was placed in the infant division. He later told a reporter that 'my childhood ended at the age of seven'. Hanwell was a thoroughly Victorian institution, based upon a regimen of formal instruction, carefully arranged days and strong discipline. In that respect it did not differ very much from the great public schools of the period. The young inmates marched from class to class, and from dormitory to dining hall. Chaplin's number was 151. In material respects, however, the children were much better cared for than their contemporaries consigned to the streets or slum dwellings. They were given warm clothes, good shoes, and a nourishing if plain diet.

But for the young Chaplin it was a place of suffering and humiliation. In later life he referred to it as 'my incarceration'. He was separated from his mother and, after Sydney was sent to a naval training ship, from his brother. He had no one else in the world. He was small, and helpless, and hopeless. He contracted ringworm, and fell into what he called 'paroxysms of weeping' when his head was shaved. He was detected in some piece of misbehaviour, the details of which are unclear. He may have peeked at a girl through her keyhole; he may have started a fire in the boys' lavatory. The stories differ. Whatever the crime, the punishment was determined in advance: he received a slash or two with a birch cane. A little while afterwards he was prescribed a laxative and consequently soiled his bed. He was punished two days later by being denied the orange and boiled sweets handed out on

Christmas Day. Yet despite his distress this was the only period of his life when he received any continuous education. He learned to write his own name and to read a little.

Hannah did not visit him for almost a year, and it seems that he felt a profound sense of betrayal. When she eventually came to him in the summer of 1897, the young Chaplin was horrified and humiliated. He told a good friend, Harry Crocker, that 'she caused me anguished embarrassment'. She may already have borne the marks of insanity that afflicted her family and had brought down her mother. He told Crocker that for some reason she was carrying an oilcan. 'Why do you come with that, Mother?' he asked her. 'Why do you come at all? They'll all see you. They'll all see you!' In *My Autobiography* he tells a different story of a fresh and fragrant woman coming to visit her lonely child. The reader must judge.

In later life he conceived a scene in which an old lady trudges up a staircase carrying a bucket of water; on the fourth or fifth landing a door suddenly opens, and a man punches her in the face. 'Oh,' he says in horror, 'I thought you were my mother.' 'You have a mother?' 'Yes,' he replies, weeping, 'I have a mother.' Chaplin never really trusted women. He always feared loss and abandonment, slight and injury, indulging in paroxysms of jealousy on the smallest provocation. With his lovers he was suspicious and difficult and angry.

Yet he survived Hanwell by making himself invulnerable. 'Even when I was in the orphanage,' he told his eldest son, '. . . even then I thought of myself as the greatest actor in the world. I had to feel the exuberance that comes from utter confidence in yourself. Without it you go down to defeat.' This invulnerability later became part of his screen persona. The Little Tramp, Charlie, is often detached and invincible. He always picks himself up and walks jauntily into the distance; in that respect, he shows indomitable energy and determination. He rarely becomes an object of pity.

So in the life of the small child we can see the seeds of the Little Tramp. In the earliest films he is often angry or cruel, wishing at all costs to take revenge on life and especially on those figures of authority who threaten him. He craves food and security. He desperately seeks love but never finds it. He has learned to cope with the vicissitudes of existence by affecting indifference. He is rootless, with no discernible home. Most of Chaplin's later films, too, concern the art of survival in a hostile or unsympathetic world.

At the age of eight the young boy was discharged from Hanwell on 18 January 1898, and returned to his mother. Sydney came home from the training ship, *Exmouth*, two days later. The family were once more together. The nature of their life now is not known, although it could hardly have been a secure one. He may have been recollecting this period when he said to a companion, May Reeves, that 'every four weeks we were evicted because we couldn't pay the rent. Each time we had to pack up and carry our mattresses and chairs on our backs to a new house.' He and Reeves were walking around Kennington on one of his nostalgic visits to his old neighbourhood. He showed her a dilapidated grocery store. 'How happy I was to be able to run there and buy something for tuppence.' Then he pointed to a shed. 'I often spent the night in there when we were chased from our lodgings. But I preferred to sleep on park benches.'

It was perhaps inevitable that on 22 July the Chaplin family arrived at Lambeth Workhouse. They had not managed to survive the outer world. The two boys were after a week transferred to the poor-school in West Norwood to which Sydney had once been consigned. A strange episode followed. On 12 August Hannah Chaplin managed to persuade the authorities that she was fit and able to look after her children. So they were released from the school into her care. Mother and children spent their day of freedom in Kennington Park, where they ate cherries on a bench and played catch-ball with a crumpled newspaper. It was a brief respite from the world that enclosed them. Hannah said brightly, at the end of the day, that they would just be in time for tea. She meant tea at the Lambeth Workhouse where they duly presented themselves, much to the annoyance of the officials who had to fill in once more all the appropriate forms. Three days later the boys were back in West Norwood. The world closed in again. Chaplin, in later life, said that parks always induced in him the sensation of sadness. He wrote, in a magazine article of 1931, 'how depressing Kennington Park is'.

At the beginning of September Hannah Chaplin was taken from the workhouse to Lambeth Infirmary, with her body badly bruised. The authorities here attested that she was suffering from syphilis, which in its third stage may attack the brain. The diagnosis was never repeated by later physicians, but it is perhaps significant that it could be made in her case. Nine days later she was moved again; she was consigned to Cane Hill asylum in Surrey, where a doctor recorded her behaviour. 'Has been very strange in manner – at one time abusive & noisy, at another using endearing terms. Has been confined in PR [padded room] repeatedly on a/c of sudden violence – threw a mug at another patient. Shouting, singing, and talking incoherently. Complains of her head and depressed and crying this morning – dazed and unable to give any reliable information.' She asked the doctors if she were dying. She told them that she was on a mission from the Lord. Then she stated that she wished to get out of the world.

Two nurses went to West Norwood to acquaint the boys with their mother's condition. Sydney finished a soccer game and then burst into tears. Charles did not cry, but began to blame his mother for betraying him. In truth she had succumbed to hereditary madness which she was too ill and weary to withstand.

It was now determined that Charles Chaplin senior had to take responsibility for the two boys. So they were driven in a van from Lambeth Workhouse, where they had once more been assigned, to an unprepossessing house at 287 Kennington Road where Chaplin lived on the first floor with his mistress, Louise, who did not welcome the arrival of unwanted children. On the frequent occasions when she was drunk, she complained bitterly of the imposition laid upon her by the presence of the boys. She conceived a particular dislike for Sydney, who avoided her company by staying away from morning to midnight.

Chaplin senior himself was in the last stages of his career; his popularity had waned and, as the bookings grew less frequent, he consoled himself with drink. On the nights when he did perform, he could be charming and expansive; he had six raw eggs in a glass of port before leaving for the hall. But he often spent all day and all evening in some of the many public houses of the neighbourhood, trying to drown his anxiety and frustration. His youngest son watched him closely; he would one day make a speciality of 'drunk routines'.

Chaplin senior's drunkeness gave rise to more bitterness in Louise, which she vented on the boys. Charles returned one Saturday morning after school to find the flat deserted and the larder empty. He waited, but nobody came. In desperation he walked into the street, and spent the afternoon visiting the various markets of the neighbourhood. He had no money, and no food. He wandered until nightfall, and then returned to Kennington Park Road; but the flat was in darkness. He walked the few yards to Kennington Cross where he sat on the kerb and waited. Two musicians, one with harmonium and the other with clarinet, were playing an old-fashioned tune outside the White Hart public house; it was called 'The Honeysuckle and the Bee' and it so enchanted Chaplin that he crossed the road to get closer to the melody. He would remember the song all his life.

When he went back to the house, he saw Louise making her way down the garden path. She was staggering drunkenly, and he waited until she had closed the door. Then he slipped in with the landlady of the house who had suddenly returned. He went up to the darkened landing. Louise came out, and ordered him to leave. He did not belong there. On another occasion a policeman reported seeing Sydney and his young brother, at three in the morning, sleeping by a night watchman's fire. This was the life which the young Chaplin was obliged to lead.

On 12 November, Hannah Chaplin knocked on the door. She had been discharged from Cane Hill, and had come to take them away. She took them round the corner to a small lodging in Methley Street, where she earned a bare income by sewing together blouses. The odours of Hayward's pickle factory behind them competed with the stench of a slaughterhouse beside them. Yet South London people were inured to smells.

The Chaplins' landlady at Methley Street recalled that 'Charles was rather a frail child with his mop of dark hair, his pale face and bright blue eyes. He was what I call "a little limb" – out in the streets from morning to night. I remember he was a regular one for finding a man with a barrel organ, and dancing to the music. He got a lot of extra money for the organ grinder and a few coppers for himself. I suppose that's how he started becoming an entertainer. Charlie was supposed to go to school in Kennnington, but he was an awful truant.'

His days at school were in fact coming to an end. His last recorded attendance there was on Friday 25 November 1898, after which date he was to be found upon the music-hall stage. He had become a professional dancer.

2

On stage

At the end of 1898 the young Chaplin joined a troupe of professional clog-dancers billed as 'The Eight Lancashire Lads'. He may
have obtained the employment through the agency of Charles
Chaplin senior since the troupe's founder, William Jackson, lived
a few doors away along Kennington Road; the boy's experience
as a street performer may also have worked in his favour. He was
given board and lodging during each tour, and Hannah Chaplin
was sent half a crown a week. She may not have considered it to
be ideal work for her younger son, but at least it provided the
family with a steady additional income.

The 'Lancashire Lads' were described by one trade newspaper
as 'a bright and breezy turn, with a dash of true "salt" in it'. They
performed for ten minutes and produced 'some of the finest clog-
dancing it is possible to imagine'. Each boy wore a white linen
blouse, a lace collar, knickerbocker pants and red dancing shoes.
Clogs were a form of footwear for hard labour in the mines and
factories of the north of England; to dance in them, with agility
and grace, was a sign of triumph and freedom from misfortune
or servitude. This might be a reflection of the young Chaplin's
spirit. He rehearsed for some six weeks, while the troupe were
appearing in Manchester, before being allowed to appear on stage
for the first time at Portsmouth. He suffered from stage fright,
and a further few weeks passed before he could perform a solo
dance.

William Jackson's son recalled that 'he was a very quiet boy at
first . . . and he wasn't a bad dancer'. He added that 'my first job

was to take him to have his hair, which was hanging in matted curls about his shoulders, cut to a reasonable length'. He also recalled that the young Chaplin was already 'a great mimic'. From Portsmouth the 'Lancashire Lads' went on to London, Middlesbrough, Cardiff, Swansea and Blackpool. They were rarely out of work. In London and other cities they would dash from theatre to theatre, in a cab or horse-drawn cart, often with the announcement that 'we must hurry along to our next hall'. It was exhausting work. The theatres had the odour of oranges and beer, of unwashed bodies and tobacco; they were loud and rowdy places, where the audience might engage in impromptu dances or violent squabbles. Prostitutes would wander at the back of the gallery. The people could be ferocious but were easily pleased; they sang along with the familiar songs, and called out the catchphrases of their favourite comedians.

Chaplin could not have had a better training in the discipline of song-and-dance. He also took the opportunity of studying the clowns and comedians who appeared on the same bill with him. He told a reporter in 1917 that 'every move they made registered on my young brain like a photograph. I used to try it all when I got home . . . My earliest study of the clowns in the London pantomimes has been of tremendous value to me.' He even considered joining another member of the troupe, a boy named Bristol, in a double act called 'Bristol and Chaplin, the Millionaire Tramps'. Comedy tramps were a staple of the stage, with 'tramp jugglers' and 'tramp cyclists' among them.

The life of the music hall was a tough and demanding one. Any single act would last for a short time, between five and fifteen minutes, in front of an often raucous audience generally animated by alcohol. Mesmerists and magicians, acrobats and comedians, would vie for applause and attention; an inattentive audience spelled death to a performer. The songs of the music hall were often devoted to the woes of the working class, to the little details of social and domestic life, to the perilous life on the edge of downright poverty; they were filled with broad humour or more subtle sexual innuendo.

The sketches of the comics and mimes were often set in pawn-shops, in cheap lodging houses, or in restaurants; the characters included waiters, tramps and men down on their luck known as 'the shabby genteel'. Some of them would dress oddly, or walk comically, or make use of such props as umbrellas and walking sticks. They would inspire Chaplin's early films. The most successful artists could sustain the same part over many years, while others preferred variety and variation. The important point was that, in the words of a music-hall paper of the period, 'originality goes a long way towards creating his [the artist's] success in life. What does originality consist of? Personality, to a large extent.' Chaplin was to make an art out of personality.

The greatest of these original artists was perhaps Dan Leno, with whom Chaplin shared a bill for fifteen weeks at the Tivoli in London; it would not have taken him long to pick up the fundamentals of the comedian's act. Max Beerbohm described Leno as 'that poor little battered personage, so "put upon", yet so plucky with his squeaking voice and sweeping gestures; bent but not broken; faint, but pursuing; incarnate of the will to live in a world not at all worth living in – surely all hearts always went out to Dan Leno.' His face was painted dead white; he often wore long baggy trousers and enormously long boots. He had large eyes with arched eyebrows, and could mimic an expression of pathos at a moment's notice. Marie Lloyd, another music-hall star with whom the young Chaplin worked, asked 'Ever seen his eyes? The saddest eyes in the whole world. Because if we hadn't laughed, we should have cried ourselves sick. I believe that's what real comedy is, you know, it's almost like crying.' In turn Stan Laurel would one day say of Chaplin that 'he had those eyes that absolutely forced you to look at them'. And so it would be with the Little Tramp, in appearance, in attitude, and in manner.

Leno was filled with a pulsing nervous energy; he could leap backwards six feet and land on the tip of his boots. He might be invoked as the true cockney spirit that Chaplin himself came to embody. In 1915, at the beginning of his film career, Chaplin was described by *Bioscope* as 'the Dan Leno of the screen'. In later life he liked nothing better than to impersonate the old stars of the music-hall stage, of whose songs he had total recall.

Chaplin said of this period that he endured his life as a clog-dancer because he believed that it would give him the opportunity for something greater and more challenging. His ambitions were unlimited. One contemporary, the young son of the manager of the Canterbury Theatre, recalled his ice-blue eyes that were the token of something intense and unbroken within him. It was the power of his will.

In this period Hannah and Sydney Chaplin were sharing their lodgings in Methley Street with Hannah's father. Charles Hill was then transported from there to Lambeth Infirmary, and in the following month was admitted to the workhouse. These were the familiar stages of decline for the impoverished inhabitants of South London who descended from destitution to death. Might the Chaplin family one day be among them?

In the last months of the young Chaplin's tour with the 'Lancashire Lads' Charles Chaplin senior began to fade away. His final booking was on 31 December 1900, at the Empire in Portsmouth. At that time his adopted son was appearing in *Cinderella* at the London Hippodrome. Chaplin recalled working with a famous French clown, Marceline, in this production. Marceline would fish for dancing girls in a large pool, with diamonds and jewellery for bait; eventually he managed to catch, with many gyrations and paroxysms, a small poodle. The dog was a great mimic. If Marceline stood on his head, so did the poodle. It was said of this clown, or 'Auguste', who never spoke but only mimed, that 'he had that terrific power of making you laugh, and at the same time of awakening your sympathy for him'. The young performer was watching.

Chaplin played a small cat in a scene with Marceline, but he could not resist adding a little piece of 'business' of his own. At one matinee he sniffed at a dog and then, in a most unfeline manner, cocked his leg against the proscenium arch; he then winked at the audience before capering off to great applause. His short routine might have amused the spectators but it angered the manager, sensitive to any hint of impropriety. It is an early indication of Chaplin's desire to stand out and be distinctive.

At the close of *Cinderella*, on 13 April 1901, Chaplin left the 'Lancashire Lads'. He was suffering from asthma, and his mother believed that the strain of stage work had materially affected his health. So she called him home. As Sydney had just taken up a job as assistant steward and bandsman on the SS *Norman*, she may have wanted her younger son for company. His condition left him gasping for breath, close to suffocation, and may in part be related to his confined circumstances with his mother. The doctor counselled that he would eventually outgrow the affliction, which indeed he did.

In the spring of this year, Charles Chaplin senior was close to death with the complications attendant upon cirrhosis of the liver. He had, while inebriated, been taken by his friends to St Thomas's Hospital. When he eventually realised where he was, he fought desperately to escape. But he was too ill to resist; his body was painfully swollen with dropsy, and the doctors tapped sixteen quarts of fluid from his knee. He had literally drunk himself to death at the age of thirty-eight. The funeral, on 9 May, was arranged by the Variety Artists' Benevolent Fund, but he was consigned to a pauper's grave in Tooting Cemetery. His obituary in *The Stage* noted that 'of late he had but poor luck, and misfortune had done much to break his health'.

Soon enough it was time for the young Chaplin to find work.

He and his mother were once more moving from lodging to lodging; Chester Street, Paradise Street and Munton Road were among their temporary addresses. He first earned a modest living from trading on his father's death. With black crêpe on his sleeve he sold narcissi in the local public houses, lamenting in a whispered voice the death of his father. Who could fail to be moved by the grieving boy? He was a success until Hannah caught him coming out of the public house with the bunches of flowers.

She was adamant, however, that he should not go back into the music hall; it had been the source of all his father's troubles. So he attempted other trades. He could be practical and business-like when it came to material survival. He was an errand boy in a chandler's shop. He took on Sydney's old job as a surgeon's assistant, acting as a receptionist in the surgery. It is recorded that he was then employed as a pageboy, but this may be a confusion with his later role as a pageboy on the stage. He became in turn a clerk, a barber's assistant, a printer's assistant in a stationery supply company, a glass-blower's assistant, and a newsboy outside Clapham Common tube station. He gave dancing lessons. He even sold old clothes at the street market in Newington Butts.

He hated, and despised, poverty. Poverty was demeaning. Poverty offered no escape. No doubt as a child he cried with frustration and self-pity and helplessness. By his own account he was often 'furious' at the world. 'Look at them,' a character says in his last film, *A Countess from Hong Kong*, 'packed together like sardines. That's what I dislike about the poor. They have no taste. They indulge in squalor. They pick the worst neighbourhoods to live in, eat the worst kind of food and dress atrociously.' The sentiment is exaggerated but on one level it reflects Chaplin's own feelings.

Chaplin recalled how in this period his mother encountered in the street a fellow artist fallen on evil times. A derelict woman with shaven head was being tormented by some urchins until

Hannah interfered. The woman then spoke. 'Lil, don't you know me? Eva Lestock?' She had been known as 'Dashing Eva Lestock', and had been described by *The Era* as 'one of the prettiest and most fascinating serio-comic songstresses we have'. Now, through illness and drink, she had been reduced to sleeping under the arches or spending the night in Salvation Army shelters. It is a measure of the perilous life of the stars of the music hall. Hannah took up the woman, and led her to the Chaplin home. Chaplin himself was angry and embarrassed at this turn of events, considering the woman to be little more than a filthy vagrant. Hannah sent her to the public baths and, much to Chaplin's discontent, Eva Lestock spent three days with them in their cramped lodging. He had no sympathy with the poor or the abandoned.

He enjoyed a somewhat happier period when he and his mother rented a room in the house of Mrs Taylor, a church member and fellow Christian. This restful interlude came to an end when his mother became irate with Mrs Taylor's daughter and, according to Chaplin himself, called her 'Lady Shit'. The episode throws an interesting light on his statement that his mother was the most refined woman he ever met.

One of the last London addresses that Chaplin shared with his mother was Pownall Terrace. In a wartime broadcast, in 1943, he said that 'I shall always remember the top room at 3 Pownall Terrace, where I lived as a boy; I shall always remember climbing up and down those three flights of narrow stairs to empty those troublesome slops.' He recalled Healey's the greengrocer, Waghorn's the butcher, and Ash's the grocer. The air of the house itself was 'foul with stale slops and old clothes' while mother and son lived in a room a little over twelve feet square; a table against the wall was cluttered with dirty plates and teacups; a little iron bed, painted white, stood in the corner. At its foot was an armchair which unfolded to become a single bed.

It was in this little room that some of the most climactic scenes of his boyhood were to take place. He came back one evening sometime in the spring of 1903, to be told by a little girl that his mother had gone mad. She had gone from door to door in the neighbourhood bearing little lumps of coal and explaining that they were gifts for the children. The detail of giving away coals as presents is highly pertinent. The earliest dictionary of slang tells us that, in the gypsy patois or 'canting language', 'cole' was the word for money.

The parish doctor had already been called by the neighbours. He immediately diagnosed insanity, as well as malnutrition, and told the young boy to take her to the local infirmary. In fact she seemed anxious to be admitted there. It was a haven. Chaplin later told a journalist that 'I saw myself, a scared, undersized, skinny kid, leading my mother by the hand, dragging her through the fog and the smells and the cold'.

When they arrived at the infirmary she was soon taken away by the nurses, but not before giving one last lingering look at her son. The records of the Lambeth Board of Guardians reveal that the young Chaplin had told the doctor that his mother had been 'mentioning a lot of people who are dead', and that she believed 'she could see them looking out of the window'; he explained that she had talked to 'imaginary people' and that she had in the past kept on 'going into strangers' rooms'. The doctor himself reported that 'she is very noisy and incoherent, praying and swearing by turns – singing and shouting – she says the floor is the river Jordan and she cannot cross it'. He added that on occasions she was 'violent and destructive'. Chaplin must have already seen much of this in his mother's behaviour.

The boy was questioned by the doctor, and with his usual quick instinct for survival, informed him that he was going to live with his aunt. He had no wish to return to an institution. In fact he returned to Pownall Terrace, where the landlady allowed him to stay until she had managed to rent the room. He avoided everyone; he stayed out all day, somehow contriving to steal or beg for food. He fell in with some wood-choppers, who worked in a mews behind Kennington Road; he helped them with their work, and at the end of the week was given sixpence.

He was anxiously awaiting Sydney's return from sea. On 9 May, a few days after his mother's confinement, his brother's ship docked at Southampton. 'If Sydney had not returned to London,' Chaplin said later, 'I might have become a thief in the London streets . . . I might have been buried in a pauper's grave.' Sydney wrote ahead to signal his arrival and, when he arrived at Waterloo station from Southampton, a dirty and tattered street urchin approached him. Chaplin recalled the incident in *Charlie Chaplin's Own Story*, published in 1916. 'Sydney, don't you know me? I'm Charlie.'

Sydney, shocked by his younger brother's appearance, took charge. He ensured that Chaplin had a hot bath and then gave him money to buy some new clothes. They had learned that their mother had just been transferred to Cane Hill lunatic asylum where they visited her. She was much changed. She was pale, and her lips were blue; she was listless and depressed, seeming vague and preoccupied as they tried to chat with her. She was to remain incarcerated, with one interval of lucidity, for the next seventeen years.

3

Keep it wistful

Even during this period of hardship and uncertainty, the young Chaplin had never lost sight of his theatrical ambitions. He had kept intermittently in contact with Blackmore's Theatrical Agency in Bedford Street off the Strand. There had been 'nothing for you' until, a month after Sydney's return, he received a letter asking him to call. Mr Blackstone had just been informed that the role of Billy, the pageboy in W. C. Gillette's *Sherlock Holmes*, was to be cast for a national tour; he had at once recalled the vivacious and energetic boy who had contacted him before.

Chaplin's good fortune, one of the great strengths of his life at times of crisis, was in fact redoubled. The actor to play Holmes himself, H. A. Saintsbury, had recently written *Jim, A Romance of Cockayne* and, as soon as he saw the fourteen-year-old Chaplin, he realised that he would be perfect for the role of a cockney newsboy; he did not know that Chaplin had played the part in real life. Saintsbury gave him the script. Chaplin took it back with him to Pownall Terrace, where Sydney drilled him in the dialogue. There was the question of salary. He was offered £2 10s. a week by the manager of the theatre, to which he replied 'I must consult my brother about the terms.' The manager burst out laughing. Yet this was the financial role that Sydney would play for most of Chaplin's life.

Jim opened in Kingston upon Thames on 6 July 1903, but closed only two weeks later at the Grand Theatre in Fulham. Chaplin, however, was already learning valuable lessons in the art of acting: Saintsbury taught him the importance of timing; he instructed him how to pause, to project his voice, to notice the right cues, even how to sit. He said that these matters came 'naturally' to him, but he may have needed a little prompting. He had a tendency to overact and to move his head too much. His work on the play had a great effect upon him; many years afterwards he could remember its dialogue word for word. He also retained something else. In later life he would tell his actors not to move their heads too much.

Even though *Jim* had not been a success Chaplin earned his first notices. *The Era* described him as 'a broth of a boy as Sam the newspaper boy, giving a most realistic picture of the cheeky, honest, loyal, self-reliant, philosophical street Arab who haunts the regions of Cockayne'. It is no wonder that he was 'realistic' since he knew the world, and the type, at first hand.

Soon enough it was time to begin the tour of *Sherlock Holmes*. The cast rehearsed throughout July and on the 27th the play opened at the Pavilion Theatre along the Mile End Road. When they travelled north to Burton upon Trent and Newcastle the wardrobe mistress, Edith Scales, was appointed as his unofficial guardian. She recalled that with his first week's income he bought a box-camera and set himself up as a part-time street photographer, taking pictures for threepence or sixpence a time. He was always intent upon making money. When the cast was staying at the Market Hotel in Blackburn Chaplin marched into the sitting room, where the farmers were drinking, and sang to his improvised audience. He then performed a clog dance, to general satisfaction. At the end of the show he went round with his hat.

Miss Scales provides other glimpses of the boy of fourteen and fifteen years. He kept two tame rabbits. While staying in Ashton-under-Lyne he witnessed his landlady's altercation with a drunken chimney sweep; Miss Scales recalled that, when he stood in the witness box during the subsequent hearing, 'no one could understand his cockney accent'. He would later take pains to erase the inflection. Miss Scales also revealed that Chaplin 'used to check every item on the bills rendered him by landladies when we were on the road'; he would then remove the costs of items he had not received.

By his own account he suffered from melancholy and loneliness in these northern towns. He was also very shy. He fell half in love with the leading lady, Greta Hahn, but on seeing her in the street he would quickly walk down a side alley to avoid any meeting. 'I began to neglect myself,' he wrote, 'and became desultory in my habits.' He received letters from Sydney, who informed him that with the failure of his theatrical ambitions he had taken work as a bartender at the Coal Hole along the Strand. 'Since Mother's illness,' Sydney said in one letter, 'all we have in the world is each other. So you must write regularly, and let me know that I have a brother.' Chaplin was always a bad correspondent.

He was playing Billy, the pageboy of the great Sherlock Holmes, and he was soon receiving good notices. The part might have been made for him. *The Era* wrote that he 'succeeds in making the smart pageboy a prime favourite with the audience'. His secretary at a later date came upon his earliest collection of press cuttings. On its opening page were two reviews of Billy in *Sherlock Holmes*. One stated that 'Mr Charles Chaplin is unusually bright and natural as Billy', while the other agreed that 'the brightest bit of acting in the play was given by Mr Charles Chaplin who, as Billy, displayed immense activity as well as dramatic appreciation'. The reviews were underscored at the time by Chaplin himself, and he kept them with him all his life.

At the end of 1903 Chaplin was able to persuade the management to allow Sydney to enter the company of *Sherlock Holmes*; he played the role of an elderly aristocrat, but was no doubt employed partly to look after his younger brother. It was on this tour that the first caricature of Chaplin was executed by an artist named George Cooke; Chaplin was apparently delighted by the novel likeness of him, and paid seven shillings and sixpence for it.

The two boys were joined a few weeks later by their mother, who had been released from Cane Hill asylum. It is not at all clear when the family were reunited; it may have been as early as the beginning of January, when the players were at Wakefield, but Chaplin himself recalls that it was towards the end of the tour, when indeed they were closer to London at Aldershot or Eastbourne. The precise location is not of great importance.

With a combined income of more than £4 a week they were able to rent a 'special apartment de luxe' complete with two bedrooms and a sitting room. For the brief period that she shared the tour with them, Hannah Chaplin shopped and cleaned the flat. It might have seemed that the old domestic world had been restored, except that Hannah was oddly uncommunicative and detached; she seems to have acted more like a guest than a mother. It was agreed, therefore, that she should move to a lodging in Chester Street, Kennington, where she would feel more at home.

The tour continued until the beginning of summer when the final curtain fell on 11 June 1904, at the West London theatre on the Edgware Road. The young Chaplin was now, in the theatrical expression, 'resting'. He and Sydney joined their mother in Chester Street. Their activities during this period of freedom are not documented, but Chaplin notes that he was relieved when he was able to join the second tour of *Sherlock Holmes* at the end of October with a new company and a new leading man. Life with Hannah was becoming ever more difficult. Sydney also took a chance at freedom and went back to sea as assistant steward and ship's bugler. He was away for three months.

Just after Sydney's return to Kennington, Hannah relapsed into madness. On 16 March 1905, she was admitted once more to Lambeth Infirmary. The doctor recorded her as 'very strange in manner and quite incoherent. She dances, sings and cries by turn. She is indecent in conduct and conversation at times and again at times praying and saying she had been born again.' Two days later she was taken back to Cane Hill asylum where she remained for seven years before being removed to a private institution paid for by the now rich and successful Chaplin. On a letter written from Cane Hill to her sons in 1905, she puts as the address at the top of the letter 'best known to you'.

The second tour came to an end at the beginning of May 1905, and Chaplin was for a while once more 'resting'. But the public appeal of *Sherlock Holmes* was apparently enormous, and by the middle of August he had joined a third company touring the play around the country. He was not impressed with his colleagues. He described the company as inferior, the members of which he proceeded to antagonise by lecturing them on how such and such a scene was done and how such and such a line should be spoken. It may have been at this time that he purchased his first violin, to which he would one day add a cello; it was for him lonely and melancholy music. Since he was left-handed, he was of course compelled to string his instruments in reverse order.

In October he was relieved to be parted from the company. William Gillette, the author of *Sherlock Holmes*, had written a ten-minute 'curtain-raiser' for the main play of the evening. *The Painful Predicament of Sherlock Holmes* was to be performed only in London at the Duke of York's theatre and its material was also, for Chaplin, very close to home. It concerned, according to *The Stage*, the irruption into Baker Street of 'a poor crazy woman, excitable, impulsive, and tremendously voluble'. The page, Billy, played by Chaplin, is ordered to call for assistance from the asylum, whereupon 'two stern-faced men in uniform appear, evidently attendants from a lunatic asylum, and the poor creature is marched off, back into captivity'. This was close to Hannah Chaplin's fate.

The Stage added that 'Master Charles Chaplin was duly boisterous as the harmless, necessary page.' Billy's last words are 'You were right, sir. It was the right asylum.'

Chaplin rarely wrote to his mother at Cane Hill, and is not known to have paid her many visits. He was troubled by her. He knew that her own mother had gone insane, and he feared for himself. His cameraman for thirty-eight years, Roland or 'Rollie' Totheroh, recalled that he believed he also 'would eventually go insane'. Other friends have remarked on the frequency with which he brooded on the possibility of madness. He liked to sing an old music-hall song:

> Oh ever since that fatal night
> Me wife's gone mad,
> Awfully queer,
> Touched just here.

At which point Chaplin would point to his own head. The fear or suspicion of impending insanity might therefore account for his dark moods and his sometimes irrational anger. One of his constant house guests in later life, Cecil Reynolds, was a neuropathologist; it might be divined that Chaplin wanted him as a consultant and a possible doctor.

The production of *Sherlock Holmes* at the Duke of York's theatre, where it had replaced *The Painful Predicament*, was a very great success with the stars of London mingling with the fashionable classes to attend its performances. Queen Alexandra saw the play, and sitting in her box were the king of Greece and Prince Christian. 'Don't tell me,' the king screeched at his son who was intent upon giving away the plot. 'Don't *tell* me!' The young Chaplin was even mentioned in *The Green Room Book: or Who's Who on the Stage* where he was described as 'impersonator, mimic and sand-dancer . . . cradled in the profession'. His reputation was high enough to be invited to the funeral of the eminent actor, Sir Henry Irving, at Westminster Abbey.

Sherlock Holmes ended its run on 2 December, after the sudden and unexpected departure of William Gillette. Chaplin had hoped to remain with Gillette, learning his trade in the 'legitimate' theatre. Instead he was for a short period out of work as he idled around pool-rooms, indulging in wine and women as the mood took him. He always had a powerful sexual instinct, and those whom he called 'whores and sluts' were readily available to a handsome young man. But he was not one meant to be indolent. Work was at the centre of his being. At the beginning of 1906 he joined his fourth tour of *Sherlock Holmes* which performed at venues close to hand, such as Peckham and Greenwich, together with some of the northern cities. By now he might justifiably have become tired both of the part and of the play.

Sydney Chaplin probably had little difficulty in persuading him to leave the tour and to join him in a company, 'Wal Pink's Workmen', that specialised in slapstick routines. For three months he performed in a sketch, *Repairs*, in which he played a particularly incompetent carpenter from the firm of Spoiler and Messit. In a scenario close to one of his later short films, decorators fall upon 'Muddleton Villa' like a whirlwind wrecking everything in sight. Paste buckets are upset; carpenters' ladders swing wildly around; paint flies everywhere.

This was where Chaplin really belonged. He had hoped to become a serious actor but he now returned to the music-hall world he knew so well from the experiences of Hannah Chaplin. *Sherlock Holmes* was one of the last stage plays in which he would ever perform. Ahead of him lay sketches, skits, stunts, spoofs and send-ups with all the general 'business' of the popular stage. *Repairs* was also the first occasion when he performed in mime.

*   *   *

While on tour he saw an advertisement in *The Era* asking for male comedians between the ages of fourteen and nineteen. Chaplin, now seventeen, decided to attend the auditions. *Casey's Circus* was a kind of variety show in which the young inhabitants of a slum court mimic the most popular music-hall acts and circus performers of the day. It was an opportunity for broad satire, smutty songs, quick routines, comic impersonations and general frenzy. This was work at which the young Chaplin excelled and he joined the new company in the spring of 1906.

He said in later life that it was an 'awful' show, but he confessed that it helped him to learn the trade of the comedian. There was, first of all, the funny run. In one sketch he had to play the part of Dick Turpin, highwayman, being pursued around and across the stage by the police. The principal comedian of the cast, Will Murray, said that 'I think I can justly say that I am the man who taught Charlie how to turn corners.'

This was the manoeuvre that Chaplin used in so many films that it became something of a trademark. He would raise one foot in the air and hop a little way on the other in order to get around a 'bend'; it could be described as a one-legged skid, and he achieved the precarious move only after many hours of rehearsal with Murray. He also had to learn how to halt in the middle of a run; he would stop suddenly on one foot and balance himself; he then had to throw out his chest in order to preserve the balance and prevent himself from falling forward on his face. He always held his head and body upright. Whenever he took a fall he took care not to land on his posterior but to roll further over so that he ended up on his back.

The next great lesson was that of impersonation. Walford Bodie was a popular music-hall hypnotist and conjuror of arresting appearance; he had a long waxed moustache, with its ends pointing upwards, and large penetrating eyes. Chaplin was chosen to parody him, a task to which he applied himself with alacrity. He studied the performer's photograph in *The Era*. Will Murray showed him Bodie's mannerisms and for hours he would rehearse them in front of a mirror. He assumed the Bodie manner with instinctive skill. It was said many times of Chaplin that he *became* the person, or even the object, he imitated; so it was on this first occasion.

Some other comic touches completed the part. He tried to hang his cane on a peg but he was holding it at the wrong end, and it clattered upon the stage. He picked it up, but his silk top hat fell off. He attempted to put the hat back on his head but its thick paper wadding fell out and the hat engulfed his face. The audience burst into laughter. He was playing the part of an earnest and serious-minded man who cannot help but behave in a ludicrous manner. It struck him that the more serious he became, the funnier he seemed to be.

Dan Lipton, a comic songwriter of the period, recalled that 'the way that boy burlesqued Doctor Bodie was wonderful. I tell you he had never *seen* the man.' Lipton added that 'he always had the most remarkable nerve, but at the same time like all real artists he was sensitive and temperamental'. A fellow performer recalled that Chaplin was 'a very earnest lad who went through his paces as though his life was dependent on it'.

He left the tour of *Casey's Circus* in the summer of 1907. Many years later, in a speech at a show-business dinner, Chaplin began to speak of Will Murray. A heckler called out 'Ask him for a pay rise!', to which Chaplin replied 'He gave me the sack.' He may indeed have asked for more money and been shown the door. He stayed in a lodging house along Kennington Road, and waited for the next opportunity. He bought lanterns and carpets for his room; he also began to read Schopenhauer, with all the enthusiasm of an autodidact. He read the philosopher, with varying degrees of concentration, for the next forty years. The young man might have been drawn to his theory of the pre-eminence of the human will but, equally, he might have agreed with Schopenhauer's claim that sexual passion is 'the strongest and most active of all motives'. How well, and how quickly, Chaplin could read is an open question.

His was still a very uncertain life and profession. At one stage in this period of enforced rest, by his own account, he took on the role of a semi-juvenile lead in a comedy entitled *The Merry Major*. The leading lady, who played his wife, was an actress of fifty who was always something the worse for gin. He then wrote and played the principal role in a slapstick comedy entitled *Twelve Just Men*; it was abandoned after three days of rehearsal. Perhaps in desperation he now decided to play the part of a Jewish comedian. He was given a week's booking at the Foresters' Music Hall in Bethnal Green, but his routine was not considered to be a success by his largely Jewish audience; they even construed some of the jokes as anti-Semitic, and he was booed off the stage to the accompaniment of orange peel and catcalls.

His older brother was rather more successful. Sydney had joined Fred Karno's performers in the summer of 1906, while Chaplin was touring with *Casey's Circus*, and had already gained plaudits and promotion. He was always willing to help his brother, however, and persuaded his employer to take a chance on the young man out of employ.

Fred Karno, a former gymnast and acrobat, had perfected a show in which various mimes and acrobats performed in silent burlesque with romantic ballet music as an ironic accompaniment; the sketches were fast and furious, complicated routines that required swift movement, split-second timing and instant reactions. Karno had built his headquarters in Vaughan Road, Camberwell, where three houses had been knocked together to create the 'Fun Factory' where all the sets, costumes and props were manufactured. From here Karno's buses set out, transporting the various acts to the many music halls of the capital. Custard pies and buckets of whitewash, trick cyclists and spinning plates, high wires and wooden stilts, spinning clubs and fire-torches were always on the bill. The sketches included bicycle thieves and boxers and drunks. It was cruel, and boisterous, and funny.

At Sydney's urging Karno agreed to meet Chaplin. The manager thought him too shy, and too frail, to excel in slapstick; but, out of deference to Sydney's urgent appeals, he agreed to try him. Chaplin was eighteen, but he looked even younger. When Karno mentioned this, Chaplin simply shrugged. It was, he said, a question of make-up. He later professed to believe that this nonchalant response got him the job.

Karno rehearsed the players endlessly, day after day, so that the confusion and mayhem could be almost militarily controlled; it was inspired chaos. It worked to an insistent rhythm, with every element measured and concentrated. Stan Laurel, another of the Karno troupe, recalled that their manager 'didn't teach Charlie and me all we know about comedy. He just taught us most of it.' In particular, 'he taught us to be precise'. Chaplin himself said in *Variety* in January 1942 that 'each man working for Karno had to have perfect timing and had to know the peculiarities of everyone else in the cast so that we could, collectively, achieve a cast tempo'. This was the speed and timing that Chaplin applied in all of his films. Karno also taught his players that humour came from the unexpected or from a sudden change in pace. He instructed them to 'keep it *wistful*'; when you knock down a man, kiss him on the head. If you hit someone hard, just look sorry for a few seconds. That makes the action funnier. Chaplin would never forget these early instructions in the art of comedy.

He began touring with the Karno Company, at the beginning of 1908, with *The Football Match*. In this he was meant only to have a minor role but, by means of additional business, he managed to catch the audience's eye; he tripped over a dumb-bell; he hooked his cane on a punchbag; he lost a button and his trousers fell down. The audience reacted with laughter, and soon enough they were greeting his initial entrance with applause. After the success of the first evening, he went out dazed into the night. He had done it. He walked out of the Empire in New Cross and somehow made his way to Westminster Bridge where he looked down into the water; then he began walking home and stopped at the Elephant and Castle for a cup of tea at a coffee stall. He was exultant. He would never be out of work again.

His new-found popularity was not to the taste of his fellow comedians, who reacted with natural jealousy. 'I have more talent in my arse than you have in your whole body,' one fellow player told him.

'That,' Chaplin replied, 'is where your talent lies.'

Karno himself recalled that 'he could also be very unlikeable. I've known him go whole weeks without saying a word to anyone in the company. Occasionally he would be quite chatty, but on the whole he was dour and unsociable. He had a horror of drink, and put most of his salary in the bank as soon as he got it.'

Stan Laurel, however, believed that he was too shy to mingle comfortably with other people. Another Karno contemporary recalled that 'he was very highly strung and given to extravagant expressions of delight when things went aright with him and his work; yet a little incident, the merest mishap to a fellow actor, for example, would crumple him completely and render further work impossible for the rest of the day'. Others noticed his 'self-absorption'.

From the early summer of 1908 Chaplin and his older brother were sharing a bill together; in a period of what was for them unprecedented prosperity they decided to rent a four-room flat at 15 Glenshaw Mansions in Brixton. Brixton was one of the areas favoured by music-hall stars, and they decided to create a suitably exotic background for their lives. The brothers carpeted the main room and put up a Moorish screen; they had a suite of furniture and a pastel representation of a female nude. As a final touch they purchased an upright piano. It resembled nothing so much as a brothel without any women. The routine of touring generally required a visit to three music halls each night, and so in this period they went from the Streatham Empire to the Canterbury Music Hall before finishing at the Tivoli.

Some of their rehearsals took place in the Montpelier Assembly Hall, in Walworth. Here in early August Chaplin met a young girl who was training to become a dancer. Hetty Kelly was fifteen years old, and seems to have been in turn thrilled and bewildered by the attentions of a passionate young man. It is the familiar tale of first love. He was melancholy and dissatisfied with life; she was innocent and beautiful. They agreed to meet at Kennington Gate on the following Sunday afternoon, from where they drove by taxi to the West End. The intensity of his emotion was already apparent but, when he called her 'my nemesis', she did not know what he meant. They walked back to Camberwell, after an evening at the Trocadero restaurant, and as they strolled along the Embankment Chaplin was 'ecstatic'. For three mornings he met her outside her house in Camberwell Road and escorted her to the Underground in Westminster Bridge Road. On the fourth morning he sensed her coldness or uncertainty and rebuked her for not loving him. There then followed scenes typical of those between immature and inexperienced youth. Were they in love? How much do you love me? What *was* love? We must part and never see each other again. Goodbye.

The difference is that Chaplin, more than fifty years later, seems to have remembered their fraught dialogues with precision and transcribed them in his autobiography. It is not clear how much sprang from wishful thinking or a melodramatic imagination but it is certainly true that his infatuation with the young girl stayed with him for a long time and may have informed his attitude towards other women. It had been for him a spiritual experience, all the more potent for being unfulfilled. Here was a girl who remained untouched and out of reach, invulnerable, all that could be desired, so to be hoped for and yet never to be attained. She stood out in explicit contrast to the women he had picked up in the pool-rooms three years before.

The touring continued at its usual frantic and fatiguing pace all over the country from Nottingham to Newcastle, Leeds to Bristol. A fellow comedian at Karno, Chester Courtney, recalls that they played twopenny poker, shared Woodbine cigarettes, enjoyed omnibus rides and became involved in 'promiscuous flirtations'. In the course of the tour Chaplin had at last achieved his ambition in playing the leading role of *The Football Match*, but first-night nerves caused an attack of laryngitis that ruined his comic delivery. The same complaint had once affected his mother. Karno might have unleashed on him the full fury of his well-known temper, but Sydney persuaded him to give his younger brother a non-speaking part in another Karno production.

Mumming Birds was a pantomime without words, in which the unconvincing acts of a low music hall are interrupted by a character known as 'the inebriated swell'. Some of the humour comes from the incompetent conjurors, ballad singers and 'strong men', but most of it derives from the staggering antics of the drunk in white tie and tails. The part of course was played by Chaplin, who knew from experience how drunks behaved. They were all around him in South London. That is why he did not need to say a word. He relied upon timing, dexterity, and the ability to take a tumble without injuring himself. He had found his metier. Mime became his single most important music-hall part, and one that eventually launched him into a film career.

In some sense the character of the drunkard took him over. In an interview at the end of his life he revealed that 'I would go on, and I absolutely was in touch with something else. It was almost a psychic sort of thing. It came, I think, with a certain boredom and tiredness that was a form of relaxation and allowed a talent or some-thing to break through. I couldn't do wrong. I remember it so well. An old music hall on Edgware Road. For about four nights that happened, and I really enjoyed this thing within me – so much so that other actors used to stand in the wings to see me.' The inebriate, swell or no swell, would become a staple of his later comedy.

He then proceeded to play the star in another comic sketch, *Jimmy the Fearless*, in which he took on the part of a boy who escapes from the drudgery of his daily life by dreaming of heroic adventures. This was a role he would also reprise in his films. The *Yorkshire Post* reported that 'his entrance alone in *Jimmy the Fearless* sets the house in a roar and stamps him as a born comedian'. At one point in his routine he absent-mindedly carves a loaf with his knife, while reading a book, and unwittingly turns it into a bread concertina. He was to use the same joke in a film of 1915, *A Jitney Elopement*. He also took part in a sketch entitled *Skating*, in which his skills on the ice were matched only by his ability in comic timing; it was remarked by a reviewer that 'his tumbling and foolery' were extremely funny. His experiences here would also be redeployed in his work upon the screen.

In the winter of 1909, he performed for three weeks with a Karno troupe in Paris. *Mumming Birds* was staged at the Folies Bergère, which had not then acquired the somewhat louche repu-tation it later enjoyed. A gentleman called for him after the performance. 'You are instinctively a musician and a dancer,' he told him. When Chaplin asked later for the man's name, he was informed that it was Claude Debussy. He had never heard of him.

He fell in love again with a young girl, Mabelle, who was in his own words, 'only ten or twelve'. He denied that their relation-ship was sexual but said that she was part of his spiritual quest for beauty. He just liked to hold her and to hug her, literally clasping at innocence. This yearning, or aspiration, would be the cause of much subsequent misfortune.

4

Making a living

In the early autumn of 1910 Chaplin signed a new contract with Karno. He was now a star performer and an acknowledged master of music-hall pantomime. The manager of Karno's interests in the United States, Alfred Reeves, had at this time returned to England in search of a new company for the profitable American circuit. It seemed inevitable that Chaplin would be one of those chosen, and only a few days after signing the contract he embarked on the SS *Cairnrona* to cross the Atlantic. 'He's old enough and big enough,' Reeves had told Karno, 'and clever enough for anything.'

Stan Laurel recalled the journey across the ocean on a ship that was little more than a cattle-boat, and in particular he remembered the first sight of land. 'We were all on deck, sitting,' he wrote, 'watching the land in the mist. Suddenly Charlie ran to the railing, took off his hat, waved it and shouted, "America, I am coming to conquer you! Every man, woman and child shall have my name on their lips – Charles Spencer Chaplin!" We all booed him affectionately, and he bowed to us very formally and sat down again.' These might seem the recollections of hindsight, but other members of the party have verified the scene. It is a measure of Chaplin's inordinate ambition and self-confidence. Stan Laurel himself of course also found great fame in the United States, when he became the thin man in the partnership of Laurel and Hardy.

The ship docked at Quebec and the new American company travelled by train to Jersey City. By the beginning of October they had arrived in New York. Chaplin was at first bewildered and a little frightened by this foreign metropolis that seemed to him too loud, too garish and too fast. Yet when he mingled with the crowds on Broadway, passing the lighted marquees of the vaudeville theatres, he began to feel more at home. This was his true setting. He was no longer the South London boy with an unhappy history; he had all the world before him.

The first production of the Karno troupe in New York, *The Wow-Wows*, was not a success. It was too brittle, and altogether too English, for an American audience. It was, in the word of Stan Laurel, 'awful'. Nevertheless they played it for the rest of the month, in the Bronx and Brooklyn as well as in New York itself, until Alfred Reeves had the happy inspiration of replacing it with *Mumming Birds* or *A Night in an English Music Hall*; this was the music-hall sketch in which Chaplin played the inebriate swell. He took up the role with enthusiasm, and the fortunes of the tour were restored.

They went everywhere from the autumn of 1910 to the summer of 1911, taking in Winnipeg and Chicago, Portland and San Francisco, Cleveland and Kansas City. Many photographs of the tour survive. Chaplin poses in a long American greatcoat which, as he said, made him look 'like a ringmaster in a circus'; he is photographed with four other players by a poster saying 'Continental Divide Elevation 6,350 feet'; he is playing a violin, left-handed, with Alfred Reeves standing by his side; he poses, nattily dressed, on a road in downtown San Francisco; he stands beside some placards announcing 'CHARLES CHAPLIN THE INEBRIATE'.

He picked up some American admirers with that act. Groucho Marx recalled that the audience was 'intent on Chaplin's every move'. He added that 'at the table was a large basket of oranges. Finally, he started to pick up the oranges one by one, and threw them right at the other performers. One of them knocked the pianist off his chair. People became hysterical. There never was such continuous laughter.' The *Winnipeg Telegram* noted that 'Charles Chaplin, in theatrical parlance, "hogs the show".'

Stan Laurel, Chaplin's room-mate for much of the tour, described him as 'very eccentric'. He noted that 'he was very moody and often very shabby in appearance', but then he would surprise everyone by dressing up in style. Laurel would fry pork chops in defiance of the rule that no cooking was allowed in the rooms; Chaplin would cover up the noise of sizzling by playing loudly on the violin.

He was reading all the time. He tried to learn Greek, but abandoned it quickly enough. He thought of yoga. He was, in other words, intent upon self-improvement. He bought a cello to complement his violin, and began to wear what he considered to be a musicianly outfit in fawn and green. Dress was clearly very important to him. As Thomas Carlyle remarks in *Sartor Resartus*, 'the Spirit of Clothes' accommodates the whole soul and intelligence of man. Chaplin's costume as the Little Tramp might be adduced as evidence here.

Laurel recalled surprising him in the bathroom of their lodgings; he was posing with his cello in front of a mirror, his hair unnaturally tousled. He was pulling the bow across the strings in grand style, just like the professional musicians of the orchestra, admiring himself as he did so. He never ceased to play a part; he had to do so in order to find himself. In the words of a later acquaintance, he was always 'on'. He was in essence unpredictable. He would perform in the sketches with great gusto and feeling; off the stage, however, he was often reserved and uncommunicative.

When Chaplin returned to England in the summer of 1912, he discovered that he had no home. Glenshaw Mansions was no longer rented. Syd had married, and Chaplin was forced to find alternative accommodation in a back room off the Brixton Road. He was not idle during the four months on English soil, however; he toured with one of the Karno troupes in England, and even made short visits to the halls of Jersey and of Guernsey.

He also managed, with his brother, to visit Hannah Chaplin in the Cane Hill asylum; she had been consigned to a padded cell after a period of singing hymns very loudly. Chaplin could not bring himself actually to see her but waited for Sydney to speak to her. It seems that his mother had been given forcible ice-cold showers, as a form of shock therapy, which had turned her face quite blue; they decided at once that with their combined incomes they could afford to place her in a private institution. Chaplin had, in addition, saved $2,000 from his American tour; he was always very thrifty. So Hannah was removed to Peckham House, in Peckham Rye, where she remained for the next eight years.

By Chaplin's own account he no longer felt at ease in England. After the United States it seemed small and tight and dismal; he variously described his moods as those of sadness, bitterness and gloom. It was in a frame of mind very like that of liberation, therefore, that on 2 October he embarked on the SS *Oceanic* for his second tour of the United States. It was now for him familiar territory. The Karno troupe opened in New York, in the middle of October, and toured continually for the next fifteen months; they were doing three or four shows a day, seven days a week. But once more he found the routine 'bleak and depressing'; these were always Chaplin's favourite adjectives.

At the beginning of April 1913, he took advantage of a rest in Philadelphia to travel back to New York; he stayed at the Astor Hotel, and indulged in the luxury of melancholy. On the first evening he wandered towards the Metropolitan Opera House, where on a whim he decided to attend a performance of Wagner's *Tannhäuser*. The experience shattered him and, at the climactic moment, when Tannhäuser falls upon the bier of Elisabeth and asks her to pray for him, he wept. It seemed to him to be the story of his life.

When he returned to Philadelphia he found a telegram waiting for him. It had been sent to Alfred Reeves. 'IS THERE A MAN

NAMED CHAFFIN IN YOUR COMPANY OR SOMETHING LIKE THAT IF SO WILL HE COMMUNICATE WITH KESSEL AND BAUMAN 24 LONGACRE BUILDING BROADWAY NEW YORK.' Chaplin believed that this was a firm of lawyers, perhaps ready to announce a legacy from a rich American relative, but he was quickly disabused.

Kessel and Bauman were the owners of the New York Motion Pictures Company, of which one of the subsidiaries was the Keystone Comedy Company. One of the Keystone comics, Ford Sterling, was threatening to leave. They needed a replacement, and believed that they had found one in Charles Chaplin. Here was a young man who had gained top billing in the Karno tours and had been almost unanimously praised by the press. He could electrify an audience. He was offered $150 a week for three months, to be followed by $175 for the remaining nine. He had never earned so much money in his life. He may have quailed at the idea of an independent life, separated from the troupe, but his decision still came quickly. He would join Keystone as soon as his contract with Karno came to an end.

The most likely instigator of this offer was Mack Sennett, the manager of Keystone. By his own account he had seen Chaplin perform in New York and had been 'more than impressed. Stunned might be a good word.' He added that 'I think I was so struck by him because he was everything I wasn't: a little fellow who could move like a ballet dancer. The next week I couldn't remember his name, but I sure as hell never forgot that wonderful easy grace of movement. I had seen nothing like it.' Sennett, a Canadian then in his early thirties, was a natural showman who had been informally trained by D. W. Griffith at the Biograph Studio, one of the earliest of its kind; he learned from Griffith how to edit a film so that it maintained its pace and its rhythm. But he also had a natural instinct of his own; he had a feeling for comedy, notably on the ground that anything which made him laugh would also appeal to the general public. With the creation of the 'Keystone Cops' in 1912 he might be said to have invented American comedy.

Chaplin himself had been entertaining vague hopes of a cinematic career. He had been growing tired of the stage. He had already discussed with Alfred Reeves the possibility of filming the Karno routines, but the idea came to nothing. Nevertheless, while on tour, he often went to the little local cinemas and stood at the back where he watched the action.

Film was in any case the coming thing. With the advent of small storefront theatres, known as nickelodeons, motion pictures of ten or fifteen minutes' duration were becoming increasingly popular. The theatres may have been unsavoury and unhygienic, smelling of sweat and tobacco, as malodorous and dirty as the 'penny gaffs' of a previous era, but the power of the medium overcame all obstacles. Even the vaudeville theatres showed 'flickers' as part of their programme. The poor and the illiterate flocked to these silent shows, to be seen at the price of a nickel or five cents. For immigrants, who could not yet read English, they provided immediate access to American life. They were filled with action and with movement, never before captured by any other medium. They offered what seemed at the time to be spellbinding realism, except that the actors moved at a speed faster than that of real life. It was part of the attraction. The members of the audience sat on hard wooden seats, and brought their own refreshments with them. Sometimes the screen was little more than a bedsheet tacked against the back wall.

Chaplin's final performance on stage was at Kansas City on 28 November 1913. He brought the cast drinks after the curtain and, although he tried to make a joke of the 'farewell', he was trembling when he shook hands with all of them. He then hurried off backstage; one of his colleagues followed him, curious, and saw him crying.

Less than three weeks later he arrived at the Keystone studio on Allessandro Street in Edendale, California. He was always to say that 1913 was his lucky year. And so it proved. He, like Shakespeare, had the inestimable advantage of being an instinctive artist in the preliminary years of a new art.

The life of the film studio was, at first, a bewildering and wholly alien experience for Chaplin. It had the ramshackle and improvised quality of all original things. The complex itself was built in the farm fields of the San Fernando Valley, beside warehouses and workshops, wooden shacks and stores, set among cacti and coarse sagebrush, palm and eucalyptus; it was essentially a noisome suburb, some five miles from Los Angeles. A four-room bungalow was used as the headquarters of the operation and a barn had been converted into dressing rooms, with a rickety green fence surrounding the complex. The long sign outside the studios read 'KEYSTONE MACK SENNETT KEYSTONE', with a row of cars in front ready to be used as comedy props.

A number of sets were created on a large wooden platform, veiled from the elements by yards of white linen; the diffused sun in the bright Californian sky was the only means of lighting. Since the films had no sound, the studio was filled with noises – of directors shouting instructions to the actors, of the cranking sound of the rolling cameras, of the performers talking to one another, of whistling and hammering, of music played by a live band or a phonograph to lend rhythm to the action. Three or four films were made at the same time. One set might be a prison interior, while another might be a fashionable drawing room. The facade of a three-storey tenement, complete with windows and a fire escape, was supported by nothing more than wooden scaffolding.

No scripts were used; the essential art was that of improvisation. If a fire were reported in the neighbourhood, the director and crew might rush to the scene in order to film the actors in front of it. An initial scenario, or idea, was followed by an extemporised sequence of absurd events that always ended in a chase. The chase was the essence of Keystone, and the ultimate in chases was known as 'the zigzag rally' in which, for example, a wild posse of policemen will never run in a straight line but rebound off invisible walls. The camera was 'under-cranked' so that the action, when projected, became much faster; Sennett also took out every fourth frame so that the characters seemed to hop or jerk, thus increasing the mechanical tension of the comedy.

The actors were toys or puppets who simply ran and ran and ran until they met an immoveable object or dropped with exhaustion. They inhabited an artificial comic universe in which anything was possible; despite the violence and destruction all around, no one was ever really hurt. They were not supposed to experience emotions other than the typical manifestations of fear or greed or passion. Everything had to go as fast as possible; the audience were not to be given the time to think. Sennett's films therefore possessed enormous pace and energy that have rarely been equalled. The comedies were either 'one reelers' or 'two reelers', a 'reel' lasting for approximately thirteen minutes. The essence of the early cinema was constant motion.

Sennett turned out short and ebullient films filled with car chases and riotous pursuits; bricks were hurled, mallets were deployed, and much pleasure was derived from what Chaplin always called 'arse-kicking'. The actions may have come out of vaudeville but the setting was largely that of contemporary America; this was essentially an urban world of saloon bars and cheap hotels, hardware stores and pawnshops, banks and barbers' shops, dirty restaurants and dusty streets in which cars competed with horse-drawn transport and where the whole drama of the burgeoning nation might be found. The films give the impression of wide open spaces somewhere around the next corner. And, like everything else in America, they were manufactured at high speed. Three films were completed each week and, in the previous year, some 140 of them came out of Edendale.

The Keystone films had a small cast of regulars who had become used to working with one another; among them were Roscoe 'Fatty' Arbuckle, Chester 'Walrus' Conklin, Mack 'Ambrose' Swain and Mabel Normand. The men wore too much make-up and their acting was wildly exaggerated; some of them looked like living gargoyles. They had no audience to which they might play and, in its absence, everything was overstated.

On his first day, Chaplin arrived around lunchtime and the spectacle of the actors streaming from the bungalow was enough to unnerve him. He had never seen anything like this before. He returned to his hotel in the city and waited there for two days until he was summoned by Sennett himself, impatient to see his new comic. Sennett then took him on a tour and introduced him to some of the key players and members of the crew. Chaplin recalled that one of the first questions was 'Can you do a funny sprawl off a stepladder without breaking your bones?' Of course he could. He had done that kind of work at Karno for several years.

When Sennett first saw Chaplin out of stage make-up, he was perplexed by his youthfulness. 'I thought you were a much older man,' he told him.

'I can make up as old as you like.'

Yet Chaplin got the distinct impression that Sennett had believed he had made a mistake in hiring the young comedian.

Sennett later recalled 'a shy little Britisher who was abashed and confused by everything that had anything to do with motion pictures'. Chaplin was not so abashed, however, that he did not look around curiously and observantly. Chester Conklin said that 'he watched everybody all the time' and said little 'except to ask a few pointed and professional questions'. Why were scenes shot out of chronological sequence? Why were the 'rushes' viewed as negatives? How am I supposed to react to another actor who isn't actually there?

He wandered for some days among the actors and sets without actually being assigned a role. It seemed that no one knew quite what to do with him. Then the moment came. Henry Lehrman, one of the young Keystone directors – it was a youthful business in which all of the participants were fresh – wanted someone to play a street-smart confidence trickster. *Making a Living*, released on 2 February 1914, was Chaplin's entrance on to the screen. He was not yet the Little Tramp; he was reprising the role of stage villain complete with cravat, top hat, monocle and drooping moustache; it was known as the 'Desperate Desmond' costume. He had become a 'dude' or seedy 'toff'. In this first film he is insidious, wheedling and oddly threatening. When he kisses a girl's hand, he then goes all the way up the arm. That is an early Chaplin touch. He was probably the first to do it on the screen. He already has a full range of facial mannerisms, twitching and smiling and scowling. He also tries out a distinctive walk, the ancestor of a more famous one.

He was convinced that Lehrman was hostile to him and had deliberately cut out some of the comic 'business' he introduced to the film. But he was also aware of his own inexperience; he was still a little stiff and overanxious. It seems that Sennett himself was unhappy with the finished product and complained to Mabel Normand that 'he had hooked himself a dead one'. Yet Chaplin had no reason to be entirely disheartened. *Making a Living* may have been standard Keystone, but the *Moving Picture World* said that 'the clever player who takes the part of a sharper . . . is a comedian of the first water'.

There is some confusion about the identity of the second film, which saw the fitful birth of the Tramp or the 'little fellow'. It is certain, however, that *Kid Auto Races at Venice* was released five days after *Making a Living*. That was the rate at which the short films were produced. It was just eleven minutes in length. Chaplin plays a weird interloper quite out of sympathy with everyone around him. He is already dressed in a distinctive fashion, with clothes that are too small for him, and might actually be viewed as a tramp; his bowler is also too small, and a large safety pin fastens his jacket. A small bristle of crêpe hair is glued under his nose. This is a tramp who demands all the attention. For the first time he executes a 'flick kick' on a cigarette with the sole of his right shoe. He may be eccentric, even a little mad, but already he is an original.

He 'hogs' the scene, serenely self-confident of his own image and aggressive to those who hinder his presentation of himself. He is bristling with the desire to perform. He gets in the way of the camera filming the races, and resists every attempt of the director to exclude him. He wants to commune with that camera but, more significantly, with the vast and unknown audience that is assembled behind the lens. He sets up a direct relationship with those who are watching him, both mocking and conspiratorial. He does not care that the auto-races are a public and communal occasion; he is absurdly solipsistic, as if to say that only he matters. Only he is worth watching. Chaplin would maintain these sentiments for the rest of his film career.

Two days later, on 9 February, *Mabel's Strange Predicament* was released. This 'short' represented the birth of Chaplin's unique style of cinematic comedy, and of the tramp universally known as Charlie. The cameraman on this occasion recalled that 'I can still see the little shack where he came out of the dressing room. He'd come out and he'd kind of rehearse himself – that walk, the cane, the hat . . . Did it look funny there and then? Yes, it did. Well it was, because it was fresh . . . And his movements, too. Wiggle the mouth and that moustache would kinda work. And the cane flapping around, swinging on his arm . . . and going around on one leg like he was skating.' He was drunk, a reminiscence of his Karno days. He stumbled over a lady, raised his bowler to apologise; then he staggered upon a spittoon, and again raised his hat in awkward apology. He shuffled, with his feet turned outwards. He twirled his cane and knocked off his own hat. He even began to perfect his expression of leering concupiscence. The technicians and performers, standing around, started to laugh. Sennett laughed. Chaplin knew that he had done it.

Mabel's Strange Predicament was the film, therefore, in which he first donned the Tramp's distinctive costume. Like all sacred relics, however, the origin and provenance of the dress are unclear. He had almost as many explanations as he gave interviews. He said once that 'I thought of all those little Englishmen I had seen with their little black moustaches, their tight clothes, and their bamboo canes, and I fixed on these as my model.' Yet he may also have recalled the large shoes and baggy trousers of many music-hall acts in England. On another occasion he suggested that he had taken pieces of other actors' costumes while waiting on set; it had been a matter of chance. But, in contrast, he also explained that his appearance had come 'by degrees'. Then he told one of his sons that he had been asked, as a juvenile, to take the place of a performer who had fallen ill; the man's clothes were too big for him but, when he appeared on stage, he raised laughter and applause. Sometimes he attempted a metaphysical explanation, with the little moustache as 'a symbol of vanity' and the baggy trousers as a 'caricature of our eccentricity, our stupidities, our clumsiness'. He may also have had in mind the 'shabby genteel' of London life whom he knew very well. Any and every explanation is possible.

The fact that he hit upon the rudiments of the costume so swiftly, however, suggests that in some obscure recess of his creative mind he had already imagined something like it. It was the epitome of all the comic tramps he had seen upon the English stage, the quintessence of the 'poor and put upon' little fellow whom artists like Dan Leno had portrayed. The costume then created the performer. In a form of intimate communion with the bowler hat, the cane, the short and tight jacket, the frayed tie, the gaping shoes, he became Charlie. He followed the lead of the character, discovering aspects of its personality all the time. In the sequence of Keystone films he completed, some thirty-five in all, he began to create the 'little fellow' as a living dimension of himself.

The movements came with the clothes. He once said that he had learned his shuffling walk, or 'duck waddle', or 'east and west feet', by imitating the gait of 'Rummy' Binks who used to hold the horses of the customers outside a public house in South London. But he could equally have taken it from a performer, Fred Kitchen, in the Karno Fun Factory.

Two or three days after finishing *Mabel's Strange Predicament* he began work on *Between Showers* in which he played against Ford Sterling, still with the company, who had already attained fame as the chief of the Keystone Cops; he was known as a 'Dutch comedian', essentially a parody of the German immigrant, and he specialised in what might be called the first wave of American film comedy with florid gestures, exaggerated expressions and a general tendency to be over-theatrical in every scene. He gave the impression that film was theatre for stupid people. Chaplin was in contrast more contained and much stiller, even though in this film he does indulge in what is known as 'cocking a snook' by putting the fingers of one hand up to the nose; this was a wholly English gesture that the young Chaplin had used constantly. It came from his training with Karno and also from his familiar acquaintance with the street urchins of South London. Yet the impression remains that Sterling had only an outer, while Chaplin possessed an inner, life.

5

The rhythm

The product at Keystone was despatched quickly. In March 1914, for example, Chaplin completed four short films. Each one lasted between twelve and sixteen minutes. In *A Film Johnnie* he plays a vagrant who stumbles upon the Keystone studio in action, with all the accidents and misunderstandings that may be supposed to follow. Charlie seems utterly bemused by his first sight and experience of the studio, just as Chaplin had been when he first arrived on Allessandro Street.

His director was now George Nichols, a veteran of fast and furious production. Chaplin would suggest various scenes or devices to Nichols, who would then invariably reply 'We have no time! No time.' The other players took Nichols's part and complained that the young Englishman was 'a son of a bitch' and impossible to work with. He was always moaning – about the director, the actors, the stage sets, the plots.

He was hardly a favourite, therefore, with cast or crew. Mack Sennett recalled that in the early days he was considered to be an 'oddball' who 'liked to be lonely'; Chaplin walked the streets 'peering at things and people' and despite earning a more than respectable salary he preferred to live in a shabby hotel. But his appetite for work was undiminished. Chaplin, according to Sennett, 'was the most interested person where he himself, his future, the kind of thing he was trying to do, was concerned, I ever knew'. He came to work at the studio an hour before the others, and stayed after they had left; he would question Sennett about his day's performance, and run over the rushes with a keen eye for his mistakes. He thoroughly learned the art of cutting and splicing.

Tango Tangles followed *A Film Johnnie* one week later. Chaplin is not dressed as a tramp but as a smart young swell. It would perhaps have been something of a shock to audiences, if they had known that Chaplin and the Tramp were the same person, to have seen how young and handsome the actor was. In truth he was still only twenty-four years old, but he seemed younger; he had the looks of a matinee idol, as well as the skills of a professional dancer. In this film he is meant to be inebriated but he plays the drunk with as much grace and fluidity as he plays the dancer; in all of his routines he relied upon perfect pacing as well as precision.

His Favourite Pastime puts Chaplin with 'Fatty' Arbuckle as two drunks who are involved in an endless struggle with a recalcitrant world of swing doors, waiters, other barflies, and steep stairs. This is the kind of routine that Chaplin could now perform in his sleep but the *Kinematograph Weekly* observed that he 'indulges in escapades which are side-splitting in their weird absurdity and their amazing suddenness'. It is confirmation of the fact that the young Chaplin represented something quite novel and unfamiliar on the screen. He was already essentially a solo performer. 'Fatty' Arbuckle himself was as his name suggests the quintessential fat man, although he was extraordinarily athletic and graceful, with a marvellous sense of comic timing. In these respects only Chaplin could equal him.

In this period Chaplin enjoyed his first Hollwood romance. Peggy Pearce played opposite him in *His Favorite Pastime*, as the object of his drunken desires, and soon enough they were close in another sense. But it came to nothing; Miss Pearce lived with her parents, and was conventional enough to insist upon marriage. This was not a state to which the young Chaplin aspired. He did manage to flirt with Mabel Normand, however, until she gave him the refusal absolute after a charity function in San Francisco. Mabel had been with Keystone since 1912. She had been discovered by Mack Sennett and quickly became his lover as well as his principal comedienne; she had a naturally expressive face, and a puckish humour, which endeared her to audiences and to her colleagues. However her rejection did not greatly affect Chaplin, who was incorrigible in making advances to other female film stars. By his mid-twenties he had in fact acquired something of a priapic reputation. He often boasted about his sexual conquests, and once confessed to having had sexual relations with more than 2,000 women. That does not seem a very high number for a rich, handsome and famous man, but it does suggest something of an incurable itch.

He could use, and discard, his partners at will. When asked by *Vanity Fair* in 1926 to describe his ideal woman, he replied that 'I am not exactly in love with her, but she is entirely in love with me.' In his films Charlie can be bashful and diffident with females whom he can only tentatively approach, but vulgar and aggressive towards what might then have been described as 'loose' women. He tips his bowler upwards from every angle when he sees a likely catch; he uses his cane to drag her nearer by the neck or by the legs. One critic noted that 'I have seen Mr Chaplin blithely performing functions in the moving pictures that even I would decline to report.' Whether life followed art, or art followed life, is an open question. It is clear, however, that he funnelled all his sexual energies into his character.

The two short films that followed *His Favorite Pastime* – *Cruel, Cruel Love* and *The Star Boarder* – do not show Chaplin at his best or most original. In the first he parodies stage melodrama, with an exhibition of histrionics in the false belief he has swallowed poison; in the second he gives what may be his first direct look into the camera, with the expectation of sympathy and complicity from his audience. In *The Star Boarder*, too, his cane and shoes are shown before he is; this would suggest that his costume was already well known enough to provoke laughter. At the time of the film's release Keystone also sold a set of four photographs of their stars; they were Mabel Normand, Mack Sennett, 'Fatty' Arbuckle and Chaplin himself. In less than four months he had become an established name.

Yet his character was not set firmly in the imagination of his colleagues. In the next film, *Mabel at the Wheel*, he reverts to the part of stage villain with drooping moustache and histrionic tendencies. His dissatisfaction at the role may have helped to inspire his sudden revolt against Keystone. Mabel Normand herself was the director, as well as the titular star, of the film. When Chaplin suggested an extra piece of comic business, she rejected his advice on the familiar ground that there was 'no time'. At which point Chaplin sat down at the side of the road and refused to carry on with the filming. 'I don't think,' he told her, 'that you're competent to tell me what to do.' The crew predictably took Mabel's part, but he refused to budge. After all, as he said, 'this was my work'.

Mack Sennett was predictably furious at the young Englishman's insubordination. It seemed likely that Chaplin's contract would be torn up and that his days in the silent cinema had come to an abrupt end. Yet on the following morning Sennett approached him in a friendly and obliging way. He had in fact heard from Kessel and Bauman that the Chaplin films were outperforming any others from Keystone, and that more orders were being placed every day.

Chaplin himself may have sensed something of this, because he took the opportunity of suddenly amicable relations to announce that he wished to direct as well as to act. He even offered to finance his first film with his own money. It proved to be an unnecessary precaution. The subsequent Chaplin films at Keystone, all of which he directed except the last, were the most successful in the studio's history.

Twenty Minutes of Love, his first attempt at direction under the supervision of Sennett, was completed in the space of one afternoon. It was scripted, as well as acted and directed, by Chaplin. It is a 'park comedy' in which an assorted array of lovers, policemen, thieves and Charlie engage in a balletic performance of feint and counter-feint before a natural landscape of trees and lawns and bushes and park benches. Of his films it is one of the purest in action, with a series of encounters that recapitulate one another in what could be an endless pattern of meetings and chases. Yet Charlie, as always, stands apart. A look of malice comes across his face when he sees two lovers embracing, and then he sets out to do everything possible to break them up. He is both thief and 'peeping Tom'. The ensuing action has all the intricacy, variety and energy of a thoroughly successful farce.

Caught in a Cabaret, his next film, is a fresh and engaging short picture in which a waiter in a 'low' tavern passes himself off in society as the prime minister of Greenland; in other copies of the film, his card reads 'O. T. Axle, Ambassador for Grease'. The *New York Dramatic Mirror* noted that it may be 'unwise to call this the funniest picture that has ever been produced, but it comes mighty close to it'. It was the first comedy of two reels that Chaplin wrote and directed, with a playing time of thirty-two minutes.

Direction was an energetic and personal affair. He demonstrated to the other actors the attitudes and expressions he wanted from them; he went through their steps and diverted them with handstands and general 'mugging' to lighten the atmosphere. The camera was anchored at middle distance, from which vantage the actors performed in full view with very few close-ups or fanciful editing; this is the way that Chaplin liked it. He always wanted to make sure from the cameraman that his feet were showing. Like a dancer he needed the full revelation of his art. He seemed to have a speed and movement that distinguished him from the other performers; as T. S. Eliot once remarked, 'he has escaped from the realism of the cinema and invented a *rhythm*'. In an interview in 1942 Chaplin remarked that 'movement is liberated thought'.

The Keystone comedies reached the screens of the nickleodeons two or three months after filming had been completed, and so there was a delay in the recognition of the young Chaplin by the public. He was being noticed but he was not yet recognised. The newspapers had different names for him such as 'Chapman' or 'Chatlin' or simply 'Edgar English'. But, as we have observed, this was the age in which a vast public was being drawn to the motion pictures. It became known as 'the age of the common man' with a technology that could cater to his needs and illusions. Chaplin unleashed another aspect of this power. All the dispossessed or lost, or those who had failed in life, saw in him an image of themselves. That was his genius – to turn his early experience of hopelessness into a universal symbol. He saw as much himself, and trembled on the threshold of his fame.

Caught in the Rain, released after *Caught in a Cabaret*, sustains his part as a drunk and philanderer. It was followed by *A Busy Day* and *The Fatal Mallet*. In *A Busy Day* he plays a violently disposed, almost insane, female in the tradition of the London pantomime dames. It was filmed during a four-hour parade in celebration of an expansion of Los Angeles Harbor, and is a miracle of quick timing and improvised performance. In *The Fatal Mallet* Charlie is an unscrupulous and brutal pursuer of women. No female has the *right* to reject him, and they must suffer all the consequences of their folly. Mabel Normand, the object of his lust, is hit with a brick in the face. He sticks out his backside so that he looks like the menacing cock of the walk. He scratches his upper torso and makes a face like that of a baboon.

So Charlie, the 'little fellow', is not altogether a benign figure; he can be cunning, cruel and hostile; he has a taste for brutality;

he bites his opponents and can engage in unprovoked malice; he can conjure up a sickly grin or the imbecilic smile of a drunk; he generally puts his hand over his mouth when he laughs, as if he has something to hide; he thumbs his nose and sticks out his tongue; he exhibits an almost elfin wickedness; he is leering and lascivious, propositioning almost every woman whom he encounters. He colludes with his audience all the time with ingratiating or impish glances; he winks and grins; he mimics exasperation and indignation towards the camera. And he enjoyed the response. He would attend the film-houses, often standing at the back, and loved to hear what he called 'the joyful little screams' that were provoked by his first appearance.

In June 1914, five short pictures were released that helped to reveal the power of motion in the Keystone films. In *The Knockout* Chaplin plays a boxing referee whose gyrations among the ropes and around the ring must have been sedulously choreographed; it was the kind of role he had played for Karno, but now with a difference. The art of the cinema was truly the art of motion; that was how it had been conceived from the beginning; these were 'motion pictures' celebrating all the possibilities of movement. No cultural form had ever been able to achieve that feat before.

In *Mabel's Busy Day*, for the first time, he rolls his bowler hat down the length of his arm and then catches it. The action is played out at a real automobile race, and once again deploys all the resources of frenetic movement. One reviewer described it as 'side-splitting'. For the first time human beings can be seen in collision with the world and with each other; the important moment is the moment of impact, with the awareness of materiality. Chaplin later revealed that the movements of all the players had been rehearsed as if they were participating in a frantically paced ballet. Charlie himself emphasises the quality of dance with his spins and turns and pirouettes.

In *Mabel's Married Life*, Mabel Normand proved that she was as expert a pantomimist as Chaplin himself. When Charlie puts his leg over Mabel's lap, one of his most emphatic sexual positions, she examines the broken sole of his shoe. It is an apt image of their relationship on film. In the concluding scenes he attacks a boxing dummy as if it were a real and dangerous opponent; each time it bobs up he launches an ever more vicious assault upon it. In Chaplin's art his rivals are both comic and sinister. This is a world of possibly brutal violence rendered harmless by comedy; that is the secret of its popularity in the real world of the audience.

The Chaplin phenomenon was now spreading beyond the shores of the United States. Keystone released the first Chaplin films in Britain, in June 1914, with an advertisement asking 'ARE YOU PREPARED FOR THE CHAPLIN BOOM?' and went on to claim that 'there never has been so instantaneous a hit as that of Chas Chaplin'. He had previously been known in Britain as a star of the Fred Karno company, but it was now agreed that he had joined the front rank of film comedians.

Laughing Gas and *The Property Man* followed, sustaining Chaplin's pre-eminence. In *Laughing Gas* he plays the part of a dentist's cleaner who promotes himself to an assistant, allowing room for all the instincts of refined cruelty that Charlie possesses. He terrifies patients with oversized pliers; he engages a female patient in what another period might describe as sexual assault; he tries to revive an anaesthetised victim with a mallet, and even manages to punch waiting customers in the mouth. His logic is always curious. This lady wants something corrected, so he polishes her shoes while she is in the dentist's chair. I have knocked out this man's teeth with a brick. They were rotten. So why is he now complaining? This might be condemned as playing to children; yet Chaplin had already noticed that, in the audiences of his early films, the children always laughed first. He takes his violence to further heights in *The Property Man*, where he kicks an elderly employee repeatedly in the face and head. In the end he aims blows at him just for the fun of it. It has become instinctive. Yet this is the violence of the animated cartoons that Chapin himself helped to inspire; it causes no hurt and produces no injury. The violence of his films, in later years, would in any case be more subtle and subdued.

His next film, *The Face on the Bar Room Floor*, went in a wholly different direction as a parody of conventional romance. One of his strongest tendencies was to deflate, mock and satirise easy or familiar sentiment; in this case an inebriate artist, down on his luck, laments to a barroom audience the loss of an early lover to a businessman. The story was taken from a poem of the same name. *Bioscope* predicted that the film 'will evoke screams of laughter'. But what kind of screams will they be? Bertolt Brecht wrote in his diary, after seeing it, that 'the film owes at least part of its effectiveness to the brutality of the audience'. The same might be said of almost all of the Keystone films.

The Face on the Bar Room Floor is not one of the most eminent of his films, except for a moment of inventive genius at its close. The Tramp sees his erstwhile lover with the businessman, now her husband, together with several small children. His relief at escaping that domestic fate is palpable. He shrugs his shoulders and turns his back to the camera; he stumbles over his shadow, and raises his hat to it. He has immense self-possession and instinctive charm. He begins a resigned walk away, enlivened by a jaunty little jump and quick-step that announces he is once more ready for the adventure of life. This walking off with a 'lift' was to become a characteristic move.

Mack Sennett had now persuaded him to leave his cheap hotel and, on a temporary membership card, to join the Los Angeles Athletic Club where he rented a large corner room for $12 a week. The room contained a piano as well as a row of bookshelves upon which he kept an array of pamphlets, booklets, and more solid volumes of what one friend called 'all the gloomier philosophers'. He had access to the gymnasium and swimming pool, together with the restaurants and bars of the establishment. It was the social centre for the bachelors and businessmen of the town.

He wrote later that he lived in the softest lap of luxury for $75 a week, but it seems that he was not willing to extend his largesse to his friends. Chester Conklin once complained that Chaplin 'was willing to let you buy him a drink . . . but I guess he had not spent much time in London pubs, where he would have learned that it was up to him to knock for the next round'. His meanness, or stinginess, was already very well known.

On 9 August 1914, he wrote what was for him a long letter, on the club stationery, to his older brother in which he expatiated on his good fortune. His name was in capital letters on the bill-boards; he was a huge box-office attraction, and was on the verge of making a great amount of money. He had become a big deal, a big shot, a big fish. He had lots of friends in Los Angeles, and even had his own valet. He was getting on well with Mack Sennett but, as he would often say in the future, 'business is business'. He was also still taking the precaution of saving most of his income.

In the film he made soon after, *The Masquerader*, we see the youthful Chaplin arriving at the studio to begin work; he is cheerful, blithe and energetic. He fools with 'Fatty' Arbuckle at the dressing table before returning to the set dressed as a woman; he is the epitome of femality, coy and inviting, prim and daring, in a series of gestures and expressions that were also characteristic of his male role as Charlie. He was of slight build and delicate features, with small hands that were often said to resemble those of a female. One friend, Carol Matthau, said of him that he 'had what only whole men have – certain feminine qualities'. Mary Pickford, a veteran performer of the early era of cinema, remarked that 'one would never say he was effeminate, but I would consider that he is at least 60 per cent feminine. You can see it in his work; he has feminine intuition.'

His performances have in that respect often been described as 'camp', but that is to mistake the nature of his role. Like all great clowns he partakes of both sexes; he is the born inveigler who goes through the world seeking sympathy and even affection. Why should he not 'come on' to men as well as to women? He puts his hands between his knees and bats his eyelids; he wriggles and pouts; he saunters and swaggers; he often flirts with bullies in order to avert their wrath; he employs all the sexual signals of a woman. He is not parading himself as a homosexual, but instinctively and unexpectedly defending himself against a hostile world.

He was by now creating much more coherent narratives with a particular attention to the eccentricities of his character. In *His New Profession* he takes a tumble and lands upon dog shit before wiping the bottom of his trousers upon the grass; then he proceeds to rob a supposed cripple of his money. Chaplin seems here to be intent on breaking cinematic taboos by creating business all of his own. He was later to confirm that he was a success at Keystone because he turned himself into a distinctive act. Sennett and others never used him in any 'chase' scenes; they knew that it would be a waste of his individuality.

His next film, *The Rounders*, displays him again in the role of a drunk. A 'rounder' was at once a rogue and a bounder, thus illuminating Chaplin's understanding of the part he has to play. In the company of an equally drunken 'Fatty' Arbuckle they stagger from comedy to calamity with equal abandon. There is a difference, however. Arbuckle is a genial drunk. Chaplin is never genial in this condition; he is self-absorbed and utterly impervious to those around him; he deals with everyone and everything in a cruel and arbitrary fashion. He is still infantile in an adult world. He is a stranger in a strange land. Arbuckle said of his acting companion that 'I have always regretted not having been his partner in a longer film . . . He is a complete comic genius, undoubtedly the only one of our time and he will be the only one who will be talked about a century from now.'

The New Janitor, released in late September 1914, shows him in full exploration of the possibilities of the 'little fellow'. The element of pathos now enters the plot. It had already been pressing for entrance, but in this film it emerges almost fully formed. The new janitor is a put-upon, disparaged, and despised, lowly employee; even the lift attendant laughs at him, and obliges him to walk wearily up the stairs. As he steps patiently and slowly, the spectator feels that he has a history of suffering and disappointment behind him. This is a new development for Charlie.

His eventual triumph, when he single-handedly foils a bank robbery, is evidence of a new form of comic drama from Keystone where suspense and sentiment play a larger role than the comic-strip surprise and slapstick that came before. It is not coincidental that *The New Janitor* took seventeen days to complete rather than the two or three days normally expended. It may be that sentimentality was inevitable for the proper creation of Charlie; in the process, he becomes human and sympathetic in ways that were not previously available to him. In *My Autobiography* Chaplin recalled the remark of an actress watching one of the scenes during rehearsal. 'I know it's supposed to be funny,' she said, 'but you just make me weep.'

This ability to convey pathos may have come to him instinctively and unexpectedly; he may not even have noticed it at the time. Certainly he did not attempt to reproduce it in his final films for Keystone. In his next film, *Those Love Pangs*, Charlie reverts to the role of a tough and verminous little brat engaged in a battle to win the charms and attentions of what seem to be prostitutes in the park. He looks disgruntled; he strikes out, preferring a kick in the chest to a punch in the face as a more defiant gesture; he bites a rival's moustache, much more luxuriant than his own.

He contemplates suicide for a moment only, but he is constitu-tionally incapable of emotional self-indulgence. He would much rather fight back.

Dough and Dynamite, like many of Chaplin's films, emerged from a happy inspiration when one day he passed a bakery with the sign 'BOY WANTED' in the window. It became one of the most successful, and most intricate, of all the Keystone comedies. An elaborate set was built, in the absence of Mack Sennett on duties elsewhere; when Chaplin discovered that he had gone over the budget he decided to turn the film into a two-reeler to recoup some of the costs. It ran for thirty-four, rather than for fifteen or sixteen, minutes. He need not have concerned himself with the returns; *Dough and Dynamite*, his thirtieth film, was three times as profitable as its rivals at the time. According to Sennett, this was the film that finally sealed the reputation of Chaplin with the general public. It was said by *Photoplay* that 'people who never went to the movies before were driven by the accounts of the new comedian'. One cinema in New York presented only Chaplin films to its audiences.

He was now coming to the end of his contract with Keystone. Sennett placed guards at the studio to prevent competitors from approaching him, with instructions to interrupt if any stranger came too close. When filming *His Musical Career*, in the late autumn of the year, so many spectators surrounded him in a street scene that the traffic was blocked for some hours. Chaplin's own style was also evolving all the time. He was now interested less in rapid cutting, in the Keystone style, than in longer scenes where his comic inventiveness could be better displayed. One reviewer noted Charlie's 'extreme seriousness, his sober attention to trivialities, his constant errors and as constant resentment of what happens to him'. All this was the fruit of long concentration and meditation.

In his August letter to Sydney, Chaplin had mentioned a long-term project that had consumed much of his attention in the summer. *Tillie's Punctured Romance* has the distinction of being the first full-length comedy ever filmed, at eighty minutes, but it does not really mark any development of his art. Chaplin simply reverts to type as a stage villain enticing and defrauding the large and exuberant Marie Dressler. Dressler herself was a vaudeville star whose hatchet-faced visage was compensated by wild exuberance and extreme overacting. It is she, rather than he, who dominates the picture. He was, as a result, less than enthusiastic about the finished product.

Two last films had been contracted with Keystone, and he got them out of the way as expeditiously as possible. *Getting Acquainted* and *His Prehistoric Past* are by no means the best of his achievements, as he was distracted by the increasing pressures placed on him by various competing interests. Every studio now wanted him. *Getting Acquainted* was the last film in which he would act with Mabel Normand, but he was intent upon moving on. There was one final piece of business to perform. When he inadvertently lifts Mabel's skirt with the hook of his cane, he is embarrassed for the sake of the cane; he spanks it and then scolds it, before giving it a placatory kiss. As he was to say later, 'If what you're doing is funny, you don't have to be funny doing it.'

He had learned a great deal from his first film studio; he had learned how to perform in front of, and direct behind, the camera. He had learned how to improvise, and to follow an inspired idea to its natural conclusion. And he had, after all, created Charlie, the 'little fellow', under the auspices of Keystone. He had made thirty-six films in one year, 1914, and as a result had become the most popular film comedian in America. To some people he *was* film. But he had already rejected the frantic environment of the studio system. He would never work again for another director, and would always write his own parts.

6

The eternal imp

Chaplin left the Keystone studios on a Saturday night in December, after cutting his last film, without bidding farewell to any of his erstwhile colleagues; he spent Sunday in his room at the Los Angeles Athletic Club and on the following day he turned up for work at the Essanay Studios in Niles, California. Of course everyone at Keystone knew about his imminent departure, but he could not bring himself to make a speech or shake hands. He just left. Sennett said later that 'as for Charles Spencer Chaplin, I am not at all sure that we know him'. He had never really been part of the team; he would never become a member of any group.

At the beginning of the negotiations for his future Chaplin had demanded $1,000 a week from Keystone; when Sennett argued that even he did not command such a salary, Chaplin pointed out that it was the name of Chaplin rather than Sennett that sold the films. He was then approached by the Essanay Film Manufacturing Company of Chicago. The 'S' and the 'A' were George Spoor and Max Anderson; Spoor was a cinema exhibitor and distributor, while Anderson as 'Broncho Billy' had become the first cowboy star in cinematic history.

Anderson had become acquainted with rumours about the young comedian's very large demands. Unlike Spoor, he was an actor rather than a businessman. He was well aware of the Englishman's enormous popularity. He may have fastened to the principle that, if he thinks he is worth that kind of money, we might as well give it to him. So through an intermediary he offered Chaplin $1,250 dollars a week with a bonus of $10,000 on signing the agreement.

Unfortunately he neglected to tell his business partner of the arrangement, while Spoor did not in any case believe that Chaplin was worth that much. For his part Chaplin wanted the fresh start that Essanay could provide him. Anderson offered him larger budgets and less exacting deadlines; Chaplin would be able to cut his production by a half, and still earn more money than ever before. Every film would be designated as 'Essanay–Chaplin Brand'.

On that Monday morning Anderson brought him by car to Niles Studios, an hour's drive from San Francisco, where the 'Broncho Billy' films were made. Chaplin did not like what he saw. The studio itself was situated in a large field, with a glass roof that kept the interior unnaturally hot and stuffy. It was soon decided that Anderson and his new employee would make their way to the less cramped headquarters of Essanay in Chicago.

On his first week in the city Chaplin was tracked down by a reporter who noted that 'during his first few days in the Windy City . . . Charlie was wanted here and Charlie was wanted there, from the time he arrived in the morning until he left at night'. Chaplin did remain in one place for long enough, however, to grant an interview in which he stated that critics did not realise that film-makers 'do things on the spur of the moment and that our minds are under a constant strain, for we must concentrate on our work from morning till night'.

The studio itself was in the industrial area of the city, and had once been a warehouse; he soon discovered that it had taken its tone from its surroundings and was run like a business. At six o'clock, whatever the state of the proceedings, the lights were turned off. He also discovered that little had been done to prepare for his arrival. The manager told him that he would find his script in the scenario department. This was the last thing he wanted to hear. He wrote his own scripts.

Eventually he met George Spoor who was still distinctly unenthusiastic about his new acquisition, and refrained from paying the bonus for as long as he could. So Spoor arranged an experiment to test the young comedian's true popularity. He paid a bellboy in a Chicago hotel to 'page' Chaplin. As the boy proceeded to shout out 'Call for Mr Chaplin' a large crowd gathered in anticipation. Chaplin used to tell the story, but it is not necessarily accurate. In his autobiography he also professed not to know the extent of his fame in this period. His recollections are generally unreliable. Whatever the truth of the matter, Spoor realised the worth of his investment when the first of Chaplin's new films had an advance sale of sixty-five copies. By the time filming was completed 130 copies had been ordered. This was unprecedented.

Chaplin made only one film in Chicago. He had left behind his old costume at Keystone, but it did not take him long to recreate the essential wardrobe of the 'little fellow'. He arrived on set in full dress, bowler and cane; it is reported that he then stopped and, in front of a crowded set of stagehands and spectators, proceeded to perform a clog dance like the one he had perfected with the Lancashire Lads. One observer noted that 'they didn't know whether he was crazy or doing it just for their amusement'. And then he shouted out, 'I'm ready!' So filming began.

His presence behind the camera soon became as prominent as his performance itself. He was always shouting encouragement, or whispering instructions. As one of the actresses, Gloria Swanson, recalled, 'he kept laughing and making his eyes twinkle, and talking in a light, gentle voice, and encouraging me to let myself go and be silly'. Ben Turpin, the Essanay veteran with the famously crossed eyes, remembered Chaplin's instructions rather differently. 'Do this, do not do that, look that way, walk like this, now do it over.' Turpin and Chaplin only worked together in three films.

His New Job is set in the film studio of 'Lockstone', very much like that of Keystone, where he plays the role of a stagehand unexpectedly promoted to the part of the 'leading man' with predictable results. It does not represent any noticeable advance on his previous work, although one reviewer came to the conclusion that Charlie was somehow a little 'nicer' than before. It is hard to see any evidence for this. He is still the mischief-maker and eternal imp of the perverse, complete with kicks and punches; instinctively he hits, bites and slaps everyone and everything in sight. For inexplicable reasons Charlie wants to take revenge on the whole world. Chaplin himself said soon after its release that 'it is the very best comedy I have ever produced . . . the greatest comedy of my life. I couldn't help laughing when I saw it on the screen.'

His popularity could not in any case be assailed, and in February 1915 *Photoplay* concluded that 'the art of Charles Chaplin defies analysis, and disarms the critic'; the journalist noticed one element in the growing subtlety or complexity of his performance, however, in the observation that he 'remains emotionless, and even absent-minded, in the very midst of his maddest escapades'. The same reporter interviewed the young man about his past, and stated that he had tried to reproduce 'exactly what he said in the way he said it'.

Among other comments Chaplin spoke of his 'highly cultivated' mother. 'That was in England,' he said, 'she died there.' He added that, after her death, 'I was apprentice to a company of travelling acrobats, jugglers and show-people' and that 'I have never had a home worth the name.' This was perhaps less than fair to his mother, who was still very much alive in Peckham House hospital, but perhaps it suited his mood at the time. The two brothers had neglected to pay the costs of her care, however, and three months after the interview the Peckham hospital threatened to return Hannah Chaplin to Cane Hill asylum; it seems that another relation came to her rescue, and was eventually reimbursed by the Chaplin brothers.

Chaplin did not like the headquarters of Essanay. It had the atmosphere of a bank. The staff were not to his liking, and he was still not happy with Spoor. He completed *His New Job* on 12 January 1915, and six days later returned to Niles Studios for the more congenial company of Max Anderson, who had implicit faith in his art. He breathed more easily, and his invention grew more rapidly, in California; it was still for him the land of the future, the furthest extension of the western world, a place of infinite promise where anything could be achieved. He was established in the state for almost forty years. Niles itself was a junction point of the Southern Pacific Railroad, with twenty-four passenger trains stopping each day to disgorge businessmen and commercial travellers; the photographs of the period show it to be a town of wide and dusty streets lined with two-storey wooden shops and dwellings. The studio itself stood at the western mouth of the Niles Canyon, in which setting many of the 'Broncho Billy' items were filmed.

Niles Studios offered Chaplin only an austere welcome. He was given one room in a bungalow that he shared with Anderson; it consisted of an iron bed, together with a rickety table and chair, and a filthy bathroom. It was noticed, by those who greeted him at the studio, that he brought with him in a cheap canvas bag 'a pair of socks with the heels worn out and an old couple of dirty undershirts', together with a worn-down toothbrush. He was still in part a child of South London.

Under the terms of his new contract Chaplin could complete a film in three weeks rather than three days, without the manager of the studio endlessly hurrying him on, and for the first time he had the luxury of allowing his comic ideas to develop. Chaplin still needed to find a leading lady, on the model of Mabel Normand at Keystone. So on the day after his arrival he placed an advertisement in the *San Francisco Chronicle* that read 'WANTED – THE PRETTIEST GIRL IN CALIFORNIA to take part in a moving picture'. Three girls arrived at the Niles Belvoir Hotel some days later, among them Miss Edna Purviance (to be pronounced as in

71

'reliance'). That is one story of her discovery. Another anecdote suggests that one of the cowboys in the 'Broncho Billy' series remembered a blonde secretary from San Francisco; Chaplin duly interviewed her. It is also possible that he met her at a reception in Los Angeles in 1914. In any event she was pretty and blonde; she was about Chaplin's height, at five feet four inches, and she had a full figure; he soon realised that she also had a sense of fun, and a natural warmth that might project itself upon the screen. And so he asked her to join him.

'Why not?' she replied. 'I'll try anything once.' She was nineteen years old and had no experience of making films, but that was for Chaplin no disadvantage. Rollie Totheroh, one of the cameramen at Niles, recalled that he preferred working with actresses 'who didn't know their ass from their elbow'. Chaplin liked to mould the clay into the shape he most desired. Soon enough he and Edna Purviance played more than screen partners. She moved into a hotel close to his bungalow and they dined together most evenings. She seems to have been as undemanding as she was unpretentious, much better than any other of his lovers at coping with his anxieties and unpredictable moods. He said later that they were inseparable companions and for a while they even contemplated marriage but hesitated on the brink.

Edna Purviance took a part in his second film for Essanay, *A Night Out*. 'After the first day in front of the camera,' she recalled, 'I came to the conclusion that I was the biggest boob on earth.' Yet she added that 'Charlie was very patient with me.' It was soon clear that she possessed a more innocent and less boisterous presence than Mabel Normand, and so her role as Charlie's heroine was a more subtle and delicate one. She was his leading lady for the next eight years in some thirty-four films.

In *A Night Out* Chaplin used Ben Turpin in the routine known as 'the funny drunks'. It is reported that they were so successful, while filming at the Hotel Oakland in Oakland, California, that they were almost arrested and charged with public intoxication. Chaplin swayed and staggered through a pantomime of inebriation that was always an instant success with the cinema audience.

He had already made a career out of drunkenness, perhaps in imitation of his supposed father or of the many inebriates of South London. On some occasions his simple needs and desires are thwarted by an apparently malicious world. Objects become animate. Nothing works. Nothing fits. Doors close suddenly. This is a world of brutality, lust and violence. Chaplin manages a lecherous grin, or puts on a false smile. He is the spirit of London.

On other occasions the drunk inhabits a liquid and unstable world where fantasy and reality are wholly mingled, and where a pleasant state of security or unawareness promotes the atmosphere of dream. It is the perfect context for the way in which Chaplin manipulates real objects for his own ends – by turning a cigarette into a key, for example, or a ladle into a ukelele – while at the same time violating all laws of social intercourse. Chaplin is engaged in wholly irrational behaviour in a wholly reasonable way.

He had gone for the weekend to San Francisco on completing *A Night Out* but, on his unexpected return, he came upon Anderson and one of the cameramen busily cutting and editing the negative. He told them to take their hands off his film. The cameraman at Niles, who had incurred Chaplin's wrath, was Rollie Totheroh. The confrontation was soon over, and amity prevailed. Rollie and Chaplin in fact soon understood each other so well that Totheroh became his principal cameraman for thirty-eight years.

At the beginning of March 1915, Chaplin addressed a letter to 'My Own Darling Edna' in which praised her as the sum and source of his happiness. In *The Champion*, the Essanay picture he was then making, Charlie is about to kiss Edna on camera for the first time; at the salient moment, however, he holds up a large mug of beer to mask their embrace. The public must be kept away. Yet his real partner in this film is a bulldog, Spike, with whom at the beginning he shares a hot dog; he is shown, in the words of the storyboard of the title, 'meditating on the world's ingratitude'. The offer of the hot dog is the first act of altruism to be seen from Charlie; the dog, after all, can give nothing back except a training in kindness. Thus were created the traces of the lovable tramp who would one day come to dominate the films. Love my dog, and therefore love me. He was experimenting with the depth and complexity of his characterisation while at the same time he was refining the subtlety and development of the comedy itself.

The Champion concerns an amateur boxing championship that Charlie wins by sheer bravado and balletic skill. The choreography of the fight was of course devised and rehearsed in exquisite detail. He seems to embody pure athleticism, despite the spareness of his build; in the world of oversized and overactive cartoon characters that populate this boxing ambience, he is a miracle of understatement.

Chaplin himself was devoted to boxing, at least as a spectator sport. He enjoyed the company of famous boxers, and was filmed theatrically sparring with them in the grounds of his studio. He would go to local matches with his colleagues, and was well known to the amateur boxers in the ring who would call out to him. It is also reported that he sometimes acted as a 'second' at the fights.

For his next two films at Essanay, *In the Park* and *A Jitney Elopement*, he took advantage of the Californian landscape. The first of them is more or less what its name implies, a quickly completed one-reeler concerning lovers, policemen, thieves and the 'little fellow'. He had spent so much time rehearsing and supervising the fight sequences in *The Champion* that he was obliged to return to the efficient formulas of Keystone for the subsequent picture.

Charlie has more poise and dash than in the Keystone comedies, however, and it is easy to understand his immense and growing popularity. Did you see what he did? What is he going to do next? His was a completely different kind of character, and the early audiences were mesmerised by his originality. They had never seen anything like it before. One reviewer of the film wrote that 'there seem to be no grey patches in his work. It is all one long scarlet scream.'

At the beginning of *A Jitney Elopement* Charlie is seen clutching a flower; this would become one of his favourite images, worked up over and over again in various situations, in which the blossom represents beauty and transience, sweetness and loss. In this film he impersonates Count Chloride de Lime in order to rescue Edna from the attentions of the real count; it ends in a motor-car chase along the Californian roads. The 'jitney' was a slang term for the Model T Ford.

It caters to the taste of the early audiences for speed and motion, but it neatly supplements a story of drama and character as well as broad comedy. Charlie's assumption of the part of the count is very dexterous; he commits many notable social gaffes without betraying any embarrassment. He is the master of the situation until the real count arrives unexpectedly; it is an exercise in subtlety rather than in slapstick. It might even be said that from this time forward Charlie himself, the 'little fellow', always possesses an aristocratic air; he is sometimes aloof, sometimes condescending; he can be haughty with those who trample on his dignity. He is fastidious, even pernickety. He is decidedly superior to those around him.

Chaplin had been monopolising the studio facilities at Niles Studios, already overstretched by his constant demands and recriminations; he disliked what he called its 'backwoods atmosphere'. So it was eventually agreed that he should rent his own space. By the beginning of April 1915, he had taken over the converted Bradbury Mansion on North Hill Street in San Francisco with his crew and cast, from where eventually he moved to the Majestic studios in Los Angeles.

A farm in California became the setting for the film that has been described as the apotheosis of Chaplin's early style. In *The Tramp* Charlie becomes the 'little fellow' with a heart made to be broken, the tramp with impossibly romantic pretensions. Having saved Edna from the attentions of a gang of thieves, he is taken by her to her father's farm where he is offered work. He is injured by an attack on the farm by the same thieves, and is wounded in the subsequent fight. He is now a small-time hero, but he mistakes Edna's admiration for love. This proves to be the source of his distress.

Chaplin knew or sensed that this film would be a defining moment in his career, and he wanted to bring it as close to perfection as he could manage. Some sequences were repeated forty or fifty times. One of the performers told Stan Laurel at a later date that 'they repeated some gags until the actors felt that if they did it one more time they'd blow their corks'. But Chaplin was relentless until he got it right.

The Tramp ends with what would become the most famous exit in cinematic history; he walks dejectedly away from the camera down a dusty country road. Then happiness suddenly breaks through: he perks up and shakes himself before jauntily going on his way. His little dance upon the road is a form of self-definition. He is free. He is essentially alone but he will never truly be lonely because he is infinitely resourceful. He is self-defined, self-aware and perhaps self-absorbed. He has the will to live in a world that may not be worth living in. The open road is an important conclusion to him; it implies an endless journey, with the Tramp implicitly in the role of Everyman. That is why Charlie was compared to Don Quixote or Sir Galahad, Huckleberry Finn or Hamlet.

At Essanay some were dismayed that Charlie had discarded comedy for pathos. But the ending of *The Tramp* is not sad at all; with the sudden onrush of optimism or high spirits, he has immeasurably deepened the possible range and expression of the 'little fellow'. 'Say,' he asked one acquaintance, 'did you see *The Tramp*? I know I took an awful chance. But did it get across?'

It had certainly required much time and invention to complete; so Chaplin decided to compensate by making a short one-reeler, *By the Sea*, which as its title suggests is concerned with some seaside antics devised by Chaplin and fellow actors. It is all performed with vim and gusto, and demonstrates how good he is at uncomplicated pantomime. As Mark Twain writes at the beginning of *Huckleberry Finn*, 'persons attempting to find a motive in this narrative will be prosecuted . . . persons attempting to find a plot in it will be shot'. But Chaplin never employed the one-reel format again. He had moved beyond it.

The next film, *Work*, represents a return to the more complex characterisation of *The Tramp*. Here Charlie becomes an abused and exploited decorating hand, a member of the proletariat rather than a tramp. Charlie never does like work. He is 'late' more often than not, and he goes through the motions of labour in a completely uninterested and disorderly fashion; when forced to apply himself, he runs about like a mechanical toy that has been over-wound. In subsequent films, in fact, he portrays the horrors of work more often than he depicts the poverty and pathos of the Tramp. He becomes a janitor, a floor-walker and a fireman; he takes the role of a waiter, a baker, a dentist's assistant, a delivery man; he plays a prospector, a policeman, an itinerant glazier, a barber, a counter assistant, a road sweeper, a mechanic on a production line, a caretaker. He even plays the role of a professional comedian. Not even the last of these satisfied him. Work is boring. Work is futile. It might be one of the lessons taught him by his London boyhood.

In *Work* itself he plays a decorator's assistant who cannot muster the elementary rules of his profession. It is a routine he had first learned in the English music-hall act of 1906, *Repairs*, but here it is invested with much greater art. In the opening sequences Charlie is dragging a heavy cart through the streets of Los Angeles, while being whipped and goaded by his employer; he manages to avoid the approaching trolley-cars but is then faced with the prospect of a steep hill. It was a novel form of visual wit and therefore provoked laughter. Originality often does. It is in fact one of the most visually arresting sequences that he ever attempted, and may in part have been inspired by the experimental techniques of D. W. Griffith's *The Birth of a Nation*, released a few months before, a film that Chaplin watched again and again. It may also have been derived from a real scene he had once witnessed where, as he recalled, the laughter had been at the working man's expense. According to the notice in the *Bioscope*, 'the humour is designed to rise in a long crescendo of screams to a climax of roars'.

Chaplin injured his wrist while filming, but such was the hysteria surrounding reports of him that it was widely rumoured he had been killed while engaged in a dangerous stunt.

The pace of his work at Essanay slowed down, as testimony to the care and attention he was now bestowing upon his films. In the first four months of 1915 he had produced some seven films; in the remaining eight months he completed six. It can be surmised that Chaplin spent a little less than two months in making a film of 1,800 feet or a standard two-reeler; for this he used 36,000 feet of negative, which meant that every scene was 'shot' twenty times. With all the trials and changes involved, this implied about fifty rehearsals for each of the scenes.

In this period he embarked upon another ambitious and elaborate project, provisionally entitled *Life*. It was to be the portrait of the lower depths of the city, a place of disease and dosshouses and destitution. Yet it was never made, and the idea is likely to have been turned down by the management on the grounds that the figure of Charlie, in the public imagination, was incompatible with low tragedy. The scene of the dosshouse and its habitués emerged in a later Essanay film, but Chaplin's proposal to deal with scenes of suffering and poverty in the manner of Dickens was never properly fulfilled.

He followed this, curiously enough, with the last of his cross-dressing comedies where for most of the film he masquerades very successfully as a woman. You might in fact say that he *is* a woman;

his is not a female impersonation but a female persona. Charlie becomes Charlotte. *A Woman* was made in the newly refurbished Majestic studios, in which Chaplin changed all the locks and introduced a new security system. He had now become so popular that competitors were more than willing to steal his material or his ideas; he also did not want to be watched when working. It is said that Essanay even built an embankment around the studio to deter competitors.

But although *A Woman* is in many respects a deft and ingenious film its successor, *The Bank,* is a more substantial work. This was the occasion when Chaplin made a deliberate decision to extend the characterisation and behaviour of the 'little fellow' whose capacity for pathos had first been shown in *The Tramp.* He plays a janitor of a local bank who has fallen deeply in love with the manager's secretary, Edna, who of course is unaware of his timid advances. It is a saga of hopeless and helpless yearning punctuated by some subtle and not so subtle comedy; it also contains a dream adventure, in which Charlie rescues Edna from bank-robbers. He had first played the valiant dreamer in the stage comedy, *Jimmy the Fearless,* seven years before.

One scene represents the culmination of this new aspect of the Tramp. He watches as Edna discards some flowers that he had left for her as a love token, and his expression of disbelief, bewilderment and grief is one of the most memorable moments of his career. His is a bleak and frightened face, wide-eyed and distraught. It is the moment when he reimagines what it is to be betrayed by a woman whom he adores, an instant that might indeed go back to his childhood. The pathos was in fact advertised in the posters for the film, where the image of the sorrowful face of Charlie is prominently displayed as the principal attraction for the public. It was clear to audiences now, if it had not been evident before, that Chaplin was no conventional film comedian.

7

Charlee!

In this year, 1915, Chaplin became the most famous man in the world.

It was now widely reported that, on Charlie's first appearance on screen in any of his new films, the audience would erupt in cheers and laughter. In a theatrical revue, *Watch Your Step*, Lupino Lane sang 'That Charlie Chaplin Walk'. Song-sheets were now rolling off the presses with titles such as 'Charlie Chaplin Glide', 'The Chaplin Waddle', 'Charlie Chaplin – March Grotesque', 'Those Charlie Chaplin Feet', 'Charlie Chaplin, the Funniest of Them All' and 'The Chaplin Strut'. Nursery rhymes were written about him:

> Charlie Chaplin, meek and mild,
> Took a sausage from a child.
> When the child began to cry,
> Charlie slapped him in the eye.

The children of Puerto Rico also had a song about Chaplin, warning one another to keep their kittens indoors; otherwise 'Chali Chaplin' would swat them with his cane. It is significant, perhaps, that children were the first to spot the violent aspect of the Little Tramp. A French film-maker said that Chaplin 'was one of the few people a child of this century would know, straight after his parents'.

Chaplin dolls and Chaplin toys, Chaplin hats and Chaplin ties, Chaplin socks and squirt-rings, Chaplin playing cards and Chaplin lapel pins, were soon on prominent display in most of the department stores of the country. There were Charlie Chaplin lucky charms and Charlie Chaplin coins to be used in slot machines. Plaster statuettes of the 'little fellow' were everywhere. Comic strips and cartoons were devoted to him. Books were published with titles such as *Charlie Chaplin's Comic Capers* and *The Charlie Chaplin Scream Book*. He was the inspiration for Felix the Cat. One cartoon depicted two news-boys in earnest conversation. 'Chimmie, who'd you ruther be – th'president or th'kaiser?' 'Aw fudge – I'd ten thousand times ruther be CHARLIE CHAPLIN.'

Cardboard images of the Little Tramp were placed outside the neighbourhood cinemas whenever one of his films was being shown, with the slogan 'I am here today!' Chaplin imitators were now the rage and in the summer of 1915 the *Cleveland Plain Dealer* reported that 'Cleveland has been getting so full of imitations of Charlie Chaplin that the management of Luna Park decided to offer a prize to the best imitator and out they flocked.' (The winner was the twelve-year-old Bob Hope.) In New York the street vendors cried out, 'Get Charlie Chaplin on a balloon!', while other hawkers sold postcards of his image. Children would save their pennies until Saturday, when they could buy Chaplin candy and Chaplin gum. At the local cinemas, according to one reporter, the antics of Charlie 'had the kids in hysterics, the kids – of all ages. Really jumping with laughter.' The craze was alternatively known as 'Chaplinitis' or 'Chaplinoia'. He had become much larger than film. He had become the emblem of popular culture.

Yet his success was by no means confined to the Unites States. The French composed songs in his honour, and Marcel Proust for a time trimmed his moustache in the Chaplin style. At a slightly later date Chaplin became the hero of the Dadaists, and an inspiration to Léger. This was the period when the French distributors rechristened him as 'Charlot' bringing him closer to the figure of Pierrot, the mute and white-faced character of the *commedia dell'arte* who has no real place in the world.

The medical wards of the wartime hospitals were showing Chaplin films as a welcome recuperative, and one critic claimed that 'such a bearer of healing laughter . . . the world had never known'. An English postcard recorded that 'everyone is Charlie mad on this side. Sing songs about him and crack jokes.' Lenin said that 'Chaplin is the only man in the world I want to meet.'

It has been estimated that from 1915 onwards some 300 million people were watching Chaplin. A correspondent of the *New York Times* in Ghana reported that a cinema in Accra was packed by 'Fanti savages from Ashanti land, up-country Kroo boys . . . Haussas from the north of Nigeria.' When Chaplin appeared on the screen, 'there was an immediate chorus of shouts, "Charlee! Charlee!"' It was the only English word they knew. He was soon known across the world from Africa to Asia, Australia to South America. In later years he would be imitated by the folklore performers of Cambodian theatre, by the puppet plays of Turkey and by the kabuki theatre of Japan. In Japan he was known as 'Professor Alcohol' because of the popularity of his impersonation of the 'funny drunk'.

He was the first human being ever to be the object of global adulation far beyond the later cult of 'celebrity'. He said himself that 'I am known in parts of the world by people who have never heard of Jesus Christ.' By an instinct of genius he had created an icon or image of common humanity that was deeply congenial to people around the globe. He seemed to epitomise the human condition itself, flawed and frail and funny.

A large number of companies asked him to endorse their products and, for an appropriate fee, he obliged. Of course Chaplin himself could not conduct all of his financial affairs while at the same time running a studio. He decided to keep the business in the family. Sydney Chaplin, at his younger brother's urging, had already come to California in order to work for Keystone. He had been the more important comic performer in England, and Sennett now hoped that he might make as great an impact as his brother in America. So the brothers were seeing each other on occasions in Los Angeles, where it soon became apparent that Chaplin's fame and profitability were not to be equalled but were instead to be professionally managed. Sydney's contract with Keystone came to an end in 1915, and at once he took up the role of his younger brother's agent.

Chaplin was looking for opportunities elsewhere. He made four more films for Essanay and in a sense they show him marking time. He was impatient to take the next step forward, thus acquiring greater freedom as well as greater resources. Yet he still had to fulfil his contract. *Shanghaied* was released at the beginning of October. It is a nautical comedy in which Charlie is pressed for service aboard a boat of villains. The interior sets were rocked back and forth on rollers to give the illusion of instability, while the scenes on deck were managed by rocking the camera back and forth; these were techniques he would put to equally good use in *The Immigrant*. The film is notable for the display of Charlie's graceful acrobatics in the face of overwhelming difficulties. He dances a hornpipe on a wildly swaying deck, and even manages a complete somersault while carrying a tray of plates. His Karno training was still invaluable. In the course of filming the cast and crew were marooned by bad weather somewhere off the coast of California; Chaplin sent a distress signal to the local town of Venice. It might have added to the sense of danger conveyed in the film itself. Essanay bought him a schooner for some of the scenes, and he blew it up at the end of the picture; the conspicuous consumption is evidence for the profitability of his films.

His next film, *A Night in the Show*, was essentially a reprise of his standard act for Karno in *Mumming Birds*. Once again he plays the role of a louche drunk who cannot help but intervene in the variously mediocre acts of a vaudeville stage. He is not Charlie here but a young aristocrat who cannot hold his drink; no rich character in his films is ever sober, suggesting perhaps his anger and resentment at the class differences that had bedevilled him in England. He intimated that this was one of the reasons he left for the United States. *A Night in the Show* is, if nothing else, a reminder of the act that impressed Mack Sennett and thereby introduced Chaplin to the world.

His penultimate film for Essanay was more ambitious. *Burlesque on 'Carmen'* was loosely based on the novel by Prosper Mérimée and the opera by Bizet, yet in fact it was more closely modelled on two film versions of the same story that had been released earlier in the year. Chaplin always enjoyed parodying the conventions of melodrama and adventure; he delighted in unnatural action and exaggerated gesture. The resigned look, the yearning look, the puzzled look, the desperate look, were all material for his wild caricatures. He could not see a person or thing without becoming it; he could not see a person or thing without spoofing it. No one could play the lover more movingly or genuinely, but the authenticity can be abandoned in a moment. In *Carmen* he is pure expression without emotion.

He was a wonderful parodist or impersonator because he believed passionately and instinctively in his performance, even though he sensed it to be unreal. For him there was no distinction between acting and living. He plays any part intensely, even though he knows that nobody is really there. The American critic, Walter Kerr, put it best in *The Silent Clowns* in his remark that 'we shall often see him collapse inwardly with regret the moment an imposture has ended, or is about to end; there is no way of sustaining it, of committing himself to it indefinitely; and he must now return to his nothingness. The coming nothingness haunts him even as he is being his most brilliantly accomplished'.

Chaplin finished working on *Carmen* even as Sydney was engaged in negotiations on his behalf with the various film producers of New York. He received an unwelcome surprise when

Essanay eventually released the finished film in the spring of 1916. After his departure from that studio, the managers tampered with the finished product; they reinstated all the scenes that Chaplin had edited out and extended the film to four reels with some added material from Ben Turpin. By turning two reels into four, they damaged the quality and coherence of the original production. Chaplin was devastated; their intervention in his work left him so depressed that he took to his bed for two days. It is an indication of how protective he was of his vision. In future contracts he insisted that no one be allowed to interfere with, or mutilate, his finished work.

In that same spring Essanay released *Police*, the last comedy that Chaplin had made for the studio. He felt, immediately on completing it, that it was the finest film he had ever created. This is in fact an accurate assessment. Charlie is here given an instinct for life, an irrepressible optimism and jauntiness in 'the cruel, cruel world'. He is infinitely expressive, with almost every conceivable human emotion passing over his face in quicksilver rapidity. He can be both coy and malevolent, for example, at the same time. He is shabby and plaintive, but unbowed; he is endlessly resourceful and adaptable; he is always being impeded but never defeated; he is bowed but not broken. In the final scene he walks away from the camera with his arms stretched out in a Christlike gesture of joy or exaltation. It is as if he is saying – look, I have come through.

He had finished with Essanay. He was now resting in Santa Monica, in a house facing the sea, where he contemplated what he called 'the future, the future – the wonderful future!' He did not yet know where it might lead him. In February, 1916, Sydney called him to New York where the offers for his services were beginning to multiply. When his train eastward stopped at Amarillo, Texas, he was astonished to be greeted by a deputation from the town; he was equally surprised by the large crowd that gathered around, and by the bunting and flags that decorated the station.

This was his first real taste of the fame that had accrued while, as it were, he was busy working. As the train travelled further east, he saw people in the fields and at the railway junctions waving towards him; it became 'the Chaplin Train'. The crowds were large at Kansas City and Chicago; by the time the train reached New York, the commissioner of the police asked him to get off at 125th Street instead of Grand Union where they could no longer control the traffic and the press of people waiting to see 'Charlie'.

His reaction to this evidence of his great fame was equivocal. He enjoyed it, of course, and the adulation of the crowd always mattered to him; he liked being famous, and became annoyed or depressed if people failed to recognise him in public places. Yet on another level the popularity drove him further into himself; he became more aware of his fundamental isolation. The thoughtless public were cheering a person, or persona, who did not really exist. Success only intensified that irritable sensation of being in need or want of something – or someone – he could not find. His egocentricity, which he himself admitted, left him in perpetual exile. He was tired and, left to himself, withdrawn and melancholy.

Sydney greeted him in New York, with a waiting limousine ready to snatch him away from the crowds. He showed him a newspaper headline, 'HE'S HERE!', and another that read 'CHARLIE IN HIDING!' He did not need to go into hiding. If he was not expected anywhere, and without his comedy make-up, he was not generally recognised. A female New York newspaper reporter, Miriam Teichner, noticed the effect. 'Well,' the clerk at the Plaza Hotel asked her, 'do you think you'd know him if you saw him?' She replied that she thought she would. 'Well, he's right here in the lobby.' She looked, and looked, but she could not see him. She asked a maid to go over to him and give him her card.

When he appeared at an actors' benefit concert at the

Hippodrome in New York he led the John Philip Sousa band to only modest applause. Who was this man? When, however, he executed a few steps of the Chaplin walk, the theatre erupted with cheers and applause.

And what did people actually see when they met Chaplin? He was not tall; estimates vary between five feet four inches, and five feet six and a half inches. Yet it was agreed that he looked very small. An acquaintance from the 1940s, Alistair Cooke, an English journalist, remembered him as being 'tiny'. His head was a little too large for his lithe and delicate body, an effect that was accentuated by his film persona. Miriam Teichner first noticed his smile, saying that 'if there could be such a thing as a smile with a man instead of a man with a smile, Charlie Chaplin's smile is it'.

He was considered by most to be good-looking, with crinkly coal-black hair always ready to curl and large eyes; he had skin like ivory and neat white teeth; his lips were firm and meaty, while his nose was prominent. His eyes were deep blue, an effect of course not seen on the screen. When they were circled with black make-up, in his films, they appear to sink down into his face like pools of sorrow. Some other salient facts might be mentioned here. He was left-handed. He was always smoking and at least until middle age generally had a cigarette in his hand. It was a sign of his nervous disposition.

On 26 February 1916 Charles Chaplin was standing in Times Square among small knots of people when he saw, on an electric sign, the news that 'Chaplin signs with Mutual at six hundred and seventy thousand a year'. He had come to New York to make a deal. Sydney managed all of the negotiations, although Chaplin himself had an acute and highly developed business sense. As Sam Goldwyn was later to observe, 'Chaplin's no negotiator – he just knows he can't take anything less.'

Several companies were naturally interested in enlisting

Chaplin's services; he was after all by far the most popular film actor of the age. The arrangement he signed with the Mutual Film Company of New York was unprecedented; at one stroke he became, at the age of twenty-six, the most highly paid employee in the world. *Reel Times* reported that 'next to the war in Europe Chaplin is the most expensive item in contemporaneous history'.

Soon after signing the contract with Mutual Chaplin told a journalist that 'I am left free to be just as funny as I dare, to do the best work that is in me, and to spend my energies on the thing that people want. I have felt for a long time that this would be my big year and this contract gives me my opportunity. There is inspiration in it.' His immense popular success meant that he now had the power to control all aspects of film production, from rehearsals to the editing room. Mutual had agreed to equip a new studio for him, and to pay for all production costs. He realised, too, that he could continue to fashion and develop the most significant screen character in the history of the cinema.

He had agreed to make twelve two-reel films, at the rate of one each month, for a subsidiary of Mutual to be called the Lone Star Film Corporation; Chaplin himself was of course the lone star. He later described this period as the happiest of his career, and it has been justly concluded that the films he made at Mutual are indeed his funniest and most joyous. He commuted each day from the Los Angeles Athletic Club, where he had once more taken up residence, to the studio south of Santa Monica Boulevard. It was described as being situated 'on the fringe of the motion picture studio area in Hollywood'; it comprised a whole block 'and is probably the most pleasant studio in California'.

It was here that he learned how to perfect his techniques of film-making. His principal cameraman, Rollie Totheroh, explained that 'he didn't have a script at the time, didn't have a script girl or anything like that, and he never checked if the scene was in its right place or that continuity was followed. The script would develop as it went along . . . He'd have an idea and he'd build up. He had a sort of synopsis laid out in his mind but nothing on paper.' He arrived every day at about nine o'clock in the morning, went into his dressing room before emerging in the costume of Charlie. He then gathered his collaborators, and gave them an account of the scene about to be played.

He relied upon intuition, instinct and inspiration; he would improvise with new props and new comic situations. 'Suppose we make him wriggle out and get away,' he might say, 'while the policeman's talking to the other fellow. That should make them laugh.' He sometimes asked his carpenters to build a set only to see if it might provoke some new idea or story. He would revise scenes or create new ones on the set. An actor might he obliged to change his or her make-up and play three or four different parts until Chaplin found the effect he wished for. Elaborate and complex scenes were shot only to be discarded, an almost unprecedented act in a film studio. 'No,' he would say, 'that's not it.' He would think of new beginnings and new endings as he worked. To misquote Carlyle on the nature of genius, he had an infinite capacity for taking pains; each shot might be taken and retaken scores of times until he believed it to be as near perfect as possible. He was as methodical and as systematic as an engineer or craftsman.

There were occasions when the development of a story seemed to pose intractable problems. He would then retire to think, to meditate, and to imagine. In these periods he could be ferocious, almost savage, in his reaction to unwelcome guests. He had to be alone, untouched, unimpeded. He became a world to himself.

The other performers were only there to complement, and to act as foils for, the 'little fellow'. They had no independent life of their own. They were not there to interrupt him. He was the only one that mattered. In a sense they became the automatons of Charles Chaplin, given no room to improvise or experiment with their roles. They followed his instructions exactly. 'Just an ever so little more in that fling of the arm, Tom,' he might say, 'yes, that's it. You've got it.' He told them, 'Above all, don't *act!*' Don't act. That was his refrain. You must think the part. You must be sincere and natural in order to be convincing. They then became a suitable backdrop for his performance.

Edna Purviance was still his leading actress but for some comic roles he brought in other performers such as Albert Austin, Henry Bergman and Eric Campbell. Campbell was the mountainous Scotsman who became the comic villain eternally opposed to the Tramp. Chaplin was staying close to his roots in English music hall; both Austin and Campbell had previously worked in the productions of Fred Karno. Chaplin made it clear to Totheroh, however, that he was always to be at the centre of each scene with the lighting and camera work arranged around his actions. As he prepared to go in front of the camera Edna Purviance would call out, 'Go on. Be cute!'

His first film for Mutual, *The Floorwalker*, had a difficult and protracted genesis. Chaplin at first had no idea whatsoever. It was his practice to walk through the streets of Los Angeles with Sydney beside him; he would spot a scene, or an object in a shop window, and Sydney would transcribe his comments on its possible comic use. One day, while searching for stories, he was present when a customer slipped and skidded down one of the new escalators. At once he had his central image. He ordered that an escalator be constructed on the set, and a department store built around it. It was a brilliant concept of his own devising; nobody had thought of using an escalator before.

The story itself is not important except as a showcase for Chaplin's various comic gifts. In one scene he creates a sketch on dual identity, with his 'double' played by another actor as if they were both standing in front of a mirror. In another scene he launches into an elaborate and graceful ballet, complete with leaps and *entrechats* and pirouettes, for the simple reason that he feels like it; as he dances he is perfectly detached from the actors around him and, at the end of the sequence, he bows to the cinema audience. If all art aspires to the condition of music, as Walter Pater suggested, than all silent film aspires to the condition of ballet.

The virtues of the Mutual contract are already apparent in this first film. The sets are more durable and realistic; the production is more accomplished, and the slapstick more elegant. The plots are also more highly developed, with a recognisable narrative structure; it was no longer comic mayhem but 'situation' comedy. With the same performers around him, in each of the pictures, he was in a position to create what can be called ensemble acting.

In May 1916, Chaplin was afforded the most important praise he had as yet received. In *Harper's Weekly*, 'The Art of Charles Chaplin' by Minnie Maddern Fiske stated that many 'cultured, artistic people are beginning to regard the young English buffoon, Charles Chaplin, as an extraordinary artist as well as a comic genius'. She compared his vulgarity to that of Aristophanes and Rabelais, Swift and Shakespeare. She went on to say that 'if it is true that the test of an artist's greatness is the width of his human appeal, then Charlie Chaplin must be entitled to a place amongst the foremost of all living artists'. Who else has appealed to the Mongolian and Slavonic races, to the Latins and the Teutons? Chaplin was flattered and elated by the praise. Inspired by the comparison he tried to read a play by Aristophanes; but he could not quite manage it.

8

Mutual relations

With fame and fortune by his side, Chaplin began to mingle more frequently with Hollywood society. He was meeting eminent émigrés such as Constance Collier, the English actress, and opulent Americans such as the first Mrs Vanderbilt. His ventures into fashionable life were now part of a larger and more prominent profile. He hired a Japanese chauffeur, Toraichi Kono, for his newly purchased Locomobile; he described him as 'my Man Friday. He is everything.' Kono, as bodyguard and servant as well as driver, remained with him for thirty years. He also employed a valet who acted as a secretary, Tom Harrington, a tall and lean man who was both confidant and amanuensis.

Fame, however, had its less attractive side. He had decided in the summer of 1914 to remain in the United States rather than to return home for the 'call-up' of conscript soldiers. It soon became known that his contract with Mutual expressly forbade him to leave the United States during his year of employment. His compatriots began to send him envelopes containing white feathers, as a token of cowardice, and some British cinemas refused to show his films. Yet other letters were being sent to him by the soldiers at the front, encouraging him to continue producing the films that still made them laugh. It was believed, by some in authority, that his contribution to army morale was far greater than any military role he could assume.

He himself would not have relished the experience. He wrote at the time to Lieutenant Clive Fenn of the Middlesex Territorial Regiment that 'I am sorry that my professional demands do not permit my presence in the Mother Country.' His real sentiments were very different. He told a friend later that the war was 'Not for me! Not for me! I'd have gone to jail rather than have gone into it. I'd have gnawed off my fist rather than get into that sort of thing.'

He continued his fast pace of work at Mutual. No sooner had he finished *The Floorwalker* than he began production of *The Fireman*, a film in which he plays an incompetent fireman. The pole, linking the upper and lower quarters of the station, inevitably has a prominent role. At an earlier date he had passed a firehouse, and had retained its comic possibilities in his mind. *The Fireman* is in some respects reminiscent of the films of the Keystone Cops, with a posse of scrambling and flailing firemen, and has more primitive slapstick than the other Mutual releases. The male bottom, for example, receives more attention than any other portion of the human anatomy in a succession of kicks and thrusts. This adds to the homoerotic nature of much of Chaplin's comedy, although its sexual nature is effectively concealed. All popular comedy, from the *commedia dell'arte* to the contemporary panto-mime, is homoerotic. A children's rhyme ran 'Charlie Chaplin sat on a pin. How many inches did it go in?'

Chaplin was in the habit of screening his latest film, unan-nounced, for the audiences attending a normal cinema programme. He would then sit among them, unknown and unseen, and gauge their reactions; if they did not laugh at a sequence, he would cut it out. It was known as 'trying it on the dog' and he was no doubt generally reassured by the wild laughter that greeted his own performances. One admirer, however, was not impressed by *The Fireman*. He wrote to Chaplin that 'I have noticed in your last picture a lack of spontaneity. Although the picture was unfailing as a laugh-getter, the laughter was not so round as at some of your earlier work. I am afraid you are becoming a slave to your public, whereas in most of your pictures the audience were a slave to you. The public, Charlie, likes to be slaves.' Chaplin kept the letter.

It may or may not be coincidence that *The Vagabond*, the third of the Mutual films, marks a departure in the nature and direction of Chaplin's art. Charlie is invested with an unusual amount of pathos when he seems to fail to 'get the girl' in the shape of Edna Purviance. He has rescued her from a gypsy encampment only to find that her affection for him is supplanted by her love for a young artist. At this point he becomes tearful and soulful. He shrugs his shoulders, and lifts his arms a little, to signal defeat or resignation. He 'makes eyes' at the camera, the eyes large and desolate in the blankness of the white make-up that Chaplin insisted on wearing as the clown. He tries his familiar jaunty walk, after Edna has apparently left him, but he cannot manage it; he slumps forward and leans upon his arm. He has exorcised the rough violence of his earlier films; now he can afford passion, and tenderness. A contemporary, who witnessed the shooting of this scene, recalled that 'there was not a tearless eye among the people who watched spellbound'. Even the crew were moved to tears.

In this film, too, he first plays the violin. The press had recently been alerted to his passion for the instrument and had written that his 'chief hobby is found in his violin. Every spare moment away from the studio is devoted to this instrument. He does not play from notes excepting in a very few instances. He can run through selections of popular operas by ear and, if in the humour, he can rattle off the famous Irish jig or some negro selection with the ease of a vaudeville entertainer.' One of the tunes he played in this film, of course unheard by the audience, was 'The Honeysuckle and the Bee'; this was the air that had entranced him as a child in South London, and one that brought back to him all the misery and pathos of his early years. It represents all the passionate melancholy of his younger self. No doubt it helped his performance.

The Vagabond is of course not devoted to pathos, and even the most sombre moments are enlivened by comic action and comic

94

detail. This conflation of pathos and comedy, of tragedy and farce, is a distinctive quality of the English imagination. It is as prominent in Shakespeare as in Dickens, with all the variations upon it played in the music halls of Chaplin's youth. It might even be suggested, in fact, that an element of Chaplin's genius lay in his transferring that unique sensibility to the art form which would conquer the twentieth century.

His next film, *One A.M.*, was a departure in every sense. With the exception of a short scene at the beginning, with Albert Austin as an increasingly impatient taxi driver, the film is entirely devoted to Chaplin. A slight deviation from the title would make 'One am'. I am. Occasional close-ups of his face emphasise his primacy. It is the ultimate expression of his belief that film was there simply to record his performance.

He plays the part of a drunken toff or swell rather than the Tramp. In this film, in a virtuoso routine, he navigates the alien and increasingly threatening objects of his sitting room and bedroom. He had always treated the world as a living thing, doffing his hat when he stumbles over a stone. In *One A.M.* he falls upstairs and he falls downstairs; he gets into an argument with various animal rugs; he picks a fight with a folding bed; the pendulum of a grandfather clock is as dangerous as a revolving table. It is the most adroit of all his acrobatic acts. It has been calculated that he falls forty-six times in a film lasting twenty minutes; the world even of inanimate objects is perilous. Chaplin, however, is a survivor of indomitable energy and resilience. That is the theme of the film.

One A.M. was not perhaps what the vast audience for the 'little fellow' were expecting. He knew as much himself when he told collaborators that 'one more like that and it's goodbye, Charlie'. It is not clear whether he was referring to himself or to his character. It was perhaps obvious to him that he could not afford to ignore popular taste in favour of his own kind of comic experimentation.

So for his next film he returned to more familiar territory. In *The Count* Chaplin impersonates an important dignitary, a masquerade he has already used in films such as *A Jitney Elopement*. It gives him scope to mimic fake dignity and spurious refinement. He loved in any case to play an impostor. The role of game and fraud appealed to him.

Charlie is a tailor's assistant, before he takes on the role of Count Broko, but he is comically unsuited for any kind of work. He does not understand this. His reaction is to laugh at his own incompetence. When he is fired, he always asks for his back wages. He cannot cope with the social rituals of the world. It may be worth reporting that he spent three weeks on filming one scene alone, in which he kicks his rival while whirling around with a partner on the dance floor. For those weeks a light orchestra was hired to play 'They Call it Dixieland' over and over again.

He was beginning to take increasingly long periods to complete each film. Each scene might now be rehearsed fifty times, and then filmed for a further twenty times. The days of creative labour and the hours of rehearsal were compounded by the strain of acting and of direction behind the camera. Upon him alone rested the success of the entire expensive enterprise. This exhausting toil was followed by the endless work in the editing room where he would choose, perhaps, between frames thirty-seven and thirty-nine before splicing together another sequence. His impatience and frustration at delays, as well as his notoriously volatile temperament, also took their toll.

It was in this period that his relationship with Edna Purviance began to fail. He had been told that she was interested in another man, a leading actor at Paramount, and he had feigned indifference. They patched up matters after an impromptu dinner, but he was aware of his own failure. He had been concentrating all his attention on his work and not on her; he had expected faithfulness without in any sense earning it. When he stayed in New York, for example, he did not write to her. When he saw her and the actor from Paramount together once more, he sensed the truth of the matter. Even though their professional relationship continued, their more intimate attachment would soon come to an end.

An unwelcome intrusion into his private life was safely averted in the autumn of this year when he managed to prevent the publication of a volume entitled *Charlie Chaplin's Own Story*. It was based upon a series of interviews he had given to a journalist from the *San Francisco Bulletin*, Rose Wilder Lane, in the previous year. Chaplin complained, through his attorney, that the book was an exercise in fabrication and fantasy. It is still an open question, however, who was responsible for the extravagant untruths. Rose Wilder Lane merely called herself a 'faithful transcriber' and 'editor', and indeed Chaplin thanked her in a note on the verso of the title page for her 'invaluable editorial assistance'.

It is in fact a work of romantic fantasy in which the narrator charts the adventures of his life in a manner not unsuited to Dickens, but there is so much local detail that it can only have come from the memory or imagination of Chaplin himself. He describes himself at one point as 'a precocious, self-satisfied, egotistic boy, able to imagine unreal things and think them true'. The impression that the book gives is in any case of more importance than the facts of the matter. The narrator is self-assured and somewhat domineering with a great sense of his own importance; he is instinctively histrionic, a born actor who treats his contemporaries and his colleagues very much as his inferiors.

He began work on his next film for Mutual, *The Pawnshop*, in the early autumn of 1916. It is one of his most celebrated and successful works, largely because it is also the most inventive. The comic business piles scene upon scene, situation upon situation. A clock becomes a tin can, a doughnut becomes a dumb-bell, and the mouthpiece of a telephone becomes a magnifying glass; he teeters wildly upon a stepladder, and turns a tape upon the floor into a high wire. He seems to create the maximum effect with a minimum of effort. Great art may lie in the concealment of art.

The Pawnshop was followed by *Behind the Screen*, where Charlie is once more a put-upon employee risking all of the hazards and obtaining none of the rewards of hard labour. On this occasion he is a prop-man's assistant in a film studio, which affords him the opportunity of satirising the clichés of the cinema; he is implicitly differentiating himself from the conventional sets and characters of his contemporaries. The film also contains the longest pie-throwing scene in the whole of Chaplin's work; this itself is a joke against some of his fellow comics.

Just after he had concluded *Behind the Screen* something inexplicable seemed to happen. The Boston Society for Psychological Research was called in to examine 'certain phenomena connected with the simultaneous paging of Mr Charles Chaplin, motion picture comedian, in more than eight hundred large hotels of the United States' on 12 November. The society concluded that 'we find beyond peradventure that . . . here existed for some inexplicable reason a Chaplin impulse, which extended throughout the length and breadth of the continent. In more than eight hundred of the principal hotels Mr Chaplin was being paged at the same hour. In hundreds of smaller towns people were waiting at stations to see him disembark from trains upon which he was supposed to arrive.'

The truth of the matter is now irrecoverable, although it was suggested at the time that the image of Charlie had so entered the popular consciousness that he had become a national obsession. One newspaper in Memphis, in the following year, noted that American boys treated him as a companion; they talked to him on the screen, registering approval or disapproval of his actions. They also 'bid him goodnight as though he was present in person.

His astral body does the same work on the screen that his physical personality is expected to do.'

His next film, *The Rink*, offered a reprise of the act that he had performed for Fred Karno in *Skating*. He soon reacquired all of his skills, and his movements upon the ice are overwhelmingly graceful and melodic; he has once more triumphed over an unstable and unreliable environment. The same fluency was not enjoyed by some of the other actors. Eric Campbell, once more playing the villain in elaborate stage make-up, had to be pushed upon the rink where he remained practically immobile until he was kicked by Charlie in the abdomen. Charlie loved to laugh at the misfortunes of others. It is also significant that the other performers did not know what he was going to do next, and had instinctively to react. It is perhaps also worth noting that Charlie gains strength and resilience *after* he has been knocked down; this effect may derive from the early experiences of his life.

At the end of 1916 Chaplin was offered a large sum to appear in a musical comedy on the stage, but he refused. He had no ambition to return to the theatre and, in any event, he had more than enough money. In *The Floorwalker*, on discovering a bag full of notes, Charlie had called out 'Spondulicks for ever!' That was essentially Chaplin's situation. He was now making $10,000 a week, most of which he put aside. His assistant, Tom Harrington, paid almost daily visits to the Los Angeles Stock Exchange in order to handle his employer's investments. Chaplin also relied upon the acumen of his brother who knew all about stocks and shares, bonds and units, and other such financial wizardries; Sydney had been working on his brother's accounts for over a year.

He was at the same time trying to 'improve' himself and there is some evidence to suggest that he informally employed Constance Collier to act as an elocutionist. She had been a famous actress in his youth, and now earned her living by training incipient Hollywood stars in performance and deportment.

The nature of his accent has always been unclear. It is more than likely that as a boy he had a strong cockney accent, although even in his first days in the theatre he may have attempted to acquire the tones of 'stage English'. His mother may also have been instrumental in teaching her talented child how 'to speak proper' in what would be considered a cultured voice. He was always a clever impersonator, and the effort would not have been prodigious. It is possible that he possessed a range of accents that he employed as the occasion demanded. In the 1920s he was described as having 'a strong English accent . . . a musical, cultivated voice with an occasional indefinable whiff of cockney'. In later years he had a decidedly theatrical tone, pitched quite high, with slightly clipped diction and a distinct American twang. He pronounced the 'a' of 'dance' as in 'bank'.

His four last pictures for Mutual, released in 1917, are some of his finest. They are the fruit of much indecision as well as contemplation, with the plot and direction of at least two of them being altogether changed in the process of filming itself. *Easy Street* is supposed to derive from East Street in Walworth, in which Chaplin believed himself to have been born. The sets for the film were otherwise designed to reproduce Kennington itself. It is reported that, in his excitement, he gave explicit instructions to his set designers to build a street and junction that were modelled on the neighbourhood of Methley Street, where he had lived with his mother beside a slaughterhouse and pickle factory. As always he wanted the work to be done immediately, and grew angry at any delay. In truth there is not much resemblance between Easy Street and Methley Street, except through the prism of an angry and overheated imagination. It seems to be just a generically rough urban street.

Charlie becomes a policeman in the film, while under the influence of a religious reformer played by Edna Purviance, and he is soon confronted by the bully of the street in the form of

Eric Campbell. The usual rough and tumble ensues, but it is marked by inimitable pace and timing; the scenes of fight and chase, for example, are exquisitely choreographed so that everything seems to move as naturally as a bird in flight. *Easy Street* is also endlessly inventive. In one scene the little policeman subdues the gargantuan bully by the simple expedient of pulling a street lamp over his head and turning on the gas. Chaplin injured himself in one of the takes of this scene but, typically, he did not react or cry out until the filming was completed.

The role of policeman may not seem to suit the 'little fellow' but, as Chaplin explained before the film's release, 'there is further contrast between my comedy walk and general funny business and the popular conception of dignity that is supposed to hedge a uniformed police officer'.

The Cure, Chaplin's next film, did not appear until three months later, an unprecedented period of gestation. He plays a 'funny drunk' who resists all the blandishments of temperance while on a visit to a health spa. Surviving out-takes reveal how scenes were dropped or rearranged, how old ideas emerged again at the last minute, and how much action depended upon chance and improvisation. It took him eighty-four takes, and a redesigned set, even to establish the opening of the film.

Chaplin hired in this period a publicist, Carlyle T. Robinson, who remained with him for the next fourteen years. When Robinson first arrived at the Lone Star Studios he quickly discovered that 'Chaplin was a very difficult person to meet, even within his own studio. I learned also that it was absolutely forbidden for strangers to penetrate into the studio, that the star did not like journalists, and did not at all wish to be bothered by old friends, even those who had known Charlie Chaplin when he played in the English music halls.' This indifference to old friendship was characteristic of him.

Robinson also discovered 'that his hours were very irregular, and most of his demands impossible to satisfy, that he had very strong likings and even stronger hatreds'. Those whom he seemed to favour were disliked by the rest of the crew, but his prestige was such that he decided all relevant issues on and off the set. Rollie Totheroh recalled, too, that 'he was the most lovable, likable person in the world when everything was going right. He could be like a Jekyll and Hyde. One day he's a swell man and then he would be mean. All he had to do is give you a look; you could feel he hated your guts.'

Chaplin's next film for Mutual, *The Immigrant*, is perhaps the most celebrated of this period. It began in the studio as a 'serio-comedy' set among the habitués of Parisian nightlife; so the opening scene originally takes place in a cheap restaurant where Charlie and Edna are customers. It seemed too tame and Chaplin decided to cast Eric Campbell as the irascible head waiter, a change which considerably altered the pace and tone of the proceedings. Charlie cannot pay the bill and is only able to find the money after a series of ingenious and intricate pieces of comic business; the sequence is a miracle of small moves, each one of them filled with suspense and anticipation.

But then Chaplin began to ask himself the reason for Edna's presence in the restaurant with Charlie. From this enquiry arose the idea of strangers in America. *The Immigrant* was therefore devised out of indirection and improvisation. In the out-takes of this film Chaplin sometimes steps out of character and shows flashes of irritation or even anger at the actors or extras. 'Stop! Stop!' he calls out at one point, with a ferocious expression upon his face.

The first 384 takes were concerned with the restaurant, while the last 345 were scenes upon the boat carrying an assembly of immigrants to New York. Chaplin seemed to relish scenes upon boats and the possibilities of sea-sickness; it was a way of creating an unsettled or fluctuating world in which the 'little fellow' must at all costs maintain his equilibrium. It was the bedrock of all his art. In the finished picture that which was filmed last, on board the boat, is shown first so that the story of *The Immigrant* flows more naturally. It becomes the narrative of strangers arriving in a strange land. Just as the Statue of Liberty comes into view, for example, the ship's officers rope off the travellers in a spirit far from libertarian. It is one of Chaplin's first statements of quasi-political satire, but it provoked no complaint. He was always in a sense an 'outsider' in American society, with a very English appetite for anarchy that saved him from self-righteous moralism. He never really fitted in anywhere.

Chaplin wrote later that *The Immigrant* touched him more than any other film he had made. It is a story of survival against the odds in a desperate world; Charlie is both trickster and trusted companion. At the end he takes Edna Purviance to a registry office in pouring rain, which aptly suggests the poignancy and ambiguity of the situation. Can they find consolation together in an alien world?

Chaplin had shot more than 40,000 feet of film that now had to be reduced to 1,800 feet for the distributors. So for four days and four nights, without intermission, he retreated to his editing room; he might view the same scene forty or fifty times, removing an inch here and an inch there.

He was so exhausted that he went to San Francisco with Sydney for a week before going on to Sierra Madre where he was to shoot a few scenes for his last film with Mutual, *The Adventurer*. He then moved to Topanga Canyon which runs down to the beach at Malibu. This was the place where, in the course of filming, he observed a large rattlesnake coiled in the road; he was apparently so unnerved by the sight that he cancelled the shooting for the rest of the day. He was a child of the city, and never did like nature. He was frightened by large moths, for example, and by the crawling things of California.

In *The Adventurer* he has escaped from prison, perhaps a metaphor for the end of his contract, and becomes an honoured guest in the household of a wealthy mother and daughter whom he has rescued from drowning. Once more he is an impostor, relying upon his quick wits and lightning speed to escape the clutches of his pursuers; in a film that contains more slapstick elements than usual, Charlie relies upon cunning and ingenuity to find his way. In one sequence he poses as a lampstand to elude the police. He refills his glass by falling upon someone else's. He stated in an article at the time that he relied upon two devices in this type of comedy. 'One was the delight the average person takes in seeing wealth and luxury in trouble. The other was the tendency of the human being to experience within himself the emotions he sees on the stage or screen.'

After completing *The Adventurer* he travelled to Hawaii for five weeks with Edna Purviance; it was the last holiday they would enjoy together. It marked also a change in Chaplin's life.

9

The little mouse

At the time *The Immigrant* reached the film-houses and nickelodeons, in the early summer of 1917, Chaplin signed a contract for
$1 million. Mutual had already offered him $1 million for eight
new films, so profitable had he proved, but now he was concerned
with more than money. He wanted all the time in the world and
the very best of working conditions. On his way to New York for
further negotiations Sydney disclosed that the succeeding Chaplin
films 'will have a continuous story running through them' rather
than a succession of humorous stunts or situations.

In fact Chaplin had already created 'a continuous story' in films
such as *The Immigrant* and *Easy Street*, but he wanted to go one step
further in the direction of independence. He wanted, above all else,
freedom from constraints. He managed this feat with First National
Film Corporation who guaranteed him an advance of $125,000 on
each film together with a direct split of the profits. Chaplin would
be his own producer, and would have his own studio, without the
interference of any executives more intent upon money than quality.
He had become an independent film-maker at last, and was free
now to experiment in ways unavailable to him before. It might also
be said that, with his permanent cast of players, he had become an
actor-manager in the Victorian theatrical tradition. The company
required a steady staple of two-reel films to satisfy the demands of
the distributors, but Chaplin's ambitions were more profound. He
was supposed to deliver eight films within eighteen months; as it
turned out, he delivered nine over a period of five years.

His studio, the first ever created for an individual performer, was erected on the corner of Sunset Boulevard and La Brea Avenue. It was decided that, in the interests of maintaining good relations with the residents, the facade would be that of a row of 'Tudor' cottages. Film studios were not necessarily welcome in respectable communities. When the building was about to be completed Chaplin put on Charlie's famous big shoes, and marked his footprints in the wet cement; with his bamboo cane he then wrote his name and the date of 21 January 1918.

The set occupied five acres of what had once been agricultural land – still interspersed with trees of orange, peach and lemon – with two large open-air stages, dressing rooms, workshops for building the sets, a film developing laboratory, a projection room and editing suite together with a tennis court and swimming pool. An old dog kept fitful guard by the studio gates.

Chaplin's own office was situated in a modest bungalow. Alistair Cooke, some fifteen years later, described it as possessing 'one small window, three straight-backed wooden chairs, an old table, about half a dozen books with peeling spines, and an ancient upright piano hideously out of tune'. Chaplin needed the security of a working environment not fundamentally different from that he had known in childhood. He also liked familiar faces. He employed Alf Reeves, with whom he had been acquainted since the days of Karno, to become general manager of the studio, in which post he remained for the rest of his life. A snatch of their conversation has been recorded.

'You're a bloody slut!'

'You're a bigger bloody slut!'

'You're a double bloody slut!'

This was now Chaplin's kingdom where he would remain for the rest of his time in the United States. Carlyle Robinson recalled that when Chaplin arrived at the studio each morning 'instantly everybody stopped what they were doing. Actors, stagehands, electricians, everybody stood in line, at attention. Then Chaplin entered the studio gates.' The luxurious car was driven by Kono, with Harrington also sitting in the front; Harrington would then jump out and open the door for his employer. This routine did not vary, and the studio typist told Robinson that 'the whole gang does that for a gag. Charlie has no illusions, but he adores it.' It is reported that the studio employees knew his mood, stormy or sunny, by the colour of the suit he wore each morning.

He still had one favourite pastime that took him out of the environment of the studio. He liked to indulge in deep-sea fishing off the Californian coast, and one photograph shows him posed beside a great fish almost twice his size with the inscription 'Merlin Swordfish Caught by Charlie Chaplin at Santa Catalina Island, 10-6-18'. It took him twenty-two minutes to land it.

Six days before the studio was formally opened, Chaplin began work on his first film for First National. *A Dog's Life* amply satisfies his concern for a clear story and precise structure to guide the action and comic business. The film opens with the Tramp sleeping in a vacant lot, all the pathos and pity of his situation captured in this depiction of the vulnerable sleeper curled upon the dusty ground like a small and gentle deer. This seems to be real dirt, in a real situation. He is more haggard and hollow-eyed than ever before. He is more fragile and more tender than the figure of the Keystone or Essanay comedies, largely because he is able to invoke the inner life of the Little Tramp who is at once tremulous and bemused. He rescues a half-starved dog, and then wins the affections of a lonely barroom singer down on her luck. The three of them join together to fight the world. Charlie himself has the indomitable energy and determination of a child, his ingenuity and inventiveness amazing.

He had for some time been looking for comedy dogs, and brought into the studio twelve of them for the production; the star of the film, however, was a mongrel called Mut whose stage name was Scraps. An entry in the accounts of the studio, 'whiskey (Mut) – 60 cents', indicates that the dog was rendered unconscious for one scene where he had to be asleep. Chaplin became

107

dissatisfied with the production three weeks after the beginning of shooting, and for a day or two considered another comedy. Then he returned to *A Dog's Life*. It was a three-reeler, Chaplin's longest and most elaborate to date. It was received with great acclaim and the French critic, Louis Delluc, described it as 'the first complete work of art the cinema has'. A more recent critic, Dan Kamin, has called it 'arguably Chaplin's most perfect film'.

Before the film was released Chaplin joined two of his Hollywood friends, Douglas Fairbanks and Mary Pickford, on a tour to rally support for what were known as Liberty Bonds used to finance the American war effort. It may have been his way of atoning for the fact that he played no other part in the First World War. Fairbanks and Pickford were by now considered to be the king and queen of Hollywood. Fairbanks had begun work with D. W. Griffith in 1915, and his athleticism and physical grace soon turned him into the swashbuckling hero of the silent cinema. By the time of the tour in 1918 he had become America's most celebrated film actor, whose aura of romance travelled with him from the screen into Hollywood life.

Mary Pickford had an earlier start, in 1909, and until the advent of sound seeemed never to be off the screen. She was known as 'America's sweetheart' or 'the girl with the golden curls'. By the time she toured with Fairbanks and Chaplin she was the most famous female actress in America, but her girlish beauty and whimsical manner concealed a sharp brain and a practical business sense. In 1916 *Photoplay* magazine described her 'luminous tenderness in a steel band of gutter ferocity'. When they set off, therefore, they were the three most celebrated stars in the world of film.

On their train journey to Washington Chaplin slept for the first two days, an indication of his exhaustion after weeks of filming; he was nervous of making public speeches but, when he had 'warmed up', he was impassioned and eloquent. He was an actor who always rose to the occasion. He became so spellbound by his own oratory in Washington that he fell off the platform and landed on the assistant secretary of the navy, then Franklin D. Roosevelt. In New York he and his fellow actors were greeted by wildly excited crowds who packed the area of the Sub-Treasury on the corner of Broad and Wall Streets. When Fairbanks hoisted Chaplin on to his shoulders, pandemonium ensued. 'Now listen,' Chaplin said to cheers and laughter, 'I never made a speech before in my life. But I believe I can make one now!' He demanded money for the troops 'so that we can drive that old devil, the kaiser, out of France!' The sentiment was enthusiastically received, and Chaplin gained some notion of the uses of fame. There are photographs of him, bowler hat in hand, and with a megaphone at his mouth.

His itinerary now took in Virginia, North Carolina, Kentucky, Tennessee and Mississippi. In New Orleans a local politician protested that his name was beneath that of a 'vulgar movie actor' on the posters; the politician drew 400 people, while the vulgarian attracted 40,000. Yet Chaplin was becoming tired of the constant travel and nervous excitement. Pleading exhaustion he returned to Hollywood by way of Texas, and was ready to start work again at the beginning of May. He had been away for almost two months. He and Fairbanks had become close friends in the interim. Both of them enjoyed huge and sometimes overwhelming popularity; like two passengers stuck at the top of a Ferris wheel, they clung to each other for support.

He had also made another acquaintance. He met Mildred Harris at a party given by the producer, Samuel Goldwyn; she was sixteen years old but had been a child actress for the last five years. Her mother was a wardrobe mistress at another film studio, and so presumably knew all the ways of Hollywood. There is no doubt that Chaplin, at the age of twenty-nine, soon became preoccupied and in the end infatuated by the girl; she had blonde hair and blue eyes, and was described by one newspaper as a 'dainty screen favourite'. Chaplin himself was young, handsome, and of course one of the richest actors in Hollywood. He was, for all concerned, a tempting prospect. He sent bouquets of roses to the Cadillac Hotel in which she was staying, and sat in his car outside the Lois Weber studio as she left work. She said later that he had been 'so fatherly' and 'acted to me as though I had been a mere child'.

It seems that soon enough, however, they became lovers. In his autobiography Chaplin claims that it was the girl who made the advances, but this is open to question. It is certainly true that Mildred Harris and her mother were ready to take advantage of the promising situation. By June reports of marriage began to emerge, only to be denied by the parties involved. Mildred Harris stated, in the familiar fashion, that 'we're just very dear friends'.

He could be a dazzling companion. Many contemporaries have recalled his routine at parties where he would imitate the manner in which the leading ladies of the day might experience orgasm. He would play the part of a bull and matador. He would dance with invisible balloons. Whenever he told a story he acted it out in mime. He had always to be at the centre of attention, even in the presence of other famous people. Yet he would soon tire of company and long for privacy; he retreated from the party in order to play the violin. On these occasions he could become nervous, withdrawn and morose. This was the side of his character that Mildred Harris had perhaps not yet seen.

He began work on his next film, *Shoulder Arms*, soon after his return to Hollywood. It was perhaps for him a natural consequence of his Liberty Bond tour, during which he had also visited army training camps. He had decided now to play the part of a soldier in battle on the Western Front. This might be considered sensitive material, if it were believed that Charlie was about to caricature the private soldiers known to Americans as 'dough boys'. Yet Chaplin resisted the objections. He knew well enough that the 'little fellow' had the ability to create a plucky, resourceful and sympathetic hero. He could become once more an Everyman, a cinematic version of the good soldier Schweik.

The first reel was to be devoted to Charlie's civilian life before being conscripted, but the scenes did not meet Chaplin's standards and were rejected. The film begins *in medias res*, with Charlie being drilled in preparation for conflict; he cannot of course get his legs and feet to combine together or to point in the right direction. Scenes at the front follow, with all the boredom and horrors of trench warfare nicely exaggerated without at any time turning them into parody. His bunker is flooded, and he can only sleep with the horn of a phonograph as a snorkel. When asked how he managed to capture unaided thirteen German soldiers, he replies that 'I surrounded them.' Behind enemy lines he puts on the costume of a tree, and in effect becomes a tree to the extent that he is hard to spot in a forest scene.

He had completed the film by the middle of September but, anxious and dispirited, he could see no comedy in it. He was about to consign it to oblivion when Douglas Fairbanks, having asked to see the picture, laughed all the way through. It occurred to Chaplin that it might perhaps be humorous after all. In fact *Shoulder Arms* became an instant success and, in the language of the time, was 'the talk of the town' with individual scenes being discussed and anatomised by critics and audiences alike. It was released in October 1918, a month before the armistice was signed; the returning soldiers appreciated it as much as the civilians they had left behind.

In the course of filming the last scenes of *Shoulder Arms* Mildred Harris informed him that she was pregnant with his child. This of course threw him into a panic; the last thing he wished for, at this stage in his life, was domestic responsibility. Of all things, he required liberty. His first thoughts were of escape. But if he refused marriage, he might expect terrible scandal to follow; he had, after all, impregnated a young girl. He asked Tom Harrington to arrange a closeted marriage at the home of the local registrar on 23 October, after the studio had closed for the day. The reaction of Edna Purviance was stoical enough. She encountered him at the studio, having read of the wedding in the newspapers. 'Congratulations,' she said. He wrote later that 'Edna made me feel embarrassed.'

He leased a house on DeMille Drive for himself and his new bride, which was described by one of her friends as a 'symphony in lavender and ivory, exquisite in every detail'. Soon after they had moved into this paradise, however, it became clear that Mildred was not pregnant at all. She had either misread her symptoms or, perhaps with the connivance of her mother, she had tricked him into matrimony. The suspicion could not have made married life any easier to bear. He knew that he was not in love with her, and very soon he was beginning to regret the union. Her presence sometimes became an irritation and he confided to Douglas Fairbanks the unremarkable news that 'she was no mental heavyweight'.

He was also distinctly unimpressed by her wish to become a film actress, no doubt trading on the name of Chaplin, but two days after the marriage she began negotiations with Louis B. Mayer of Metro-Goldwyn-Mayer. This led to an angry quarrel between husband and wife. Harris wrote in an article later that 'I think he was right. But he ought to have had a little more patience and consideration of youth.' Patience and consideration were, with Chaplin, always in short supply. She had wanted the glamour and excitement of the film colony; he needed space and time to work for himself. She was given her own chauffeur, servants and unlimited credit at the shops or department stores she frequented. He could not give anything of himself. He walked out of the house early each morning. He became irritable and moody in her company. By November, however, the new Mrs Chaplin was indeed carrying his child.

His matrimonial difficulties actively impeded his work on the next film for First National, *Sunnyside*. He agonised and despaired over the process of filming. There were occasions when he closed down the studios and went on excursions with favoured friends, but not with his wife; he might be away for a day or two at a time without informing her.

It was not a happy time for anyone concerned with Chaplin. At one stage Mildred entered the Good Samaritan Hospital where she remained for three weeks; it was reported that she had suffered a nervous breakdown. Towards the end of the year she was ordered, for the sake of her baby, to take a complete rest cure at a sanatorium north of the city, to which place Chaplin did not accompany her. When she eventually returned to Los Angeles, Chaplin spent very little time with her. She once complained that 'Charlie married me and then he forgot all about me.' A photograph of him at the time shows him to be weary and unshaven. 'I hate this picture of me,' he commented. 'I look bleary-eyed, like a murderer. No wonder!' In *Sunnyside* itself he also looks noticeably gaunter.

There was talk of his mother leaving her asylum in England and travelling to the United States to be with her sons, but Chaplin did not approve of the idea. He cabled his brother, who was then staying at a hotel in New York, with the message 'SECOND THOUGHTS WILL BE BEST MOTHER REMAIN IN ENGLAND SOME GOOD SEASIDE RESORT. AFRAID PRESENCE HERE MIGHT DEPRESS AND AFFECT MY WORK.'

His problems were compounded by his growing unease with First National. He said later that 'the company was inconsiderate, unsympathetic and short-sighted', by which he meant that they refused to comply with all of his demands. He was already supposed to have delivered eight new films, but had in fact finished only three and embarked upon a fourth. It meant nothing to First National that *A Dog's Life* and *Shoulder Arms* had been instantly popular and profitable; they knew only that Chaplin had not fulfilled the terms of his contract. He asked for larger advances to maintain the quality of his work, but his appeal was rebuffed. He threatened to turn over five short comedies to meet his contractual demands, but he could not guarantee their quality. His threat did not work. They no doubt surmised that the name of Chaplin would be enough to sell anything.

It was in this period, therefore, that he opened negotiations with D. W. Griffith, Douglas Fairbanks and Mary Pickford to open their own studio without the demands of an overweening management. They had decided that it would be more profitable to invest their own money, produce their own films and distribute the finished product themselves. They would then become truly independent. Eventually their association was named United Artists. Yet, before he could begin work on this new enterprise, Chaplin still had to complete five films for First National.

Sunnyside was released in June 1919, and was not greeted warmly by the critics. An article in *Theatre* was entitled 'Is the Chaplin Vogue Passing?' It is in truth an unremarkable comedy that makes some attempt at satirising the pastoral idyll which was one of the constituents of the American dream. Charlie is the overworked and presumably underpaid hired hand in a rural farm that also acts as a hotel, local store and barber's shop. The setting makes room for some of his familiar comic business. He is in love with Edna Purviance once more, and the presence of a threatening rival accommodates moments of farce and pathos. Yet they seem somehow forced.

It contains one remarkable dream sequence in which Charlie dances a pastiche version of Nijinksy's performance in *L'après-midi d'un faune*. Some critics have suggested that this was a serious attempt to represent Chaplin's skills as a dancer, but it is clearly nothing of the sort; it is a parody of the gestures and attitudes of the ballet dancer in his more overwrought moments. There is no real reason for the sequence to be part of the film, however, thus violating Chaplin's own strict laws of comic relevance and continuity. It is symptomatic of a film that is essentially aimless and insubstantial.

As soon as *Sunnyside* was completed he began serious work on *A Day's Pleasure*. He had worked on it before, in a sporadic fashion, but now he wanted to reduce the number of remaining pictures for First National. It is an uneven and unconvincing film concerning a boat excursion made by Charlie and family, in which he returns to one of his favourite themes of seasickness. This is combined with the antics of an unruly Ford car that is closer to Keystone than to genuine Chaplin. In the unusual role of paterfamilias Charlie has a stern and implacable quality; it is as if he had put on the mask of an idol. The actor who played Charlie's youngest son, Jackie Coogan, recalled that Chaplin 'kind of sloughed that picture off. You will notice if you see it, that it gets very jumpy. He lost interest in it.' Under the circumstances this loss of enthusiasm is understandable.

Even as he was working on *A Day's Pleasure*, on 7 July 1919, Mildred gave birth to Chaplin's son. The child was malformed, and died three days later. The death certificate recorded the 'rudimentary development of the large intestine'. The chauffeur, Kono, recollected in simpler terms that the infant was born with 'its stomach upside down'.

The production report on the new film for 10 July notes 'Did not shoot. Norman Spencer Chaplin passed on today – 4 p.m.' On the following day the entry read '11 July. Cast all absent . . . Did not shoot. Norman Spencer Chaplin buried today, 3 p.m., Inglewood Cemetery.' On his gravestone was carved 'The Little Mouse'. Sydney Chaplin described how the death of Norman tipped his brother into 'terrible depression'. Mildred Chaplin recalled later that 'Charlie took it hard . . . that's the only thing I can remember about Charlie . . . that he cried when the baby died.'

The period of reconciliation between husband and wife, if such it was, was brief since the essential components of their marriage remained the same. They could not remake the past. Although they lived in the same house, they rarely saw each other. Eventually he moved out and took up permanent residence at the Los Angeles Athletic Club. It may be that one or both of them blamed their incompatibility, or mutual resentment, for the sad fate of their child. The death of their son effectively marked the end of their marriage. Chaplin was for a day or two inconsolable.

10

The ostrich egg

Eleven days after the death of his son Chaplin was rehearsing some children for a part in his newly projected film, tentatively to be called *The Waif*. It was eventually entitled *The Kid*, and is one of the central works of his career. In one of its earliest scenes Charlie finds an abandoned baby and, after some internal debate, decides to rear it himself. Chaplin, after losing one infant, encounters another in his imagination. In that process is Norman Spencer Chaplin somehow restored to life?

Chaplin already had a young actor in mind for the central role. Immediately after finishing *Sunnyside* he had visited the Orpheum Theatre in Los Angeles where he had watched a comedy dance act by a vaudeville artist known as Jack Coogan; at the end of the performance Coogan introduced his four-year-old son, Jackie, who then went through his own brief dance routine based upon the steps of his father. Chaplin seems immediately to have been impressed and entertained by the exceedingly young performer. Jackie Coogan may have reminded him of his own youthful self on the music-hall stage.

Chaplin then met the Coogan family quite by chance in a Los Angeles hotel, where he took advantage of the occasion to become better acquainted with the boy. He asked him what he did. 'I am,' Jackie replied, 'a prestidigitator in the world of legerdemain.' This was no doubt one of the lines he had learned for his short act, but it delighted Chaplin. He told Jackie's parents that 'this is the most amazing person I ever met in my life'.

He was soon contemplating the comic possibilities of Charlie and the small boy, and soon enough the secretary of his studio visited the Coogans with an offer that could hardly be refused. 'Of course,' Jack Coogan is supposed to have said, 'you can have the little punk.' Chaplin used the boy briefly in *A Day's Pleasure*, a film that seemed to have had an interminable long process of production, before he turned his attention to the filming of *The Kid*.

He worked at white heat through the August and September of 1919. In these early scenes Edna Purviance plays the part of an unwed mother who is discharged from the charity hospital with the infant in her arms. The title of the sequence describes her as 'the woman – whose only sin is motherhood'. Chaplin may have been considering here the plight of his own mother many years before.

Other memories also intrude. When Charlie finds the abandoned child he takes him to his little room at the top of a lodging house. It is hard to be exact about the particulars, but there is a strong possibility that Chaplin here reconstructs the room he and his mother had once shared in Pownall Terrace or in Methley Street. It has a narrow bed, a table and some old chairs; the floor is made of bare boards, and the paper on the walls is peeling from damp. This is the setting for the little boy who, now grown from a baby, accompanies Charlie on his peregrinations. It is the first time that Charlie has ever been seen in any kind of home, a dwelling apparently secure from the outside world.

These attic scenes seem to have been shot very quickly. Jackie Coogan proved himself to be an excellent mimic as well as actor, and Chaplin had no difficulty in guiding him through his part. He did the action, or the expression, and the young boy copied it perfectly. This paradoxically rendered him a charming and subtle performer. As Chaplin noted, 'the mechanics induced the emotion'. He was the performer of whom Chaplin had always dreamed, a veritable extension of Chaplin himself, who might then become once more a child, releasing all the private experiences of his younger self, while at the same time Jackie Coogan took the place of Norman Spencer Chaplin buried beneath the earth. This may account for some of the power of *The Kid*.

There is one famous scene in which the young boy is being taken away from Charlie by a welfare worker and is thrown into the ophanage van, at which point the boy breaks down in hysterical tears. Jackie Coogan recalled that 'the musicians, of course, helped a lot. We had music on the set. And Chaplin used to talk, as every director did, while the shot was in process, being silent pictures. He'd say, "Now you really love this man, and he's gone, and they're going to take you . . ." It works on you.' The open van may have worked on Chaplin, too, as a reminder of the baker's wagon that had taken him at the age of seven to the orphanage at Hanwell. When Charlie rescues the boy, the audiences were shocked by his tears; the 'little fellow' had never cried before on the screen.

Another boy actor, Raymond Lee, recalled that many takes were necessary for a fight scene between himself and Jackie Coogan. '"You know," Chaplin said in the tones of a schoolmaster, "we've shot this scene exactly fifty times. I've been keeping count!"' Lee wrote that Chaplin then walked around in a circle. 'Then a stop. A thought. A smile with every tooth in it. And doing his best to look simple, Charlie Chaplin closed in on us with confessional intimacy. "Boys," he told us, "this is a very simple scene. Very simple. Two boys fighting. All boys fight . . . But boys, you aren't fighting. You're dancing with each other."' Lee concluded that Chaplin was always in search of simplicity – a smile, a half-tear or a simple look. He remarked that 'have you ever realised that Chaplin always looked at you from the screen – no matter what the action – he looked at you, the audience, as if he knew you, was about to tell you a secret'.

At the beginning of April 1920, in the course of filming, Mildred Chaplin began divorce proceedings against her husband. Her situation had not been helped by Chaplin's frequent affairs with other women; at this time, for example, he was engaged in a relationship with a young actress called Florence Deshon which was in turn followed by a fling with another actress. Chaplin was unwilling to allow his young wife any measure of independence, and even now he was attempting to overturn her contract with Louis B. Mayer on the grounds that she was still a minor. He had also recently refused her permission to adopt a child. She had at the beginning cited only his desertion but a few days later changed the charge to one of cruelty. She wished to 'tell everything. I shall let the world know how he failed to provide for me and how he sent an employee to my house and took away certain of my papers. He humiliated me before the servants. Isn't that cruelty?' Three days later Chaplin and Louis B. Mayer started a fight in the Alexandria Hotel in which both men fell to the ground.

In the course of the subsequent divorce proceedings Mildred Chaplin augmented her charges of cruelty.

'*Question*: Then what occurred?

'*Answer*: Then the next day was Christmas Day, and he would not get up all Christmas morning, and I went downstairs and took him up his presents, and he was very angry at me for making so much over Christmas . . .

'*Question*: What did he say or do with reference to your friends if he should find them in his house, what was his conduct toward them?

'*Answer*: He was not nice to them; he wouldn't come home if I had them.

'*Question*: When you had your friends he would refuse to come to the house if he found it out?

'*Answer*: Yes, sir.

'*Question*: How often did that occur, Mrs Chaplin?

'*Answer*: All the time. He would never tell me when he would be at home; he said he had to be free to live his own life and do as he pleased . . .

'*Question*: Did he give you any reason why he stayed away?

'*Answer*: No. He said I had disgraced him by going out . . .

'*Question*: Now you allege that subsequent to the time that you went to – went out some place, Mr Chaplin employed some detectives to watch you?

'*Answer*: Yes, sir . . .

'*Question*: Tell the court what happened at that time?

'*Answer*: I cried and begged him to come back home and I fainted and he said that I was acting silly and I had disgraced him and he didn't see why he should come back . . .

'*Question*: What was his method of talking to you? Was it kindly or otherwise?

'*Answer*: No, it was not kindly . . .

'*Question*: What did he say?

'*Answer*: Well he said that he knew he did not want to live with me any more; that he had tried to change me and make me live his way and be different, and he saw that it was impossible and that I wasn't good and that he couldn't trust me, and that I was – everything.'

It occurred to Chaplin himself that, in preparation for a divorce settlement, efforts might now be made to secure his business assets against future possible payments; among those assets was the negative of the film that had already been shot for *The Kid*. He also believed that First National had come to an arrangement with Mildred's lawyers so that they might legally acquire the film for which they had been waiting so long. For the first time in his career, no Chaplin film had been released that year.

At the beginning of August the cameraman, Rollie Totheroh, was aroused at three in the morning by Alf Reeves with an urgent request to get the negative out of town. It was packed into coffee tins and then transported by rail in twelve wooden crates. Chaplin had in fact filmed more than fifty times the length of the completed picture. Reeves and Totheroh were met by Chaplin and Tom

Charles Chaplin senior, *c.*1885

Hannah Chaplin, *c.*1895

Hanwell Schools, 1857

On the way to
New York, 1910.
Chaplin is inside
the lifebelt

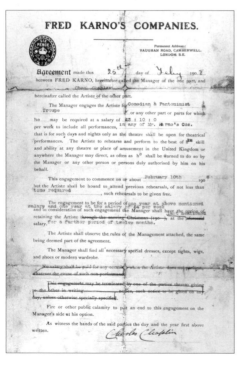

Chaplin's contract with
Fred Karno's company, 1908

Studio portrait of Chaplin, 1910

Chaplin signing his first contract with Keystone, 1914

Chaplin on the set of
Kid Auto Races at Venice, 1914

Keystone Studios,
1915

RED LETTER PHOTOCARD.

(Charles Chaplin.) Charlie and the Bulldog. (Champion Charlie.)

Picture postcard
showing Chaplin
with the bulldog from
The Champion, 1915

Chaplin and Edna Purviance in
a still from *The Cure*, 1917

Chaplin and Edna Purviance
in 1918

Chaplin signing the United Artists contract with Mary Pickford, Douglas Fairbanks and D. W. Griffith, 1919

Chaplin on the set of *The Kid* with Jackie Coogan, 1921

Mildred Harris, 1923

Chaplin and Pola Negri announce their engagement, 1923

Chaplin marrying
Lita Grey, 1924

Chaplin as
Adenoid Hynkel
of Toumania in
The Great Dictator, 1940

Chaplin as the Jewish barber
in *The Great Dictator*, 1940

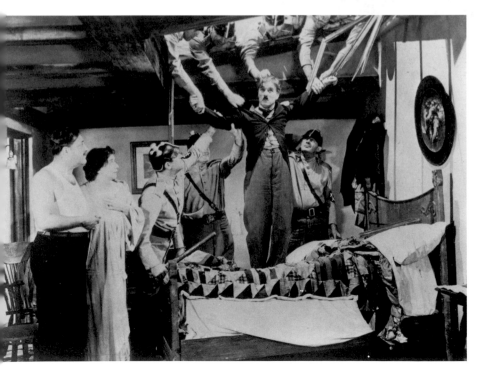

Chaplin and Oona O'Neill
on their wedding day, 1943

Chaplin receives his
knighthood, 1975

Harrington at Santa Fe from where they travelled on to Salt Lake City beyond any possible Californian jurisdiction.

At a hotel in Salt Lake City a bedroom was transformed into an editing suite where Chaplin began cutting *The Kid* into improvised shape. He and his colleagues then took the train to New York and found a studio in New Jersey where they could complete their work. Chaplin booked into the Ritz in order to conceal himself from the process servers working for Mildred Chaplin's lawyers.

While in New York he became acquainted with a group of *soi-disant* socialist intellectuals who inhabited the apartments and bars of Greenwich Village. Despite their dismissal of fame and fortune as bourgeois values, they were no doubt secretly thrilled to be in his company. In turn he enjoyed the society of intellectuals largely because he was not one. So he talked politics and art and literature. Rollie Totheroh once said that 'he can talk on pretty near any subject. But if a person really was educated on the subject he was talking on, they'd see the errors that he made.' Toraichi Kono can remember his employer 'talking volubly on a subject about which he knows practically nothing, and leave his listeners convinced that he is amazingly intellectual'. It was really just a matter of impersonation.

But he was also flattered by the attentions of those whom he considered to be more intelligent and knowledgeable than himself, and accepted their interpretation of his art as an affirmation of the common man. The Little Tramp could be seen as a working-class hero battling against the rich and the privileged. It was not the first time he had been taken by the perceptions of enthusiastic admirers. In later years, however, his association with the radical cause would create problems for his career.

In the middle of November a settlement between Chaplin and his wife was made out of court, and the divorce granted. Mildred Chaplin, at the age of eighteen, was granted $100,000 and a share of family property; but damage had been done to her. The actress Marion Davies is reported to have said that 'Mildred Harris was no saint, but she wasn't really a bad kid, and Charlie, God bless him, loused her up good.'

Robert Florey, who directed Mildred Chaplin in later days, recalled Mildred saying to him that 'it is hard for a girl to be the wife of a genius. I did not always understand him, and I felt inferior to him. He was short-tempered, impatient and treated me like a cretin. Yet I still admire him. He could have taught me so much.' The public exposure of the court proceedings had wounded Chaplin himself, who was in many respects a withdrawn and secretive man. He became more nervous and more cautious; his hair had started to turn grey.

In an interview he gave at this time he remarked that 'solitude is the only relief. The dream-world is then the great reality, the real world an illusion. I go to my library and live with the great abstract thinkers – Spinoza, Schopenhauer, Nietzsche and Walter Pater.' An element of posturing is plainly to be seen, together with the influence of the Greenwich Village intellectuals. He no longer wanted to be known as just a comedian. He added that he would like to 'retire to some Italian lake with my beloved violin, my Shelley and Keats, and live under an assumed name a life purely imaginative and intellectual'. His desire for seclusion may at least have been genuine. The interviewer concluded that 'I have never met an unhappier or shyer human being than this Charles Spencer Chaplin.'

His emotional temperature had been further raised, in the later stages of filming *The Kid*, by his meeting with a twelve-year-old actress. Lillita MacMurray had been hired to play a street urchin, but she seems at once to have caught Chaplin's attention. He asked a studio artist to paint her and, according to her own later account, he told her that 'I've been peeking at you, my dear, when you haven't been looking. I've been more and more drawn to those fascinating eyes of yours.' It may have been for her sake that he added what has always been a controversial dream sequence towards the end of *The Kid*. It is a puzzling intervention in the film, when Charlie sleeps and has a vision of his neighbourhood populated by angels. The young girl is cast as 'Sin' and, in Chaplin's fantasy of paradise, sin and jealousy always take over. It was an apt prophecy.

The Kid opened in New York on 6 February 1921, to great acclaim. It was Chaplin's longest, and best received, film to date. It marked a leap in the public and critical awareness of his art, so that now he was being openly compared with Dickens; he had in fact created a pure urban fable, like that of *Oliver Twist*. It has been said that it announced the coming of age of the cinema; film had become a world art form. In the process Charlie himself had become a fabulous creature outside the ordinary dimensions of human life. The world of the 'Chaplinesque' had been created. An English critic, James Agate, wrote that 'I do not laugh at Charlie till I cry. I laugh *lest* I cry, which is a very different matter.' The sensation was perhaps best expressed in a letter by Laurence Sterne, almost two centuries before, in which he wrote that 'I laugh till I cry, and in some tender moments *cry till I laugh*.'

An affinity has often been found between Charles Chaplin and Charles Dickens. Both experienced childhood neglect and suffering; both of them implicitly or explicitly blamed their mothers for their state. But they also owed an enormous debt to their mothers. Elizabeth Dickens, like Hannah Chaplin, was described as having 'an extraordinary sense of the ludicrous, and her power of imitation was something quite astonishing'. The two men came from the lower middle class; they were ambitious and energetic. They both had an experience of unfortunate first love that left them bereft and wounded for many years. Both men achieved uncommon fame at an extraordinarily young age – Dickens at the age of twenty-four, with *The Pickwick Papers*, and Chaplin at the age of twenty-five with the Keystone comedies.

Dickens drew much of his strength from the theatrical tradi-
tions of London; he haunted the minor theatres or 'penny gaffs'
which were the immediate predecessors of the music halls in which
the young Chaplin performed. They both loved the pantomimes
of their respective eras. Both men had imbibed with what might
be called a London vision in which farce and sentiment, melodrama
and pantomime, are conflated. Chaplin's oldest son has recalled
his father's love for *Oliver Twist*, which Chaplin read again and
again. It was as if in that novel he had found the key to his own
past. This in turn led to his film of threatened childhood, *The
Kid*, just as *Modern Times* is a distant successor to *Hard Times*.
City Lights, the story of a blind flower-seller rescued by the Little
Tramp, is altogether Dickensian in sentiment and expression. Just
as Dickens clothed London in a veil of comedy, pathos and poetry,
so did Chaplin in the haunted city of his films.

Chaplin, like Dickens, was driven, relentless, overwhelming.
Both men had always to be in control of the world around them;
they had an almost military manner in relationship to their families,
and were often accused of being dictatorial and domineering. They
seemed to be convivial and gregarious in company but they were
invaded by sudden terrors and inexplicable fears; they were both
very wealthy men who feared that their riches might be stripped
away. So there is a strong affinity. It might even be suggested that
Chaplin was Dickens's true successor.

Chaplin was even now thinking of his next film. *The Idle Class* is
not in the same inspired category as *The Kid* but his dual roles in
the picture, of both tramp and rich man, are the source of some
humour. Chaplin, the millionaire who played the part of the 'little
fellow', was of course both. It is a very ingenious and sophisticated
comedy. The rich patrician receives a letter announcing that his
wife has left him; he turns away from the camera and, with his
arms in front of him, begins trembling and shaking. It seems that

he has become distraught but, when he turns around, the audience sees that he has been vigorously employing a cocktail shaker.

Six weeks after the beginning of filming Hannah Chaplin finally arrived in the United States. She was accompanied by Tom Harrington, but neither of her sons greeted her at Ellis Island. 'So you're the mother of the famous Charlie?' an immigration official asked her.

'Yes,' she replied. 'And you are Jesus Christ.'

Chaplin had not seen her for nine years, but she recognised him at once. He had bought her a bungalow in the San Fernando Valley, near the sea, where she was in the company of a trained nurse and a married couple. She seemed to visitors to be perfectly settled for long periods; she would sing music-hall songs and reminisce about her old life in London. Like her son, she could create vivid impersonations of the people whom she had known. She enjoyed playing draughts, and kept up her old expertise in sewing. She liked to be taken in her car on shopping expeditions, on which occasions she was sometimes very extravagant; one day she came back with yards of coloured silk, of no particular use, and her son remarked that 'the poor soul has been longing for such things all her life'.

There were times when she was not altogether sane. The daughter of Alf Reeves remembered an occasion when she stepped back briefly into the shadows. She recalled that 'one day I was sitting beside her at lunch, and I noticed a mark on her arm. And innocently I said, "Nan, what's that?" And immediately she drew her arm away and hid it; and then started putting bits of bread all about herself, and on her head. The nurse, Mrs Carey, said, "Come with me, Nan" and took her off into another room. When Mrs Carey came back she said that the mark was a tattoo from the workhouse. She said it brought back the days when they had not had enough to eat; and she was putting the bread away for Sydney and Charlie.'

Chaplin's two sons recalled many stories that he and Sydney told them of their grandmother. When she went to a department store in Los Angeles she asked the clerk for 'shit-brown gloves'. When a pair was brought for her perusal she complained that 'No, no, that's not shit brown.' It is reminiscent of the occasion in Chaplin's childhood when she described a young woman as 'Lady Shit'. On the rare occasions when she visited her son's house it was said that she danced and raised her skirt so high that it became clear she was wearing no underwear.

On one occasion, according to her younger son, she was taken to the local zoo where much to the surprise of the public an ostrich had laid an egg. Chaplin recalled to one of his then lovers, May Reeves, that 'my old mother's nurse brought her there also. An attendant placed the egg in the visitor's hands so she could appreciate its weight but, thinking that this might be a trick, the good old lady threw the zoo's treasure to the ground, exclaiming "I don't want your egg." As a result the residents of Los Angeles had one young ostrich less.'

Chaplin himself did not visit her often; she still made him weary and despondent. She reminded him of a past, and of a life, he had left behind. His oldest son revealed that 'he could never see her without feeling a depression that was sometimes as acute to him as physical pain, that would last for days afterwards, preventing all concentration on his work'. No doubt he thought it enough to pay her bills and to ensure that she enjoyed a life of ease. Yet those who saw them together noted the strong resemblance between them in the eyes, the smile, and the gestures of the hands. She never seemed to be aware of his great fame. When she visited the studio and saw Chaplin in his tramp's outfit, she is supposed to have said, 'Charlie, I have to get you a new suit.' In one photograph Chaplin stands at a formal, or respectful, distance from his mother with his hands folded in front of him.

By the summer of 1921 Chaplin had begun shooting his next film for First National that would eventually be entitled *Pay Day* on the subject of builders and building sites. He shot the first scene, but he could get no further; in a subsequent memoir dictated to a reporter, *My Trip Abroad*, he recollected that 'I was feeling very tired, weak, and depressed. I had just recovered from an attack of influenza. I was in one of those "what's the use" moods . . . all the time there was the spectre of a nervous breakdown from overwork threatening.' Then he received news that *The Kid* was about to open in London. This was the stimulus that he needed. He had been thinking of London, his memories no doubt stirred by the presence of his mother. He had started a correspondence with H. G. Wells and was curious to meet the famous novelist. There was, above all, the undying attraction of the city of his childhood.

He closed down the picture and asked his press agent, Carlyle Robinson, to buy the tickets. His rapid departure surprised his friends and colleagues, let alone his studio staff. He left Los Angeles by train on 27 August, cheered on his way by a large crowd of Hollywood well-wishers, and was met at New York by Douglas Fairbanks and Mary Pickford who were there for the premiere of *The Three Musketeers*. When he attended the event, his fame had already overtaken him. He recalled that 'I felt a draught. I heard machinery. I looked down. A woman with a pair of scissors was snipping a piece from the seat of my trousers. Another grabbed my tie . . . My shirt was pulled out. The buttons torn from my vest. My feet trampled on. My face scratched.' He was then carried over the heads of the crowd into the lobby of the theatre.

On 3 September he left New York on the *Olympic* en route to Cherbourg and London, accompanied by Tom Harrington and Carlyle Robinson. If he had hoped for some respite from public attention on board the vessel, he was soon disabused. A film cameraman had been hired to follow his movements, and his excursions on deck were avidly watched by his fellow passengers; he was even asked to perform at a sailors' fund concert, which honour he declined much to the dissatisfaction of its organisers. Many of the other travellers brought up their children to be introduced to him but, without the costume of the Tramp, he felt a little fraudulent; he was like Santa Claus without the beard. In any case he was nervous with children knowing that they 'detect our insincerity'.

The *Olympic* docked at Cherbourg on the evening of 9 September, where reporters and cameramen invaded the ship. Confronted with questions in French he made a short impromptu speech in which he said that 'this is my first holiday for years, and there is only one place to spend a holiday long overdue, and that is at home. That is why I intend to go to London. I want to walk the streets, see all the many changes, and feel the good old London atmosphere again.' He was going back to the source of his life and inspiration.

11

Home again

Charles Chaplin was on the train from Southampton to London.
The crowds that greeted him at the port were smaller than he had
anticipated, and he suffered what he called 'a tinge of disappointment'. Nevertheless one newspaper had the headline 'HOMECOMING
OF COMEDIAN TO RIVAL ARMISTICE DAY'. And so it proved.

When he arrived at Waterloo he was mobbed by thousands of
Londoners. The cry came up, 'There he is!' The newsreels of the
day show him surrounded by policemen, reporters and cameramen.
The crowd surged towards him. 'Here he is. He is there, he is. That's
him.' Chaplin recollected in *My Trip Abroad* that 'this also thrills
me. Everything is beyond my expectations. I revel in it secretly.' As
he makes his way with difficulty through the mob of cheering and
waving people, he hears them calling out 'Well done, Charlie', or
'Charlie! Charlie! There he is! Good luck to you, Charlie! God bless
you!' It was a spontaneous outburst of enthusiasm from the people
of the city, and for Chaplin almost overwhelming.

When he reached the station exit, he could hear church bells
ringing and could see handkerchiefs and hats being waved in the
air. He was hauled and lifted into a limousine, with three policemen
on the running board each side. There is a photograph of him
standing up, surrounded by a sea of cloth caps and bowler hats,
straw boaters and floral hats. He made a short speech to the crowd,
which was of course greeted by wild applause, before his car
managed to make its way to the Ritz. The hotel had been locked
to prevent the crowd from storming the lobby; once he was pushed
and pulled within its doors, he was raced to his room.

The crowds were calling for him, so he went over to the window from which he waved and blew kisses. Then he grabbed a bouquet of roses and began to throw the flowers, one by one, to the people below. A police officer came into the room. 'Please, Mr Chaplin, it is very fine, but don't throw anything. You will cause an accident. They will be crushed and killed.' Chaplin had encountered, and indeed created, a wholly new phenomenon. The crowds had come out at the funerals of Dan Leno and of Marie Lloyd but the fame now generated by the new medium of film was unprecedented in human history. No one before had experienced the amount of acclaim and even adoration that now swept over him; he had no preparation or training for it. He simply had to cope with it as well as he could for the rest of his life.

His instinct was now in any case to go back, to return to the streets of South London where he had played and worked. With appropriate excuses to those who were with him, he went out of the Ritz by a back door. He walked quickly out into the street and hailed a cab, asking the driver to take him to Kennington; fortunately the cab-man did not recognise him. When he passed the Canterbury Music Hall, just after the bridge on Westminster Bridge Road, he recognised a token of his early youth. It was a blind man begging by a wall, who had hardly changed since Chaplin had last seen him. He was a symbol of the stony London that never changes, to put against all the hysteria of Chaplin's welcome. Chaplin was experiencing once more the reality of the city that inspired his art.

He then re-entered the streets of Kennington which were for him now 'another world, and yet in it I recognise something, as though in a dream'. They would have seemed smaller to him now, the change of perspective exaggerated by his time in the apparently limitless spaces of America. He saw the stone trough outside a pub where he used to wash himself. He passed a barber's shop where he used to be the lather boy. He decided to leave the taxi and walk through the lanes and thoroughfares.

A girl came up to him in Lambeth Walk. 'Charlie, don't you know me?' She had been a small servant girl in one of the cheap lodging houses where he had lived; she was still in the same neighbourhood, as he said, 'carrying on with all the odds against her'. He discovered then that a crowd of local people was following him, keeping at a respectful distance of about five yards, and he could hear them whispering 'There he is,' and 'That's 'im.'

He began to grow concerned about the number behind him. He went up to a policeman. 'Do you mind?' he said. 'I find I have been discovered. I am Charlie Chaplin. Would you mind seeing me to a taxi?'

'That's all right, Charlie. These people won't hurt you. They are the best people in the world. I have been with them for fifteen years.'

They had been unwilling to disturb his solitude but, now that he had company, they became bolder. 'Hello, Charlie!', 'God bless you, Charlie!', 'Good luck to you, lad!' They were no doubt proud to consider themselves part of the neighbourhood from which he had sprung. He noted that 'the little cockney children circle around me to get a view from all sides'. The policeman summoned a taxi, and he was driven away. On his route back to the Ritz he passed Kennington Park, where once his mother had taken him and Sydney on a day's escape from the workhouse. He passed Kennington Gate, where he had once arranged to meet Hetty Kelly; this was for him a poignant moment, because he had been told on his return to England that she had died. He stopped the cab and revisited the Horns public house, where as a boy he used to watch the stars of the music hall. Now he in turn was being watched, as he drank a glass of ginger beer.

'That's 'im. I tell you 'tis.'

'Ah, get out! And wot would 'e be a-doing 'ere?'

He was driven back along Kennington Road towards the bridge and glimpsed Kennington Cross, where he had once heard two street musicians playing 'The Honeysuckle and the Bee'. This was for him sacred ground.

Two or three nights later, he returned to the neighbourhood with some friends who had gathered about him in the Ritz. Once more he was absorbed in his memories. It was as if he was trying to discover the source of his identity and being. He recognised an old tomato-seller whom he had first seen about twenty years before, still standing in the same pitch; the young Chaplin used to watch him as he shouted his wares, but the tomato-man had fallen silent in these later days.

He then took his friends to Pownall Terrace, where he had shared a room with his mother on the top floor; it was also the room in which she had first succumbed to insanity, and from which he took her to the asylum. It may also have been the room, as we have observed, on which he modelled the Tramp's attic in *The Kid*. Mrs Reynolds, a war widow who lived there at the time of Chaplin's visit, was surprised by a knock on the door one evening. Carlyle Robinson announced Chaplin's name and with some misgivings she opened the door to reveal, according to Robinson, 'a small room illuminated by an oil lamp'. It was low and narrow, with a slanting roof, and shadows gathered in its corners. Chaplin himself seems to have been embarrassed and at a loss for words; he simply looked around the room where, as he said on the pavement after they had left, 'Syd and I clung on to life with our mother.' Mrs Reynolds asked him to come again, but of course he never returned. He had seen enough.

Chaplin was eager to meet some of the more famous inhabitants of the city. He met J. M. Barrie at a lunch in the Garrick Club where, as he put it in *My Trip Abroad*, 'I laugh at anything and dare not speak.' Yet he then spent a convivial evening in Barrie's apartment. Chaplin had come to England with the ambition of meeting H. G. Wells, and soon enough had also made his acquaintance. It is not at all clear what one made of the other, and Chaplin himself seemed not to know; he wondered 'if Wells wants to know me or whether he wants me to know him'. Wells also introduced him to his mistress, Rebecca West, who commented that he was 'a darling . . . a very serious little cockney' with 'a serious little soul'. Chaplin later boasted of having seduced her.

He had also determined on meeting the author Thomas Burke, whose collection of stories *Limehouse Nights* seemed to him to be close to his own vision of dark London. The two men, starting off at eleven o'clock one night, spent six hours exploring the streets of East London; on two occasions, at Mile End and at Hoxton, he was recognised and a crowd surrounded him calling out 'our Charlie'. Yet it seemed to Burke that Chaplin was not so much delighted at the adulation but frightened and bewildered by it. He was not Charlie at all; he had not a trace or movement of the 'little fellow' about him.

Burke was a quiet and inscrutable man, but one with great powers of observation. He believed that Chaplin 'was not much interested in people, either individually or as humanity . . . There is nothing, I think, that he deeply cares about.' He noticed Chaplin's extraordinary vitality and vivacity but 'catch him in repose, and you will catch a drawn, weary mouth and those eyes of steel'. He compared him to a 'brilliant' or gem, and added that 'the bulk of him is ice'. At no point did 'the metallic artist' sitting before him resemble the forlorn and futile figure of Charlie. That may have been the reason for Chaplin always referring imperson-ally to the Little Tramp as 'he'. Burke also observed that 'he is first and last an actor. He lives only in a role, and without it he is lost. As he cannot find the inner Chaplin, there is nothing for him, at grievous moments, to retire into.' Millions of words have been written on Chaplin, but perhaps none as pertinent as these.

His wayward habits surprised some of the socialites and famous people whom he encountered in London. One of his English friends, Edward Knoblock, who had written the screenplay of *The Three Musketeers* for Douglas Fairbanks, later wrote that in England 'where the whole social system is run on punctuality and sense of obligation to others, his neglect of all such rules caused offence. I fear he hurt himself a great deal with many of his admirers by turning up late when he was expected, or at times not even turning up at all.'

After spending ten days in London he took ship to Paris where he received another tumultuous welcome. The figure of 'Charlot', as he was known, was perhaps more revered in France where the art of the mime had become a national tradition. When Chaplin visited a circus the audience became aware of his presence, and an acquaintance recalled 'a high-tiered human monster, suddenly shouting *Charlot!* with a thousand throats'. He noted that 'the police formed a phalanx about him and he was shuffled out into the Place Pigalle. But the cry *Charlot!* had got there first. The square, the boulevards that lead to it, turned into a magnetised mob; thousands came pouring, pushing, shouting. Men touched him; women tried to kiss him.' Eventually he and his friends made an escape in a taxi. 'It's *all nothing*! It's all a joke,' he said. 'It can all be *explained*, I tell you. It's all – nothing.' Yet the evidence suggests that he craved the adulation of the crowd, even when he knew that it was hollow, and grew fretful when it was absent.

From Paris he travelled by train to Berlin, a city that he found somewhat depressing. This may have in part been due to the fact that, as he put it in *My Trip Abroad*, 'they don't know me here. I have never been heard of. It interests me and I believe I resent it just a bit.' At the Palais Heinroth, however, he encountered Pola Negri. Negri was a Polish screen actress who played, in art and in life, the part of a femme fatale. Unfortunately she knew no English, and could say only 'jazz boy Charlie'.

Negri remembered the occasion very well. In her *Memoirs of a Star* she wrote that 'a little man with a sad sensitive face fought his way up to our table. Were it not for his odd appearance, so dapper and so pathetic, I would not have noticed him. He had such a strange physiognomy, with tiny feet . . . and an enormous head that made him seem top-heavy . . . The only physically attractive thing about him were his hands, which were never without a cigarette.'

He returned to London at the end of September, where once more he met H. G. Wells and other notables. Yet every second thought was now of Los Angeles and of his studio. He had experienced 'complete satisfaction', as he put it, at the crowds that had greeted him in London and in Paris. Work, however, was still the centre of his life.

He sailed back to New York, where he saw his old acquaintances and no doubt vividly rehearsed the triumphs of his return. On his last day in the city he arranged to meet the English editor and journalist, Frank Harris, whom he accompanied on a visit to Sing Sing. Harris had come to the prison in order to see a union activist, Jim Larkin, who had been sentenced to five years on the charge of attempting to overthrow the government. Chaplin was fascinated, and appalled, by the conditions he found in the prison – the old cell blocks, the small and narrow stone dungeons, the whole architecture of inhumanity. He discussed with a prison doctor the various cures for syphilis, on which Chaplin himself appeared to be an expert, and he visited the Death House or place of execution by means of the electric chair. He was allowed to look down into a small yard where a condemned man was walking. 'Did you see his face?' he whispered to Harris. When asked by some of the convicts to give them a talk, he replied 'How can I talk to you? What is there to say except that we are all pals in this life, and if I can make you laugh, by God you can make me cry.' He added that 'If we're free, it's only because we've not been found out. Good luck, boys!' He travelled back to Los Angeles by train, dictating on the way his recollections of the trip to a journalist.

He had an unlikely companion in this period. Clare Sherdian was an English painter and sculptor who, after the death of her husband, had come to the United States with her small son. Chaplin had met her at a dinner party immediately on his return, and over dinner they agreed that she should make his bust. She had already made portrait busts of the most prominent Bolshevik leaders; she was also a niece of Winston Churchill and had married a descendant of the playwright Richard Brinsley Sheridan. So she interested him. He sat for her in a house he had rented, at Beechwood Drive in Hollywood, but he was by no means patient. He changed the colour of his pyjamas and dressing gown to suit his mood; he played his violin; he turned on the gramophone and conducted an imaginary orchestra. She finished the work in three days and, contemplating it, Chaplin said that the head might be that of a criminal. He went on a short camping holiday with her and her son, complete with cook and chauffeur, but it was abandoned when the happy party was invaded by children and reporters. The affair, if such it was, lasted only a few more days.

By the end of November 1921, he was about to recommence *Pay Day*, the film he had summarily dropped before travelling to England. 'I must get back to work,' he had told Clare Sheridan, 'but I don't feel like it. I don't feel funny.' Yet he had to complete the quota of films for First National. This was the eighth out of nine, and he was close to regaining his freedom. It is a two-reeler, short by his recent standards and the last he ever made of that length, but it is inventive and entertaining with the additional benefit of some night scenes made possible by artificial lighting. The streetcars glide through the darkness with their heavy burden of passengers.

The film opens on a building site with Charlie as a quick-witted labourer; unusually for Chaplin it uses trick photography to emphasise Charlie's prowess at catching bricks. It moves on to scenes of nocturnal revel where Charlie spends his wages in the well-known fashion, and it closes as he tries to avoid the wrath of his morose and hatchet-faced wife. There was plenty of opportunity for somewhat familiar comedy, therefore, which he duly took. *Photoplay* noticed, however, that '*Pay Day* made even the ushers laugh in the theatre where we saw it.' This was a notable compliment.

On the day before *Pay Day* was released Chaplin began work on his final film for First National. *The Pilgrim* seems to have been the first film in which Chaplin prepared written notes; he was ready to work more cautiously, if not more economically, and he may have feared quite unnecessarily that his comic powers were diminished. 'Think – think of it,' he had told Clare Sheridan, 'if I could never be funny again.'

Since *The Pilgrim* was the final film of the contract, it was perhaps no accident that Charlie is first shown as an escapee from prison. The convict then poses as a minister, having stolen the clothes of an unfortunate cleric who has gone swimming, and must convince a local congregation of his piety. It all goes horribly wrong, of course, with Charlie treating the church as a combination of barroom and courtroom; he performs with histrionic energy a sermon on David and Goliath in front of the congregation, before giving a bow and twirl at the end of his act. It is all genuinely funny, with Chaplin giving one of his most memorable performances as the counterfeit minister.

Women, meanwhile, were never far off. They were plentiful, and almost too ready to be seduced by the most famous man in the world. He himself was willing and eager to take up all offers. The hired house in Hollywood might as well have had a revolving door. It was about this time that he began to wear a perfume, Mitsouko, largely compounded of benzoin and musk.

While working on *The Pilgrim* he was engaged in what he himself described as a 'bizarre' relationship with a rich and much married lady. Peggy Hopkins Joyce might be described as the queen of alimony; she had married five millionaires, and it is believed that the word 'gold-digger' was invented in her honour. She refused to allow one of her husbands into the bedroom until he had signed her a cheque for $500,000; on a later occasion she hit the same man over the head with a champagne bottle and, as she recalled, 'he seemed to like it'.

It is reported that on first meeting Chaplin she asked 'Charlie, is it true what all the girls say, that you're hung like a horse?' She was rough, vulgar and energetic or, in other words, a bit of a handful; she was blessed, however, with a sense of humour. She had pursued her men in Europe as well as in America, and in the course of their two-week affair she told Chaplin many stories about her adventures in Paris. She would thereby become the indirect inspiration for his next film.

And then came Pola Negri, the Polish actress whom he had encountered in Berlin the year before. He met her once more at a charity event in the Hollywood Bowl, where he remembered her as saying 'Chaarlee! Why haven't I heard from you? You never called me up. Don't you realise I have come all the way from Germany to see you?' Her command of English had obviously much improved since their last meeting. Since she was about to begin a Hollywood film career, devotion to Chaplin cannot have been her only reason for crossing the Atlantic.

Pola Negri was woken at three the following morning by the sound of a Hawaiian band hired by Chaplin to serenade her. She invited him to a lavish party a few nights later where they began what he described as an 'exotic relationship'. In her memoirs she described him as a patient listener ready to advise her on her burgeoning career; she even appreciated his occasional withdrawals from the world into silence or reticence. He was, after all, an artist. It is also possible that she appreciated his fame and wealth as well as the many film 'contacts' he could pass on. When he presented her with a bracelet of diamond and onyx, 'I was told there could be no greater indication of the seriousness of his intentions, for he was notoriously miserly.'

He had recently purchased six and a half acres of land in Beverly Hills, close to the estate of Douglas Fairbanks and Mary Pickford. He began to build a two-storey mansion that he designed himself in a Spanish style which he described as 'California Gothic'; it comprised some forty rooms, together with a small cinema and steam-room without which no Hollywood house would be complete. The outside swimming pool was created in the shape of a bowler hat, just like the one worn by the Little Tramp, and a vestibule off the hall contained a large pipe organ on which he often played. It was reported that he used some of his studio workmen in the construction, but they were more accustomed to temporary sets; as a result some parts of the house were more fragile than others, and the neighbours named it 'Breakaway House'. Nevertheless he was happy here, and lived at 1085 Summit Drive for the rest of his time in Hollywood.

The mansion was surrounded on three sides by woods, and on the fourth side a lawn sloped down to the swimming pool and a tennis court. A two-storey hall ran the length of the house, and a winding staircase led to the second floor. His oldest son noted that his father kept a full-sized suit of oriental armour and a brass gong in the hallway. In the living room was a Steinway grand piano, and a copy of *Webster's Dictionary* which he often consulted; he had a habit of memorising the meaning of difficult words which he would then introduce into conversations. In the same room was a large fireplace in which Chaplin burned coal, in the English fashion, rather than wood. In the nightstand by his bed he kept a .38 calibre automatic weapon, complete with bullets. His son recalled that Chaplin also possessed a powerful telescope mounted on a tripod, but he generally trained it on the houses of his neighbours rather than on more celestial regions.

Pola Negri herself made suggestions about the interior of the mansion, as it was being completed, and even paid $7,000 for oak and eucalyptus trees to be transplanted so that she might hear the wind among their leaves. It was clear enough that she already imagined herself as mistress of the house in a union that would eclipse that of Pickford and Fairbanks, the queen and king of Hollywood.

On Christmas Eve 1922, Chaplin bought her a large diamond that he had not had the time to set within a ring; nevertheless it was a token of their engagement. A week later, on New Year's Eve, he invited her to an intimate dinner at his own mansion. This was the night, according to the actress, when their relationship was fully consummated. She described how 'he started moving towards me, moving in a gait that was a parody of seductiveness'; his passion was expressed in 'an uproarious dumbshow of rolling eyes and waving hands'. Yet he prevailed. It was only then that serious rifts began to appear between them. They argued, with Chaplin accusing her of unfaithfulness; this was his standard complaint against the women closest to him. He was himself, of course, pursuing other young women at the time.

The engagement itself was largely played out in the headlines and gossip columns of the newspapers. In March 1923, he declared that he was too poor to get married. Pola Negri then announced that the engagement was cancelled. The *Los Angeles Herald Examiner* summoned up the affair with 'POLA NEGRI JILTS CHAPLIN'. 'I end!' she was reported to have said, 'Just like that! I am very extreme.' In an interview with the *Examiner* she complained that 'he is too temperamental – as changing as the wind – he dramatises everything – he experiments in love'. Chaplin pleaded, and Pola Negri prevaricated, but the Hollywood romance had nowhere to go. It began, and ended, in illusions. Their affair had been conducted in a house of mirrors.

Soon after seeing Negri at the Hollywood Bowl he began work on his first picture for United Artists, the association between Douglas Fairbanks, Mary Pickford, D. W. Griffith and Chaplin himself. Their association had begun with the 'Liberty Bond' tour, but they began to seriously consider a formal association in 1919 when studio demands on artist's salaries and schedules seemed to represent intolerable interference. The four of them held 20% each of the stock, with a further 20% going to a lawyer, since they had decided that it would be more profitable to invest their own money, produce their own films and distribute the finished product themselves. They would then become truly free of managerial control, and their independence represented a major episode in film history.

His colleagues at United Artists no doubt anticipated another comic masterpiece like *The Pilgrim* that would considerably help the finances of the new company. Yet Chaplin never followed anyone's wishes or instructions. His business partners were soon informed that he was making a serious drama about a kept woman, and that he himself would not be appearing in the film. There was to be no Charlie and precious little comedy. He was restless and disenchanted with the figure of the Little Tramp, and wanted to escape him for a while.

He had hit upon the title of *Destiny*, and for some weeks he relied upon notes and details to fashion the work. He had worked out the scenario in his mind and did not need a script. *A Woman of Paris*, as it was eventually titled, is the story of a woman who, apparently abandoned by her young lover, travels to Paris where she becomes the mistress of a rich gentleman; the young lover providentially arrives in the capital and, after a series of misadventures, shoots himself at the prospect of losing her. It is the merest melodrama, in terms of plot, but out of the story Chaplin creates a memorable and in some respects magnificent film.

He wanted Edna Purviance to play the leading part. Her career as a comic heroine seemed to be coming to a close; she was drinking, and had become too heavy for the ingénue. But he believed that in the title role of the film he could turn her into a serious actress. Her rich lover was played by Adolphe Menjou, who from that time forward made a career out of playing wealthy and quizzical Frenchmen. He said later that he had learned more from Chaplin than from any other director. 'Don't sell it,' Chaplin told him. 'Remember, they're peeking at you.' He did not want his performers to act in any conventional sense; he wanted them to remain as unforced and natural as if they were in a real situation. The audience was very close to them, only a hair's breadth away, and any exaggeration would be instantly recognised. In this realisation Chaplin was ahead of his contemporaries, many of whom still favoured the more theatrical actions of the earliest film stars. 'Think the scene,' he told Menjou. 'I don't care what you do with your hands or feet, If you think the scene, it will get over.' This was also of course his own method. He praised an actor's simplicity and restraint above all else. Silent film itself is best at conveying simplified feeling in a look, a gesture or the simple act of lighting a cigarette. In one scene the whole action is conveyed through the expressions of a masseuse pummelling the back of a customer; Chaplin would have rehearsed for her the precise manner in which she raised an eyebrow or pursed her lips.

He sometimes goaded an actor or actress into a good performance. In one scene the mother of the young man is given the news of her son's death by a policeman. Chaplin wanted no expression from her at all but, the actress, Lydia Knott, could not oblige. So he shot and reshot the brief scene eighty times until Knott, in the words of an assistant director, 'got so angry that she swore at us and just went through this scene in such a temper that we got it'. Another short scene, in which Edna Purviance throws down a cigarette and refuses to go out, consumed two days and ninety takes. He wanted to reach a purity of expression. Chaplin had great patience in unfolding his vision. 'I don't know why I'm right about the scene,' he said during the making of the film. 'I just know I'm right.'

The naturalism of the performers was allied in *A Woman of Paris* with an overall economy of movement and gesture. He had noticed that in the more dramatic moments of life men and women attempt to conceal rather than to express emotion; it is a mechanism of self-defence. This was the technique that he used in the film itself to create an unusually realistic style; much of the action was casual and informal. It came as a profound shock to the audiences of the time, who did not quite know what to make of it. Yet other directors took the point immediately. Ernst Lubitsch and Michael Powell reported themselves to be overwhelmed by the experience, and began to imitate it in their own ways; Powell remarked that 'suddenly there was a grown-up film with people behaving as they do in real life'. It might be said, therefore, that Chaplin established a new cinema of social manners as well as a novel style of acting. Menjou himself noted that 'the word "genius" is used very carelessly in Hollywood, but when it is said of Chaplin, it is always with a special note of sincerity. If Hollywood has ever produced a genius, Chaplin is certainly first choice.'

The novelty of the film, and the absence of Chaplin from the cast, ensured that *A Woman of Paris* did not match the commercial success of his earlier comedies. Its subtlety and ingenuity were lost upon contemporary audiences. He was immensely hurt by its lack of popularity and, as soon as possible, withdrew it and buried it in his private vaults. Edna Purviance made only two more films before retiring from the screen. In an interview a week after the film's release he revealed that 'unless my feelings undergo a marked change, I am going right back to comedy'.

12

Why don't you jump?

In the autumn of 1923 Fairbanks and Pickford invited Chaplin for breakfast partly to discuss his next film for United Artists after the relative failure of *A Woman of Paris*. After the meal was over he began to leaf through a number of stereographic views, one of which pictured a long line of gold prospectors climbing in single file the Chilkoot Trail in Klondike during the gold rush of 1898.

His imagination was excited by the image and very soon afterwards he picked up a book on the plight of some immigrants to America in the middle of the nineteenth century. They had found themselves stranded in the snowbound wastes of the Sierra Nevada where, in conditions of famine and death, the survivors resorted to cannibalism in order to stay alive. They had also eaten dogs and saddles, as well as their own shoes.

So the germ of *The Gold Rush* was planted. He worked on the first rough draft of the scenario for approximately two months and by the beginning of December, 1923, he had applied for copyright on 'a play in two scenes' set in the ice and tentatively entitled *The Lucky Strike*.

He himself would of course return in his familiar role as the 'little fellow'. His experience with *A Woman of Paris* had in that sense been a salutary one, and he knew that he could not forsake the Tramp if he wished to retain his popularity. Yet now Charlie would be given a wholly new setting. He would no longer amble along the streets of the city but among the rocks and glaciers of the mountain range. Chaplin also remembered saying to himself that 'The next film must be an epic! The greatest!' If the 'little fellow' is obliged to fight the great forces of nature, as well as the great human emotions of avarice and despair, he might develop in wholly unexpected ways and thereby create a wholly new kind of comedy. It may also have occurred to him that he might thereby transcend his contemporaries, among them Buster Keaton and Harold Lloyd. The lugubrious mastery of Keaton, and the brash gymnastics of Lloyd, were as much part of silent comedy as Chaplin himself; yet he knew that he had always to stand out.

He had also to find a suitable heroine, Edna Purviance being now considered unsuitable for the role. He began shooting the film on 8 February 1924, and three weeks later he signed Lillita MacMurray as his new leading lady under the professional name of Lita Grey. The young girl had entered his life four years earlier when she had played the part of 'Sin' in the dream sequence of *The Kid*; it was clear even then that despite, or because of, her youth he was profoundly attracted to her. The difference in time had made her even more desirable. Lita Grey said to the assembled journalists, at the time of signing her contract, that 'I have held firm to my ambition to go into pictures, but I felt that I didn't want to work with anyone except Mr Chaplin. Patience has its reward.' The studio declared that she was nineteen years old, when in fact she was not quite sixteen.

The unlucky party of immigrants in Sierra Nevada had been stranded outside the town of Truckee, and as a result Chaplin decided to use that territory for his location shots. He and the crew, together with Lita Grey and her mother, travelled north by train; since Chaplin did not know precisely how he was going to fashion the story, he needed his young actress there in case of extemporised close-ups. Lita Grey remembered the bitterly cold weather, and the fact that Chaplin caught influenza and was confined to his bed for four days; she also recalled that this was the time when he first made an advance towards her. In her own account he pushed himself upon her, and was only diverted when he believed that he had heard

145

noises outside the bedroom door. He then casually announced to the young girl that 'when the time and place are right, we're going to make love'. He fulfilled his wish some weeks later in the steam-room of his mansion in Beverly Hills. It has often been said that Vladimir Nabokov's *Lolita* is in part inspired by the story of Lita Grey.

At the same time he was engaged in a liaison with Rebecca West, the mistress of H. G. Wells whom he had already met and seduced in England. West later told her sister that he wished to sleep with her 'because he had suddenly become terrified of impotence and wanted to see if it were so'. He was later in the year often seen in the company of Marion Davies, the mistress of William Randolph Hearst. The gossip columnist of the New York *Daily News* reported that 'Charlie Chaplin continues to pay ardent attention to Marion Davies . . . There was a lovely young dancer entertaining that evening. And Charlie applauded but with his back turned. He never took his eyes off Marion's blonde beauty.'

The film crew of *The Gold Rush* went back to the studio after a few days in Truckee, but then in April they returned to the ice and snow in order to begin actual shooting in the locations Chaplin had chosen. The set of a mining camp was built, and a pass through the snow created by professional ski-jumpers who carved steps out of the frozen snow on the side of Mount Lincoln; a company of 500 derelicts from Sacramento had been brought by train and, in what became the first scene of the film, in single file they climbed the slope of the frozen waste. It is as momentous a setting as anything in the films of DeMille or Griffith. It seems that Chaplin shot all the external scenes on location but then, remarkably, decided to keep only two of them in the finished film. One of them was the famous opening.

From May to September 1924 the landscape of *The Gold Rush* was recreated in the studio, with mountains and glaciers constructed out of hundreds of tons of salt and plaster as well as hundreds of barrels of flour. Here was the mining town in which Charlie falls in love with a dance-hall singer only to be rejected by her. Here was the hut where Charlie and his companion come close to starvation and madness. In these scenes dark circles were painted around the Little Tramp's eyes to emphasise his plight, making him seem even more like a character out of *commedia dell'arte*. In the most famous sequence of the film Charlie cooks a boot for himself and his companion as a delicious delicacy in the hour of need, and then eats it as if he were dining at the Ritz. Hunger, the source of many childhood woes, becomes the spring of humour. The boot was in fact made of liquorice and so many 'takes' were filmed, with so many different boots, that he and his fellow performer, Mack Swain, became violently ill for some days.

At the end of September, just as he was completing these scenes, Lita Grey announced that she was pregnant with Chaplin's child. The members of her family were predictably indignant and, facing charges of sex with a minor that might cost him thirty years' imprisonment, he was bound to accede to their demands that he marry the girl. He was duplicating his relationship with his previous wife, Mildred Harris, but it may be unwise to speculate about the reasons for this strange re-enactment. There is no reason in passion. Need knows no law. He was sometimes as blind as he was mercurial, and as unyielding as he was unpredictable; he only knew what he wanted, and what he wanted he must have at all costs. His will, and his desire, overcame his judgement.

It seems that he suggested to Lita that she have an abortion, a proposal which her Catholic mother indignantly rejected. He then suggested that a willing young man be chosen as her husband on payment of a dowry of $20,000. This, too, was turned down. He claimed subsequently that 'I was stunned and ready for suicide that day when [Lita] told me that she didn't love me and that we must marry.' He added that 'her mother deliberately and continuously put Lita in my path'. At a much later date he told friends that Lita Grey had said to him, 'You'll marry me. I've never gotten a kick out of you, but you'll marry me!'

This is the context for the strange story that has itself inspired several books and one film. In November William Randolph Hearst and Marion Davies, had invited a group of acquaintances on board his yacht, *Oneida*; among them was a producer, Thomas Ince, and Chaplin himself who was at the time still infatuated with Marion. On the following day Ince left the yacht at San Diego on a stretcher, having apparently suffered a heart attack, and died soon afterwards. The conflicting stories of the party aboard, and the absence of any inquest, aroused suspicions in the notoriously gossipy world of Hollywood. It was soon rumoured that Hearst had shot Ince after catching him with Marion; it was then further supposed that the magnate had shot Ince in the belief that he was in fact Chaplin. From the back, Ince resembled the comedian. The truth will never be found at the bottom of this well, but it is perhaps significant that a week after the incident Chaplin agreed to marry Lita Grey. It may be that the union was designed to reassure Hearst that Chaplin had no further designs upon his mistress.

The ceremony was to be conducted in the deepest secrecy, and it was agreed that the wedding party would travel by train to Mexico; if anyone was asked the reason for this journey, he or she was to say that Chaplin was investigating new locations for *The Gold Rush*. Some journalists did follow them, to the town of Guaymas, but Chaplin managed to elude his pursuers by dashing in a car to the home of a local justice of the peace. The ceremony was soon over, and Lita Chaplin recalled later that Chaplin puffed nervously on a cigarette throughout the proceedings; at the conclusion, he made a quick exit to go fishing.

He made it clear that he thought nothing of the bride, or the bride's family. He had already called her a 'little whore', and in her first autobiography she records his words to her soon after the ceremony. 'The whole point of the "little fellow" is that no matter how down on his ass he is, no matter how well the jackals succeed in tearing him apart, he's still a man of dignity. He can still look down on you and your whole bloody bunch of money-hungry scum.' She may not have perfectly recalled the words, but the hatred and bitterness behind them are nevertheless evident.

On the train back to California he is supposed to have told his companions that 'this is better than the penitentiary, but it won't last'. When they were alone in their compartment, she asked him for water. 'Aren't you,' he asked her, 'afraid that I might try to poison you?' He then suggested that she might get some air in the observation car. When she stood on the platform of the car, he came up to her. 'This would be a good time to put an end to your misery,' he told her. 'Why don't you jump?' We must rely on Lita Chaplin's own memory here, but the incident is certainly striking enough to be recalled without effort even many years later. Her account has the ring of authenticity, and it is substantially repeated in her second autobiography. On the newlywed couple's return to Beverly Hills they were once again met by representatives of the press. Chaplin remarked angrily that 'I've been trying to avoid this! It's awful!'

Lita Chaplin, at the age of sixteen, now found herself the mistress of a large mansion and a body of servants. She was still young enough, however, to be obliged by the school board of Los Angeles to continue her education; so Chaplin hired his wife a tutor. The American humorist, Will Rogers, commented that 'this girl don't need to go to school. Any girl smart enough to marry Charlie Chaplin should be lecturing at Vassar on "taking advantage of your opportunities".'

With the marriage now behind him, he threw himself into his work on *The Gold Rush*. With Lita Chaplin soon to become visibly pregnant it was imperative that he find a new leading lady. It was announced that his new bride wished to devote all her time to her wifely duties, and therefore chose to abandon her acting career. No mention was made of her pregnancy. He had, fortunately enough, filmed only a few scenes in which she had appeared and his new choice for the part, Georgia Hale, at the age of nineteen, already had much experience of acting. She recalled his manner as a director. He would 'press his lips together, straighten out his arms between his knees and rock back and forth, uttering little baby sounds of coaxing and teasing'.

She professed later that she was already in love with him, despite having been warned by one his closest friends, Henry Bergman, to 'never fall in love with Chaplin, Georgia. He's a heartbreaker.' Chaplin told her in these days of filming that 'I've been thinking too much of you lately, even away from the studio. Do you ever think of me?' She replied that she thought of little else. 'That's all,' he said, 'I wanted to hear.' Yet she kept her distance from the married man.

The woes of his marriage meanwhile became ever larger. Sydney Chaplin tried to console Lita by explaining that his younger brother's 'instincts are good. It's just that he doesn't understand himself very well.' She later revealed that he 'was a human sex machine' who could make love six times a night without noticeable fatigue; he was a strenuous lover without necessarily being a good one. His vigour, however, led her to suspect that he committed adultery whenever he found the opportunity to do so.

A son was born to the Chaplins at the beginning of May 1925; since it was only six months after the wedding it was deemed advisable to keep mother and baby away from the prying eyes of the press. They were despatched to a cabin in the San Bernadino Mountains, and then to a house at Redondo Beach in Los Angeles County. The doctor who attended was bribed to falsify the date on the birth certificate, so that 'Charles Chaplin' was registered as entering the world on 28 June. It could at least then be

considered a premature birth. Chaplin had at first resisted the
baptismal name, on the grounds that a famous name would prove
a handicap to his son; Chaplin junior himself believed that as a
consequence of his father's 'tremendous ego' he did not want two
Charlie Chaplins in the family. He never held the baby in his
arms.

By the beginning of July he had completed the editing and
cutting of *The Gold Rush*. The film had taken seventeen months
to complete, with 170 days of actual filming. At a cost of little
under $1 million it was the most expensive comedy of the silent
era but, with earnings of $6 million, it was eventually the most
successful.

At the end of the month he travelled to New York for the
premiere. Just before the opening he became the first actor to be
placed on the front cover of *Time*, but that was just the beginning
of the adulation. *The Gold Rush* opened at the Strand Theatre on
16 August and, in *My Autobiography*, he recalled how the audience
began yelling and applauding as soon as he appeared on the screen;
the 'little fellow' blithely steps around a precipice with a bear
apparently in pursuit of him. It was the perfect combination of
comedy and terror. It also conveys one of the principles of Chaplin's
comedy. Laughter relieves the mental strain of the dread we feel
for Charlie in the world.

The image of the Little Tramp was now fixed forever in the
public imagination. His yearnings are now as palpable as his bowler
hat and cane; he needs food, money and love in that order. In
this sense his fate is inseparable from that of common humanity.
In *The Gold Rush*, and the films that follow, his role combines
pathos and dignity together with an unbreakable strength of spirit.
He holds himself upright before the camera, sometimes with almost
military severity. The single most published photograph of
Chaplin's career is that of the Little Tramp in the snowbound
cabin, shivering and hungry, looking directly at the spectator with

an expression both melancholy and steadfast. When Chaplin eventually released the film, with a narrative spoken by himself, he always referred to him impersonally as 'the poor little fellow'.

The film was an immediate, and then an enduring, success. It has always been the most popular of his films, and is generally regarded as the most coherent and the best constructed. He himself said many times that 'this is the picture I want to be remembered by'. One reviewer noted that Chaplin, in his role as the Little Tramp, had 'the unique ability to enlarge himself. We cannot see the end of him. When we make his acquaintance we go on a journey which may be long, but is not exhausting, and has a great variety of views. Such men are rare.'

After the celebrations were over he returned to his hotel suite where he collapsed. It seems to have been a case of nervous exhaustion. The doctor recommended that he leave New York immediately, and he took the train to Brighton Beach. He wrote later that, on the way, 'I wept for no reason.' He checked into a hotel beside the ocean but, as he sat at the window inhaling deep draughts of air, a crowd gathered to cheer him. He retreated into his room. When eventually he returned to New York, he remained in the city for the next two months without much apparent consideration for his wife and newborn child.

He indulged himself here in the exploitation of his fame, no less with bohemians and intellectuals than with women and society hostesses. He took a suite at the Ambassadors Hotel and began an affair with a young actress, Louise Brooks, who described him as 'the most bafflingly complex man who ever lived'. He had a fear of contracting venereal disease, naturally enough, and Brooks confided to her biographer that 'he had studied the matter and was firmly convinced that iodine was a reliable VD preventative. Normally he employed only a small local application but one night . . . he was inspired to paint the sum of his private parts with iodine and come running with a bright red erection' towards the squealing Louise Brooks and a female companion.

He returned to his round of restaurants and cocktail parties, soirées and visits to the theatre. He was surrounded by crowds wherever he went. 'It isn't affection,' he told a companion, 'it's egotism. None of these people cared a damn about me. If they did, they wouldn't embarrass me. They were thinking about themselves, feeling bigger because they had seen me and could go and brag about it.'

He entertained his friends and acquaintances in New York with endless stories and imitation. Brooks recalled that he was 'doing imitations all the time'. As Isadora Duncan he danced among streams of toiler paper and, as John Barrymore, he picked his nose. He said, one evening, 'Look, Louise, guess whom I'm imitating.' It was Louise herself. She learned then that 'everything is built on movement'.

We can capture Chaplin in conversation. Anthony Asquith, the English director, reported that his face became 'a spontaneous, improvised dance'. Another acquaintance, Stark Young, said of him that 'when you talk with him you sense at the very start an impulse to make the connection between the two of you direct and alive'. Young also made the very perceptive point that 'he does not take his colour from me, but from my colour he takes what he needs to express himself to me. He says what he wants me to believe of what he is telling me and, at the same time, I can see that it is what he himself wants to believe of it through me.' His air of frankness and conviction is genuine but 'one of its secrets is that it cannot do without you'.

The philosopher Theodor Adorno believed that 'his powerful, explosive and quick-witted agility recalls a predator ready to pounce'. He noted that 'he acts incessantly . . . Any time spent with him is an uninterrupted performance. One scarcely dares speak to him, not from awe of his fame . . . but rather from fear of disturbing the spell of the performance.'

He liked nothing so much as impersonation so powerful that it seemed more vivid and intense than the real thing. Asquith remarked that 'it was not a question of mimicry or verbal description, it was an act of creation. He himself disappeared, leaving a kind of ectoplasm from which the people, the setting, the event, materialised.' He could become two housewives gossiping in a Lambeth slum. He could become a famous politician or a notorious criminal. One friend, Robert Payne, remarked that if you gave him a lace handkerchief he would become 'an old dowager, a senorita, a Russian noblewoman'. He *was* the dowager and 'brought with her the air she lived in, the whole furniture of her mind, her hobbling walk, the delicate way her fingertips touched the furniture in her room'.

Another glimpse of Chaplin's temperament can be found in an incident at a story conference during the filming of *The Gold Rush*. A fly had been buzzing around him and, calling for a swatter, he made several unsuccessful attempts to kill it. After a few seconds a fly landed on the table beside him. He raised the swatter for the final blow, looked at the fly, and then lowered his weapon. When asked why he had changed his mind he replied that 'It isn't the same fly.'

'Enjoy any Charlie Chaplin you have the good luck or chance to encounter,' one friend, Max Eastman, suggested. 'But don't try to link them up to anything you can grasp. There are too many of them.' Sam Goldwyn, a man who knew Chaplin well in the early years, deduced that he 'loved power' and hated anything that interfered with his personal freedom. He would accept invitations and then not attend the party or dinner to which he had been asked; he would forget appointments, or arrive very late; once he promised to be the best man at a friend's wedding but never turned up. He took up people only to drop them again. Toraichi Kono said of him, through an amanuensis, that 'he is one not always to be depended on . . . he conceals disdain of individuals with an engaging charm; he cloaks his distrust of most men with a disarming smile'.

The overwhelming impression is one of detachment or unconcern that is directly linked to the phenomenon of his self-absorption. In 1925 he told a film critic, Mordaunt Hall, that 'I never get away from the notion that I am watching myself in the passing show.' He said at a later date that 'I think a very great deal of myself. Everything is perfect or imperfect, according to myself. I am the perfect standard.' Even his oldest son regarded him as 'egocentric'. Only his movements and his character are important upon the screen; he is always at the centre and, as he said, 'I am the unusual and I do not need camera angles.'

An employee from United Artists, Louis Berg, conceded that he found him 'cold, haughty, and completely indifferent to his associates . . . He smiled rarely and sourly, and seemed in every way the complete opposite of his screen impersonation. His reputation was that of a tough and unyielding executive. People were unquestionably afraid of him. And his "no" was the coldest and sharpest I have ever heard in my life.' The problem was, for Berg and for many others, that 'Chaplin is not as amiable, as modest, as warm as the little fellow on the screen'.

What is the relationship between Chaplin and Charlie? As Chaplin became more powerful in life, Charlie became less assertive and more subservient. As Chaplin incurred the wrath of his public for his philandering, Charlie became less libidinous. Chaplin became a millionaire, while Charlie was always impoverished. Chaplin was a dedicated and professional film-maker, whereas Charlie could settle down to no employment. Charlie was Chaplin's shadow self or alter ego.

Yet close resemblances between artist and character also existed. Chaplin relied upon intuition and improvisation in the same manner as the 'little fellow'. Chaplin reacted strongly against poverty and social deprivation just as Charlie is always intent upon acquiring food and finding money. Chaplin was a fervent individualist who despised any attempt at social systematisation; Charlie himself became the true symbol of such an attitude. Chaplin's self-absorption is also reproduced in the Little Tramp, abstracted from the world and yet invulnerable. Charlie has a self-regard, or self-sufficiency, so strong that nothing can challenge it. He will lean his elbow on a man's lap, or forcibly pull a young woman towards him with his cane; in his early films other people are so many objects of his lust or displeasure. He has no sense of feelings other than his own. The rest of the world must adjust to his needs and his desires. Like Chaplin himself he is both playful and detached, unwilling to participate in the lives of other people.

Yet mystery always surrounds the Little Tramp. Where has he come from? Where is he going? Chaplin himself said that 'even now I don't know all the things there are to be known about him'.

13

The edge of madness

After his triumph in New York he returned to Los Angeles in the middle of October 1925, to be greeted by the news that his wife was once again pregnant. This was a cause of dismay rather than of delight, since it seemed to tie him further to a doomed marriage. He became even more distant towards her, and he began to act in an erratic manner. Lita Chaplin wrote later that her husband was taking seven or eight showers a day. This may have been under the suspicion that he had contracted some kind of venereal disease in New York. He had become an insomniac, and at night would patrol the grounds of the house with his pistol. He arranged for some of the technicians at his studio to install a listening device, channelled through a dictaphone, into his wife's bedroom. He was having an affair with his wife's erstwhile best friend, Merna Kennedy, whom he had recently hired as the leading lady of the new film that he was contemplating. He spent all day, and much of the evening, at the studio.

One evening Chaplin came home unexpectedly and found his wife had arranged an impromptu party for some of her friends. His reaction, recalled by Lita Chaplin, was perhaps predictable. 'Get that crowd of bloody drunks out of my house at once! At once!' He then addressed the gathering. 'You pack of whores and pimps would've all been at one another all over my furniture. Not *her* home. *My* home!' Then he added to his wife, 'Get this filth out of here! You can get out with them, too, if you think you're too high class to waste your time milking me any more!'

Their second child, Sydney, was born on 31 March 1926, but

Chaplin professed not to know if he was really the father. *She* said that in this period his threats and rants against her became ever more violent. *He* said that she began to smoke and to drink. Chaplin also claimed that she began to spread slanderous stories about him to whomever would listen. At the end of November Lita Chaplin left the house on Summit Drive, and took the two children with her.

Throughout this period of marital disaffection Chaplin had been engaged on the fim that would follow *The Gold Rush*. He had begun work on it soon after his return from New York but he had been preparing for it a great deal longer; four years before, he had said that 'my greatest ambition is to make a fim about a clown'. *The Circus* was to become that film. He had hired a new assistant, Harry Crocker, whom he took on what might be called a working holiday to Del Monte, a luxury resort in the eastern part of Monterey, where they could discuss the project. In fact Chaplin talked at Crocker for twenty-eight hours without interruption.

He no doubt discussed with his young colleague the projects he had shared with other aquaintances in this period. He had a desire to play Jesus Christ or Napoleon. He was obsessed with Napoleon all of his life, perhaps as the paradigm of the small man who obtains mastery over the world; many photographs show him in Napoleonic pose, one hand tucked into his jacket. Yet he wished to present the French general in a unique light as 'a sickly being, taciturn, almost morose, continually harassed by the members of his family'. He would similarly wish to portray Christ as one always surrounded by crowds that 'would throng around him in order to feel his magnetism. Not at all a sad, pious and stiff person, but a lonely man who has been the most misunderstood of all time.' Where did Christ end and Chaplin begin?

Crocker had been told, on first arriving at the studio, that 'If you're smart you enter Chaplin on your books as a son of a bitch.

He isn't always one but he can be one on occasion.' Another employee told him that 'Charlie has a sadistic streak in him.' For reason or reasons unknown he had already discharged his previous leading lady, Georgia Hale, and had hired Merna Kennedy in her place; Kennedy had no real dramatic talent, but she had been a close friend of Lita Chaplin. This may have added spice to their subsequent romance.

Chaplin began as always with little notion of the story, or the characters, of *The Circus*; these would develop naturally as he went along. Charlie is the 'little fellow' who by accident becomes a circus clown; he is naturally funny and inventive, but fails miserably when asked to perform the standard routines of the circus. This may be an allusion to Chaplin's own career as a film comedian, in which he had defied the conventional repertoire. The Tramp can never yield to order or regimentation; he must always be free to express his own quixotic and mercurial nature. Charlie then falls in love with the ringmaster's daughter, but is supplanted by a young and handsome trapeze artist whose routine he attempts to imitate. The ringmaster is played as a ruthless and autocratic bully, whose behaviour is perhaps modelled on that of Chaplin himself.

The film was beset by mistakes and misfortunes. Just as filming was about to begin, in December 1925, a violent storm tore down the circus tent which had been erected. So work had to be postponed. Chaplin had decided that he would learn how to walk the tightrope for the climactic scene in the film; he had prevously dreamed that he was walking a tightrope when he was attacked by two monkeys. This may have been some muddled image of his domestic situation. He persevered in this self-imposed and difficult task until, in the Chaplin manner, he had attained perfection on the wire. Within three weeks the scene had been completed; but then the daily rushes were discovered to be marred by scratching. The material was abandoned, and in his rage Chaplin fired all of the laboratory technicians. Filming began once more, but some of the initial verve and energy had necessarily disappeared.

In the autumn of 1926 a large fire broke out on the set, destroying the circus tent and most of the props. Chaplin was becoming more morose and depressed than ever, a situation made infinitely worse with the news that the Internal Revenue Service were investigating him for underpayment of taxes and for possible criminal fraud. He suspended work on the film and retreated to the house he had built on the north side of the studio lot where he refused to see anyone but a few intimates. It is reported that he was paralysed with fear and indecision, fearing a possible jail sentence as well as the seizure of his assets.

On 9 January 1927, he was smuggled aboard a train to New York. On the following day Lita Chaplin filed for divorce in a statement that covered fifty-two pages. She charged him with calling her a 'gold-digger' and a 'blackmailer'; he had told her that 'if she had not been selfish and had loved him, she would have "gotten rid" of said baby – as many other women had done for him'. In particular Chaplin had told her that one actress had undergone two abortions for his sake; the woman was not named, but it was widely assumed to be Edna Purviance. Lita Chaplin also accused her husband of having pulled a gun on her and threatened her, of having changed the locks while she was out of the house, and of having insisted that she accompany him to the house of 'a certain motion picture actress'. This might have been the residence of Marion Davies; his motive being to provoke jealousy on his young wife's part.

More salacious and dangerous material was to come. Lita Chaplin stated that 'throughout the entire married life of said parties and at times too numerous for plaintiff to more particularly specify, defendant has solicited, urged and demanded that plaintiff submit to, perform and commit such acts and things for the gratification of defendant's said abnormal, unnatural, perverted and degenerate sexual desires as to be too revolting, indecent and immoral to set forth in detail in this complaint'. Specific allusion was made to Section 288a of the Californian penal code that outlawed, even within marriage, the practices of sodomy and oral sex. He had said to her that 'all married people do those kinds of things. You are my wife and you *have* to do what I want you to do.'

The fifty-two pages were instantly seized upon by a voyeuristic and sensation-hungry public, and *The Complaint of Lita* was within a few days being sold on the street corners of Los Angeles at twenty-five cents a copy. While on the train to New York, Chaplin issued a statement that 'I realise that I am temporarily under a cloud, but those who know me and love me will not pay any attention to the charges, as they will know they are untrue.'

On 16 January his doctor issued a statement that his patient was 'suffering from a serious nervous breakdown'. A short sequence of film taken at this time shows him ill at ease, his face twitching. His Japanese chauffeur, Toraichi Kono, told Rollie Totheroh that Chaplin had tried to jump out of the window of his hotel bedroom in New York. So Kono kept watch by his bedside for four days and nights. The doctor had forbidden newspapers from reaching his patient, but Chaplin insisted on seeing the headlines concerning his unfortunate case. Kono believed that he derived some melancholy pleasure from being attacked, just as Pola Negri had observed that he found some satisfaction in being violently criticised by her. Chaplin always believed that he was under threat from certain enemies who were plotting to destroy him, but in truth his own actions were largely responsible for his troubles.

He managed somehow to overcome his mental crisis, and made brief expeditions from the security of his hotel. Through the agency of his lawyers he came to a tentative and temporary agreement with the IRS. Eventually, too, a settlement for the divorce was proposed. Lita Chaplin's lawyers had threatened to reveal the names of the six actresses with whom Chaplin had slept after his marriage. One of these was Marion Davies. Such an exposure was unthinkable. Chaplin at once accepted his lawyer's advice to settle as quickly as possible. Thus, on 22 August, Lita Chaplin was awarded $625,000 and her sons were protected by a $200,000 trust fund. It was the largest divorce settlement in American history, but the only damaged reputation was that of Chaplin himself. The humorist Will Rogers complained on the radio that 'I left Hollywood to keep from being named in the Chaplin trial, and now they go and name nobody.'

Chaplin went back to work on *The Circus* at the end of August, after a delay of eight months. It was remarked by the workers of the studio that, as a result of the troubles with Lita, his greying hair had now turned completely white. It was a tribute to his stamina and his vision, however, that he was still determined to finish the picture and to maintain the same scrupulous attention to detail. The final scene, in which Charlie is seen to be alone in the ring where the circus had once stood, was filmed on location in what was then the Los Angeles suburb of Sawtelle. He shot the scene again and again. At three o'clock in the morning of 10 October he watched himself in the rushes. 'He should do that much better.' 'He doesn't ring true.' 'He has his derby down too far over his eyes.' 'They have burned his face up with those silver reflectors.' It was all to be done again. He had always said that his way of working was 'sheer perseverance to the edge of madness'. The film was released three months later.

He rarely discussed *The Circus*, no doubt as a result of the personal misfortunes that accompanied it, but it is one of the most animated and engaging of his films. The early sequences, in which the 'little fellow' enters the circus and unwittingly entertains its audience, are as inventive as anything he had ever achieved before. He is trapped in a house of mirrors while being chased by the police; he inadvertently sabotages a magician's act; he enters a lion's cage and cannot get out. All of these scenes are in themselves little triumphs of the comic art, masterpieces proving that the most hilarious comedy can spring out of the most distressing private circumstances.

In the final scene of *The Circus* Charlie is somewhere outside the world; he does not accept the invitation to return to the company of the other performers, and therefore remains essentially aloof and inviolate. He is intrigued and sometimes affected by the passions of others, but he refuses to participate in them. The scene was deliberately shot in the early morning light so that the lines on Chaplin's face could more clearly be seen. He remains alone as the circus moves on. In the end, he has no need for anybody.

14

The beauty of silence

Even before the premiere of *The Circus*, at the beginning of 1928, he set to work on his next film. He was so eager to begin *City Lights* that he might have been trying to make up for time lost in the previous year. Yet, in the interim, the cinema had altogether changed. In the autumn of 1927 *The Jazz Singer* had proved the possibilities of synchronised sound, and in the following year *Lights of New York* became the first all-talking picture. By the end of 1929 8,000 cinemas had been wired for sound, and the audiences for what was essentially the new medium of the talkies multiplied.

Chaplin opposed the introduction of sound from the beginning. He believed that it would mean the end of his art. In an interview at the beginning of 1929 he complained that 'they are spoiling the oldest art in the world – the art of pantomime. They are ruining the great beauty of silence. They are defeating the meaning of the screen.' As far as his comedy was concerned, 'it would be fatal'. He was a mime of genius and, by definition, a mime did not speak.

The advent of sound dealt him a double blow since the audiences might now find Chaplin outmoded and his great art a temporary or passing phenomenon. Yet how could the 'little fellow' speak? What kind of voice could he be given? The Tramp had become Everyman, an emblem of the human world, and Everyman can have no language. If he spoke English it would affect his reception by foreign audiences who would no longer have the direct and unmediated contact with the figure on the screen. Chaplin explained that 'the Chinese children, the Japanese children, the

Hindu, the Hottentot, all understand me. I doubt whether they would understand my Chinese or my Hindustani.'

It was a financial as well as an aesthetic consideration. His film rights in Japan alone covered the cost of his productions. The use of sound equipment on set would in any case require a complete change in the nature of the performance and the style of production; it would also be highly expensive. Chaplin was, in terms of his art, a traditionalist and never became used to developments in cinematic art or in filmic technique.

He said in another interview that 'for years I have specialised in one type of comedy – strictly pantomime. I have measured it, gauged it, studied it. I have been able to establish exact principles to govern its reactions on audiences. It has a certain pace and tempo. Dialogue, to my way of thinking, always slows actions, because action must wait on words.' He seriously believed that the talkies themselves were simply a passing phase, and that the cinema would once more embrace the purity of silence.

In the spring of 1928 the principal performers of United Artists – Mary Pickford, Douglas Fairbanks and Chaplin himself, now joined by John Barrymore and Norma Talmadge – took part in a wireless broadcast so that the audiences could hear their voices. A journalist from *Variety* spoke to Chaplin immediately after the broadcast and reported 'that he nearly died while doing it through mike fright, and was worried as to how he did'. Chaplin also told the studio director that he was so anxious that he had lost nine pounds in weight during the ordeal. The experience did not endear him to the new medium. At a later date he was offered more than $500,000 to make twenty-six wireless broadcasts of fifteen minutes duration. He refused on the grounds that 'I have to remain a little remote and mysterious. They have to romanticise me. I would lose more than that at the box office if I made myself real and familiar over the radio.'

He closed down the preliminary production of *City Lights* for some weeks, however, so that he might carefully consider the problem. He tried to imagine how the scenes would be improved with dialogue, and decided that sound would have only a deleterious effect. His mind was made up. No force on earth could have changed it. So he continued the preparations for his latest silent picture when all around him the actors were talking and the bands were playing. He put the case for silence to an English journalist. 'Why have I refused to talk in *City Lights*? I think the question should really be: Why *should* I talk?' He also told him, concerning his decision, 'I began to feel like the boy on the burning deck whence all but he had fled. I confess to some worry, but never to doubt.'

He had begun making notes and creating plot lines before the premiere of *The Circus* in New York, but it was almost a year before he began any actual filming of *City Lights*. The central characters were Charlie himself, a blind flower-girl and a millionaire; when drunk the millionaire adopts the Tramp as his bosom companion but, when sober, he does not recognise him. In collusion with the drunken millionaire the Tramp becomes the girl's benefactor, but in her blindness she believes that he is her generous patron. She falls in love with one whom she considers to be a suave and handsome stranger. The comic possibilities were evident to Chaplin from the beginning, just as the 'little fellow's' love for the blind flower-girl gave him the opportunity of mingling pathos with comedy in the familiar manner. Yet in *City Lights* they are lent maximum intensity. He wished to convey the fact that silent film was supreme in the art of human expressiveness.

Even as Chaplin was preparing the film, in the summer of 1928, his mother died. She had been admitted to Glendale Hospital with an infected gall bladder. It seems that he had visited her every day and had tried to revive her flagging spirits, but she suffered a great deal of pain. On his last visit to her she had relapsed into a coma. When told of her death he went immediately to the hospital where she was still lying in her bed. He revealed to an interviewer that 'I couldn't . . . I couldn't touch her. No, I couldn't touch her.' At the funeral he was expected to step forward and say farewell to her just before the lid was placed on the coffin, but 'I said no: I couldn't.'

The work upon *City Lights* continued. For the part of the blind flower-girl he chose Virginia Cherrill, a young woman whom he had seen in a ringside seat of a boxing match; she had no acting experience but that, for Chaplin, was always an advantage. He could fashion her in any shape he wished. Virginia Cherrill was a society girl, living on alimony, and agreed to take part in the film on a whim. But she also had the advantage of poor sight, and seemed effortlessly able to feign blindness. Chaplin advised her 'to look inwardly and not to see me'.

The details of their opening scene together, when Charlie purchases a flower before realising that she is blind, took two years and 342 takes to assemble. Chaplin said in an interview that 'she'd be doing something that wasn't right. Lines. A line. A contour hurts me if it's not right. And she'd say, "Flower, sir?" I'd say, "Look at that! Nobody says *flower* like that." She was an amateur . . . I'd know in a minute when she wasn't there, when she'd be searching, or looking up just too much or too soon . . . Or she waited a second. I'd know in a minute.' When she asked why her pronunciation of words was so important in a silent film he replied, according to her own account, that 'all he asked – this was said loudly and slowly, as if he were addressing someone hard of hearing – was that she should do as he asked. Was it really so difficult?' He also demanded that she achieve the perfect gesture as she offers the flower to the Tramp. 'When you offer the flowers, *bend* your arm, make a nice movement, don't be quite so threatening.' A short film was shot of Chaplin directing this scene; he is tense, sitting upright in a canvas chair, waving his hands; he is brusque and dissatisfied. The scene itself was filmed on a set that looked uncannily like that of the street and railings outside St Mark's Church on Kennington Park Road; the resemblance is not coincidental. He was once more going back to the landscape of his childhood, from which he drew his inspiration.

He told Alistair Cooke that in this period 'I was a terror to be with.' He flew into sudden and violent rages; he refused food; he called his assistants late at night and ordered them to join him for consultations. Waldo Frank, the novelist and literary critic, composed a portrait of Chaplin at this time. He wrote that 'Chaplin's eyes are a blue so darkly shadowed that they are almost purple. They are sad eyes; from them pity and bitterness look out upon the world. They are veiled; while the man moves forward with irresistible charm, his eyes hold back in a solitude fiercely forbidding. No one who sees the eyes of Chaplin would feel like laughing.' He added that 'Chaplin does not wish to give himself to any emotion, to any situation, to any life.'

In this highly charged state it was understandable that disputes and angry arguments erupted between Chaplin and Cherrill; on one occasion Cherrill interrupted a scene to announce that she had an appointment with her hairdresser. Chaplin was so furious that he abandoned shooting, and took to his bed for several days. At one point he fired her before realising that she was in fact indispensable to the film. They never really liked or understood one another and, after the filming of *City Lights*, went separate ways. At the age of twenty she may have been too old for him.

At a later date Virginia Cherrill recalled her days at the studio. She recorded that 'Charlie even took control of what we ate. One time, we couldn't have anything but vegetables; another week, he wanted us living on cheese and fruit.' On his style as a director she commented that 'Charlie acted out every single part, you see, every glance, every movement, just as he wanted it to be played. You found yourself thinking that he was you, and that he was also that person he wanted you to be. It wasn't easy.' At a later date, in a television interview, she volunteered the information that 'he was a dervish' and that 'Charlie was always acting. He was always "on".'

Chaplin fell ill at the end of February with ptomaine poisoning that progressed into influenza, and he lost the whole of March in recovery; nevertheless the cast came to the studio each day in case he should suddenly reappear. His debility may also have had something to do with his generally nervous and overanxious state during the making of the film. He came back to the studio on 1 April, where he insisted on working further on the opening scene with the Tramp and the flower-girl. He was once again working six or seven days a week, from morning until night, performing and editing, directing and writing. 'I did it all,' he told an interviewer, 'which very few in my day did, you know. They didn't do it all, you see . . . And that's why I was so exhausted.'

Yet exhaustion did not necessarily prevent him from entertaining guests. Winston Churchill visited the set. The Spanish director Luis Buñuel used to come up to the house on Summit Drive; Buñuel later recalled that his host had tried to set up an 'orgy' for him with three prostitutes. Sergei Eisenstein also stayed at the house; he wrote to a friend that 'we often go to Chaplin's house to play tennis. He's really nice. And extremely unhappy (personally).' He made a less cryptic comment about the artist rather than the man when he wrote that 'the true, the humanly inspiring "chosen man of God", of whom Wagner dreamed, is not Parsifal bowing down before the Grail in Bayreuth, but Charlie Chaplin among the trash-cans of the East Side'.

Ivor Montagu, an Englishman who was then an assistant producer at Paramount, recalled a tea party in the garden of Summit Drive where 'all was incredibly decorous and English county'. Chaplin played tennis with his guests, on his own court, with a ferocity and will to win that were unequalled. Montagu said that 'Charlie was a very good tennis player. He seemed to be able to attain any skill he wanted.'

He finished filming *City Lights* by the autumn of 1930, but his labours were not over. He had determined that, in the absence of sound, he would write the musical score for the picture. It is music that might have been inspired by 'The Honeysuckle and the Bee', the song that he had heard one night in South London. The score incorporates the music of the Victorian theatre in its sentimental aspect, therefore, but it is composed with an elegance and simplicity that carefully accompany the mood upon the screen. Chaplin's music in general is sometimes lush, sometimes jaunty and sometimes lyrical; it includes stirring brass and haunting violins. It has passages derived from the waltz and the tango, as well as pleasurable intimations of seaside bands. It can be excitable, sweet, playful and melancholy.

He said in a radio interview that the early acts of the Karno Company, in which 'comedy tramps' appeared, were accompanied by 'very beautiful boudoir music, something of the eighteenth century, very lush and very "grandioso", just purely as satirical and as a counterpoint; and I copied a great deal from Mr Fred Karno in that direction'. His compositions are all the more remarkable in light of the fact that he had absolutely no musical training. He would hum or sing a tune while a notator would transcribe it. Yet music was in his being. All of his subsequent films had scores of his own devising.

City Lights opened at the end of January 1931, in Los Angeles. Chaplin was nervous about its reception. He told Henry Bergman that 'I don't know so much about that picture. I'm not sure.' On his way to the theatre he murmured, 'I don't think it's going to go over. I don't think they're going to like it . . . No, I just feel it.' It did indeed represent a tremendous risk; this was a silent film in the new age of sound.

In the event it earned a standing ovation. At the opening in New York, a few days later, it was greeted with the same enthusiasm and celebration. His publicity manager came into his hotel bedroom on the morning after the premiere. 'Boy you've done it,' he told him. 'What a hit! There's been a line running round the block ever since ten o'clock this morning and it's stopping the traffic! There are about ten cops trying to keep order. They're fighting to get in. And you should hear them yell!' It was widely considered to be a masterpiece of what was now an old medium, and it reminded audiences of what had been lost in the transition to sound.

It was subtitled 'A Comedy Romance in Pantomime' and is by any standard a remarkable film, breathtaking in its range and variety of feeling. Chaplin satirises pathos at the same time as he indulges in it; he introduces a number of comic scenes, such as a farcical boxing match, without at any point compromising the emotional current of the narrative. The film was released at the beginning of the Great Depression, a period of distress and destitution when the figure of the hungry and dishevelled Tramp becomes more pertinent than ever before; although Chaplin makes no allusion to the national calamity, it provides the context for the relationship between Charlie and the impoverished flower-girl. It rendered the sentiment more immediate, and more engaging.

The closing scene is perhaps the greatest triumph of his art. The blind girl can now see but she has never known the identity of her benefactor. The Tramp, more degraded than ever, encounters her; she takes his hand, to give him a coin, and at that moment understands who he is. 'You can see now?' he asks her. 'Yes, I can see now.' That is where the film ends, with a look of exaltation and also of terror on the Tramp's face. The critic, James Agee, concluded that 'it is enough to shrivel the heart to see, and it is the greatest piece of acting and the highest moment in movies'. *City Lights* remained Chaplin's own favourite among his films.

On the day after the premiere Chaplin left Los Angeles in order to attend the film's opening in New York. But that was just the beginning of a more extended journey. A week after the screening in New York he boarded the *Mauretania* for the voyage to London with Toraichi Kono and his publicist, Carlyle Robinson. He told a news reporter that 'I am looking forward to seeing once more the haunts of my boyhood, and finding out if the hot saveloy and crumpet man is still going around ringing his bell.' Yet he also wanted to rest; he stayed in his cabin for most of the journey and did not mingle with the other travellers. After the success of *City Lights*, in fact, he fell into a depression; he asked his friends, 'What am I going to do next?'

He arrived in England to an even more exuberant welcome than that he had received almost ten years before; the Great Western Railway put an observation car at his disposal at Plymouth, and it was at once surrounded by admirers. His arrival at Paddington was described by a journalist from *The Times*, who noted that 'Dickens knew something of popular enthusiasm, but could he have beheld the press of people gathered . . . in honour of Mr Chaplin he might have rubbed his eyes in astonishment.' The reporter observed that Chaplin was as excited as the applauding crowd and that 'he promptly scrambled on to the roof of the car and, waving his hat and returning the shouts of the crowd, he was borne in slow triumph out of the station'. The premiere of *City Lights* was held, a week after his return, at the Dominion Theatre in Tottenham Court Road; he had to use a side entrance in an alley, one hour before the proceedings began, in order to avoid the crowd. At the end of the performance, however, he appeared at an upstairs window where his figure was picked out by searchlights.

Immediately on his arrival in the city he began a round of social calls that lasted a fortnight. He stayed with Winston Churchill at Chartwell, and visited H. G. Wells on several occasions. He had dinner at Chequers with the prime minister, Ramsay MacDonald; when Chaplin tried to discuss economic matters with him, Macdonald merely nodded with a quizzical expression upon his face. He discussed unemployment with David Lloyd George but, as Chaplin himself recalled, 'I could not help noticing a stifled yawn.' Chaplin was full of financial plans to shrink the government, to control prices as well as interests and profits, and to abolish the gold standard; yet nobody was really interested in the economic theories of an actor.

He also discussed politics with John Maynard Keynes and George Bernard Shaw at the house of Nancy Astor; when he entered the drawing room of Lady Astor's mansion in St James's Square he said that 'it was like stepping into the Hall of Fame at Madame Tussaud's'. It was perhaps still a little unreal for him, when he noticed the newspaper placards announcing that 'Charlie Is Still Their Darling'.

He also made a more private and desolate journey when he returned to Hanwell Schools, the establishment for orphans and destitute children to which he had been consigned at the age of seven. He arrived alone and unannounced, perhaps savouring the solitariness of his approach; yet his presence soon became known to the teachers and children who were told to assemble in the dining hall. A reporter from the *Daily Express*, having spoken later to those who had seen him, recorded that 'he entered the dining hall where four hundred boys and girls cheered their heads off at the sight of him – and he entered in style. He made to raise his hat, and it jumped magically into the air! He swung his cane and hit himself in the leg! He turned out his feet and hopped along inimitably. It was Charlie! Yells! Shrieks of joy! More yells!'

Carlyle Robinson recalled that Chaplin wept when he returned to his hotel. Chaplin himself told the writer Thomas Burke that 'it had been the greatest emotional experience of his life'. He added that 'being among those buildings and connecting with everything – with the misery and something that wasn't misery . . . The shock of it, too. You see, I never really believed that it'd be *there*.' When the taxi turned off the main road, 'then, all of a sudden, *th-ere* it was. O-o-oh it was there – just as I'd left it. I've never had a moment like that in my life. I was almost physically sick with emotion.' When Burke remonstrated with him for this hapless return to past misery he replied that 'I like being morbid. It does me good, I thrive on it.' His salmon-like instinct for home led him to visit the old music halls of the capital, the Star at Bermondsey, the Royal at Stratford, the Paragon in Mile End Road and Seebright on the Hackney Road among them. He stopped at a coffee stall in the Elephant and Castle, a few yards from his childhood home, and ordered stewed eels.

Yet his moods did not last for very long. He had promised the orphan children he would return in the following week with the present of a cinema projector. On the date of the planned visit, however, he was lunching with Nancy Astor and was not in a nostalgic mood. So he ordered Robinson and Karno to carry the projector to Hanwell in his place, much to the disappointment of the children and of the crowds who had assembled to see him. It is an indication, if nothing else, of Chaplin's mercurial and unreliable character. He excused himself later by confessing that he could not bear to repeat the painful experience.

Chaplin travelled from London to Berlin, and then to Vienna where he received perhaps the most rapturous reception of his life; news-cameras show him being carried over the heads of the crowd from the railway station to his hotel. The adulation was the same in Paris and in Venice. But he had decided now to rest properly and journeyed south to the French Riviera where he might play the role of the playboy of the western world.

In Cannes he met a Czech girl, Mizzi Muller, otherwise known as May Reeves, who became for a while his latest paramour. It was the usual story of passion and high spirits interspersed with jealousy and coldness. She had already been warned that he 'stifled the personality of all those who drew close to him'. She recalled in a memoir that 'the radiant Chaplin' was shadowed 'by another Chaplin who was his nervous double, irritable and sullen'. In her account he could also be morbid and sadistic. She noticed how his mood could change instantaneously from exhilaration to depression.

Every situation became for him the occasion of drama. In conversation he would continually repeat, 'if one day I lose all my money'. This fear of poverty may have been the reason for his reluctance to part with ready cash; he would on occasions go on shopping expeditions with Reeves and return without purchasing anything at all. He seems to have enjoyed watching his image in the mirror and, according to Reeves, would remark that 'For my age, I'm still well preserved' or 'Don't you think I'm in very good shape?' 'I don't care a rap for it,' he said, after refusing to attend a banquet in his honour. 'I'm a world-famous figure.' He was perhaps following the lead of his brother who, according to Reeves, continually used the phrase to excuse Chaplin's odd behaviour.

In the company of May Reeves he spent the autumn in London, where he received unfavorable publicity for declining to appear on stage during that year's Royal Variety Performance; it was construed to be an insult to George V. He told a young tennis partner that 'they say I have a duty to England. I wonder just what that duty is. No one wanted me or cared for me in England seventeen years ago. I had to go to America for my chance, and I got it there.' He added that 'patriotism is the greatest insanity the world has ever suffered'. Unfortunately the tennis partner turned out to be a journalist, and Chaplin was surprised and annoyed by the headline 'Charlie Chaplin No Patriot'. Yet he never changed his opinion on the subject.

In London he continued his ritual encounters with the rich, the powerful and the famous. He was often in the company of the Prince of Wales, dined with various members of the nobility, and one afternoon visited Mahatma Gandhi who was staying in lodgings along the East India Dock Road. He also travelled to the north of England in order to see once more the places he had visited while on tour with *Sherlock Holmes* in the early years of the century. He was still intrigued by the adventures of his early self. Finding Manchester at three o'clock on a Sunday afternoon 'cataleptic', he drove to Blackburn where he visited the public house in which he used to lodge for fourteen shillings a week; he ordered a drink, and went unrecognised.

Yet for him holidays were essentially empty days. If he could not work, he was only half alive; he was frustrated and without purpose, all the time contemplating his future as an artist. He knew now that he could never return to wholly silent films, but what was to take their place? He had determined to return to California via New York when a telegram arrived for him from Douglas Fairbanks. Fairbanks was staying in St Moritz and begged his friend to come to him. So with May Reeves he joined Fairbanks and company for several weeks of entertainment.

Sydney Chaplin was also of the party and at his suggestion Chaplin decided to return to the United States by way of Italy, Japan and the Far East; Sydney could then organise the premiere of *City Lights* in Tokyo. It was clear that May Reeves was not to join them on the voyage from Italy, and she was left on the quay-side at Naples as Chaplin sailed away in March 1932. She never saw him again.

The two brothers travelled first to Singapore, where Chaplin succumbed to fever. Then they sailed on to Bali, partly with the intention of ogling the semi-naked native women of the island. It is not perhaps a wholly delightful picture of two middle-aged men.

On their arrival at Bali they became acquainted with an American artist, Al Hirschfield, who was living in the village of Den Pasar. Hirschfield's houseboys did not recognise Chaplin, in a locality without a cinema, and so in the words of his host he 'decided to carry out an experiment'. He decided to become Charlie for the moment and, in the absence of the requisite bowler, picked up a sola topee. Hirschfield recalled that 'Charlie put the pith helmet on his head and it sprang crazily into the air, seemingly with a will of its own. Undaunted, and with a wide-eyed look of nonchalance, he tried it again. And again the hat flew off his head.' It was an old trick from the music hall but 'the natives howled with laughter, thinking his hat possessed demonic powers'. He could never resist an audience, however small.

From Bali the Chaplin brothers sailed on to Japan. On his arrival at Tokyo Chaplin was escorted by policemen through the cheering crowds. He found it impossible to get out of the hotel by normal means, so great was the press of people waiting to glimpse him, but he and Sydney made their escape by sliding down the drainpipes in Karno fashion.

He in turn was excited and delighted by what he saw of Japanese culture. Of the tea ceremony he remarked that it might seem quaint or trivial to a westerner but 'if we consider the highest object of life is the pursuit of the beautiful, what is more rational than applying it to the commonplace?' He was entranced by the kabuki, also, and attended many performances of this ancient theatre; he was intrigued by the elaborate make-up and by the formalised gestures of the performers, so close to the nature of his own art. Just as the kabuki actor might take up a stylised pose in order fully to establish his character, so Chaplin relied upon posture and movement to define the 'little fellow'. The performers put on a characteristically thick white make-up, concocted from rice powder; in his later films, Chaplin's face became so ethereally white that it resembled a mask. He had stumbled naturally upon techniques that were already hundreds of years old.

In Tokyo he became inadvertently involved in a conspiracy. On the day after his arrival, in the middle of May, the prime minister of Japan was assassinated by a band of officers from the army and navy. The men had also planned to kill Chaplin. One of the leaders of the plot was interrogated.

'Judge: What was the significance of killing Chaplin?

'Koga: Chaplin is a popular figure in the United States and a darling of the capitalist class. We believed that killing him would cause a war with America and thus we could kill two birds with a single stone.'

It is not clear that Chaplin would have appreciated the description of him as 'a darling of the capitalist class'. He sailed from Yokohama to Seattle at the beginning of June. His world tour had come to an end, and he had observed much that had depressed him but nothing so much as the spectacle of the hordes of the unemployed. This was the real scourge of humankind. When he was told that human labour would soon become so cheap that it could successfully compete with the machine, he believed that this was 'deeply cruel'. He would reflect upon these matters in the preparation of his next film. He was about to begin work on *Modern Times*.

15

The machine

He had begun making notes for *Modern Times* while sailing back to the United States. He had also completed an 'economic solution' to the financial problems of the world that obliquely touched upon the nature of the film; it was not a very convincing solution, based upon the creation of an international currency, but it demonstrates that he was seriously considering the plight of contemporary industrialism.

He was still uncertain how to begin the film. On his return, he had found Hollywood greatly changed. Those stars of the silent era who had not made the transition to sound had retired or been replaced; as far as he was concerned, the studios had become industrial plants with the new technology hindering what he considered to be the free spirit of the cinema. The new cameras were elephantine, the sound equipment bulky and obtrusive, while the performers had to manoeuvre themselves between acres of wires and switches. There were times, by his own account, that he thought seriously of selling up and emigrating to China. This was another element in the conception of *Modern Times*.

One last battle still had to be fought with his ex-wife, Lita Grey. In the summer he filed a petition to the Californian courts objecting to his sons working in motion pictures. He did not wish them or the Chaplin name to be exploited, in which cause he was successful. Charles Chaplin junior was now seven, and Sydney Earle Chaplin was a year younger. Now that the two boys were of an age to be interesting or entertaining, he began to see them regularly. Charles junior recalled that his father would show them his early films in the private screening room of the house. 'There he is now, there comes the little fellow,' he would say, rubbing his hands with glee and anticipation. 'Yes, there he is, with the big fellow with the bandaged foot. That means trouble. Watch it, boys.' Sometimes father and sons would visit the amusement pier at Ocean Park where 'the honky-tonk, hurdy-gurdy air of the place always excited and delighted him'.

Charles also recalled the protean character of his father who could be in turn 'the strict disciplinarian, the priceless entertainer, the taciturn, moody dreamer, the wild man of Borneo with his flashes of volcanic temper'. Sydney simply described him as 'constipated'. The older brother also noticed other aspects of his father's character. Chaplin would always tip the waiter ten per cent of the meal, nothing more or less, but then he might tip a barber $5 for doing a good job.

He noted that his father would save scraps of paper and the stubs of pencils; Chaplin read pulp detective magazines, a stack of which were beside his bed; he preferred solidly English food, roast beef and baked potatoes; he ordered tea and crumpets every Sunday afternoon at four; he generally spoke of himself in the third person; he suffered from a nervous stomach. At table he ordered his sons to sit up straight and not to speak unless spoken to. Charles also concluded that 'the violence of his anger was always so out of proportion to the object that had stirred him that I couldn't help being frightened at it'.

Chaplin had already met his new leading lady. He was first introduced to Paulette Goddard on a yachting holiday with a mutual friend, and almost at once she became 'the pretty little ray of sunlight' for which he had been searching. She was then a minor actress who had completed one film for Samuel Goldwyn and was about to join the Hal Roach Studios. Chaplin remembered her first words to him. 'Mr Chaplin, I've been married, I'm divorced.

I want to meet and get on with the greatest actor in Hollywood, and that's you.' She was pretty; she was intelligent and high-spirited with a penchant for 'fooling around' that endeared her to Chaplin. She had told him that she was seventeen, but in fact she was already twenty-two. Nevertheless he bought her jewels and, at her urging, he purchased a yacht that was perhaps aptly named *Panacea* on which he sailed with visitors and house guests to the island of Catalina twenty-two miles off the coast of California.

She soon moved into his mansion and together they would enjoy nightclubs and boxing halls and the general paraphernalia of urban life. Paulette Goddard also helped in the relationship between father and sons. The Chaplin boys adored her from the beginning and began to think of her as their big sister; in turn she helped to arrange family outings and celebrations. Their father even allowed them to sleep in the same bed with her, at least up to a certain age. Goddard in fact took over Chaplin's domestic affairs and arrangements to such an extent that his chauffeur and manservant, Toraichi Kono, felt obliged to leave his employment after sixteen years of service; Chaplin was not sentimental about such matters.

One question agitated him. Why was he not at work? Goddard helped him to resolve the problem. He soon divined that she had a natural talent for comedy, and that her gamine demeanour would naturally complement the role of the Little Tramp. And so it proved. Chaplin bought out her contract with Hal Roach, made her change back the colour of her hair from platinum blonde to its natural brown, and arranged for her to have coaching in dance and voice.

The inspiration for *Modern Times* came from several quarters. He had for years been talking about a film that would satirise the factory system, but nothing had emerged. In this period, however, he recalled a conversation with a journalist from Detroit who told him that some workers in the car factories suffered from nervous collapse. More particularly he is said to have been intrigued by a rubber belt, in a Los Angeles restaurant, that transported the dirty plates to a dishwasher; he must have seen the comic possibilities of such a device, just as he had once used an escalator as the central motif of *The Floorwalker*. He may also have recalled an incident from his early childhood when he had gone to work at a firm of printers and stationers; he was put in charge of a printing machine that 'started to roll, grind and grunt; I thought it was going to devour me'. This is precisely what happens to the little hero of *Modern Times*. He said later that the film 'started from an abstract idea, an impulse to say something about the way life is being standardised and channelised, and men turned into machines'.

In the summer of 1933 Chaplin's new film was announced to the press with the news that 'it will be laid in the lower part of any big city with factories'. Various titles were suggested, among them *Commonwealth* and *The Masses*; early notes for the scenario suggest that Chaplin's interest in economic matters had led him to create a film that was serious or didactic in intent. Scenes would be 'shot in factory, men pull machine apart. Men could conspire to destroy the machine. They put me to work for the purpose, but I am innocent of their plan.' It was important that the Little Tramp remained an innocent abroad.

Yet his intentions seem to have changed in the course of the subsequent two years. When a newspaper reported that Chaplin was about to satirise President Roosevelt's economic programme as well as the factory system, Chaplin issued a statement that he was 'a great admirer of President Roosevelt and in entire sympathy with his policies'. He had no desire to antagonise his audience, comprised largely of conservative Americans, and he declared that he was creating 'a comedy picture with no endeavor to comment or satirise on social or political affairs'. He wished only to provide entertainment. He emphasised the role of Goddard as a 'waif' or 'gamine' against a background of waterfronts and dance halls. In a programme note he described the relationship of the Tramp and the young girl as 'two joyous spirits living by their wits'. There was to be 'no romance in their relationship, really two playmates – partners in crime, comrades, babes in the wood'.

It may have been that he could not, in the spring of 1934, see his way through the narrative. His son, Charles Junior, states that in this period 'his dark moods became more pronounced, his flashes of anger more frequent'. The son blamed this upon his father's 'fear of failure'. His hesitations about the use of sound were still considerable, but he prepared a script with dialogue and shot one scene with synchronised speech:

Tramp: No – oh well, where d'ya live?
Gamine: No place – here – there – anywhere.
Tramp: Anywhere? That's near where I live.

He did not believe the experiment to be a success, however, and instead of voices he created a soundtrack that could be used with comic intent. His oldest son also recalled that 'everyone in Hollywood thought my father was crazy . . . He was finished in pictures – you heard that all over town.'

Chaplin began filming *Modern Times* in the autumn of 1934, and took approximately a year to complete it. The interior of the factory, the setting for the first scenes of the film, was constructed on the studio lot at a cost of $50,000; the wood and rubber machinery, in which the 'little fellow' is devoured, was painted to simulate the sheen of steel. Chaplin also rented a five-acre lot near Los Angeles Harbor in order to create an industrial landscape. The costs were so high that he worked from a prepared scenario; he knew that delays or changes of direction would be very expensive. Goddard recalled that on her first day she turned up in 'the full glamour rig' for her debut on *Modern Times*. 'Charlie took one look at me, shook his head, and said "That's not it. That's definitely not it." He told me to take off my shoes, change my suit and remove my make-up. Then he threw a bucket of water all over me.' Many actors were in fact terrified of working with him. When he lost his temper while in costume, he would shout and gesticulate with all the mannerisms of the Little Tramp.

He showed a rough cut of the film in the summer of 1935 to the head of the Soviet film industry, Boris Shumyatski, who promptly told the American *Daily Worker* that *Modern Times* was to be 'a sharp satire on the capitalist system'. He even claimed that he had persuaded Chaplin to change its ending in order to demonstrate to the cinema audience 'the necessity for active struggle'.

This was not the kind of publicity that Chaplin needed and the general manager of his studio, Alf Reeves, was obliged to issue a statement that Shumyatski 'reads deep, terrible social meanings to sequences that Mr Chaplin considers funny'. He added that 'I can assure you that this picture is intended as entertainment, and perhaps it might be said, too, that Mr Chaplin's purpose in making this picture is to make money.' Chaplin, in other words, was not in the least opposed to the capitalist system. In the marketing campaign for the film Chaplin shoes, Chaplin hats, and Chaplin banners were provided; Chaplin lookalikes were hired to parade outside cinemas with the sign 'I'm back again!'

Musical differences bedevilled the last stages of editing. In the early autumn of 1935 a young man of twenty-three years, David Raksin, was hired to be Chaplin's orchestrator. It was not for him a happy experience. He recalled that 'like many self-made autocrats Chaplin demanded unquestioning obedience from his associates'. When Raksin dared to disagree with his employer, he was promptly fired. Raksin had simply said, 'I think we can do better than that.' Chaplin was persuaded by Alf Reeves, however, to re-employ him.

Chaplin would come to the studio in the morning with one

or two musical phrases in his head; Raksin would then transcribe them and together they would work upon a score. Chaplin would say 'A bit of Gershwin might be nice there' or 'What we need here is one of those Puccini melodies.' They still argued, Chaplin more stubborn and combative than ever, and on occasions Raksin would walk out. 'I can't go back,' he told a studio assistant, 'I'm going to punch him on the nose.'

Chaplin also quarrelled with Alfred Newman, the director of music at United Artists. He demanded rewrites and on occasions the orchestra had to play the same part twenty or thirty times. Newman himself worked sixteen-hour days and slept five nights a week at the studio. When Chaplin accused the orchestra of 'dogging it', or playing in a tired and mediocre fashion at a rehearsal, Newman threw down his baton and declared that he would never work with Chaplin again. Raksin took Newman's side, thus incurring Chaplin's wrath once more. In his search for perfection, he wore them all down.

Modern Times opened on 5 February 1936, at the Rivoli theatre in New York; a week later it was first shown at Grauman's Chinese Theatre in Hollywood. It was an immediate success. The critic of the *New York Times* remarked that Chaplin had been 're-elected as king of the clowns' while a journalist from the *New Masses* 'came away stunned at the thought that such a film had been made and was being distributed'. He called it 'an epoch-making event'. Yet the public was not so enthusiastic, and the film was by no means a financial success; it covered its production costs only after it had been released to the rest of the world.

Upton Sinclair, the American author, wrote that he had just seen *Modern Times* and that 'the part about the factory was very interesting, and charming, but the rest just repeats Charlie's old material'. By which he meant that the inventive and imaginative opening sequences, in which the Little Tramp suffers a nervous breakdown while working frantically on a production line, are by far the most impressive. Their power may derive from the fact that in the struggles of the 'little fellow' with the latest technology Chaplin was adverting to his own problems with the new world of film.

Yet in a larger sense the factory represents the modern world in which the figure of the Little Tramp is perhaps obsolete; he generally represents a 'shabby-genteel' figure from the turn of the century. So he tried to reinvent himself as a worker on the production line. Some of the subsequent scenes, however, are part of Chaplin's familiar world of slapstick, with scampering gangsters and prisoners, stern policemen and incompetent waiters, escalators and rollerskates. The emphasis in the film upon food, and the process of eating, is a reprise of one of his oldest obsessions. It might be said that faced with the complications of the modern world, he reverted to the world that he knew best.

Yet there are still some magnificent sequences. In one scene Charlie picks up a red flag that has fallen from the back of a van, waving it to attract the owner's attention, when he suddenly finds himself leading a demonstration of striking workers. Towards the close of the film Charlie 'speaks' or, rather, recites a nonsense song in an invented polyglot language:

> La spinach o la busho
> Cigaretto porto bello.

That was his response to the challenge of sound.

Then at the close he reverts to silence, as the Tramp and the gamine make their way upon the long and winding road towards the rising sun. The final words are 'Buck up, never say die! We'll get along.' It was also the last appearance of the 'little fellow'. That is perhaps why in *Modern Times* Chaplin repeated so many familiar scenes from his previous films; it was a way of saying farewell.

In this last walk into the distance it is clear that Charlie will never have a home and will always be a wanderer. He had once been violent and lascivious; he then became gentler and more ingenious; at a slightly later date he grew into the figure of human-kind; at the end he is a romantic, filled with pathos. In whatever incarnation, he was somewhere outside the world and a stranger. Chaplin also knew that Charlie's days were done.

After the premieres in New York and Los Angeles Chaplin wanted to escape once more; in February 1936, he sailed away on the SS *Coolidge* to Honolulu with Paulette Goddard and her mother. They were away for five months, during which period, according to Chaplin, they were married. Goddard also recalled that 'we got married and travelled . . . Bali, Indochina, China, those sorts of places'. Despite the declarations of both parties, no evidence for such a marriage has ever been found. It may simply have been a ruse to guarantee Goddard's respectability in Hollywood. Their elliptic comments, however, suggest that the vacation was not an overwhelming success.

He had busied himself with other projects while travelling. He had written the story for a film concerning a poor Russian countess who stows away on an ocean-going liner where she falls in love with an American millionaire; the plot would surface thirty years later in *A Countess from Hong Kong*. He was also once more contemplating a film about Napoleon, played by himself. He had already bought the film rights to a period novel entitled *Regency*, perhaps in the belief that Goddard might play the spirited heroine of early nineteenth-century London society. The projects came to nothing.

Goddard said that 'when we came back he was going to write another picture for me. But you know Charlie, it can take him forever!' She was too ambitious, and too impatient, to wait indef-initely for his inspiration. She was now seriously in contention for the part of Scarlett O'Hara in *Gone With the Wind*, even though

Chaplin disapproved. After an unsatisfactory screen test, in the autumn of 1937, she was not chosen for the role. He was still looking for the right vehicle for her and wrote three different scripts which were for various reasons not right. She was still waiting.

They seem now to have been seriously at odds. A contemporary recalled that Chaplin had become a virtual 'recluse', while another described him as 'on edge and bitter'. After a period of acrimony he decided to go with a new friend and tennis partner, Tim Durant, to the coastal resort of Pebble Beach in California; Durant later became his personal representative at United Artists. Chaplin stayed there for the early months of 1938, and tried at first to remain aloof from the somewhat louche and bizarre inhabitants.

Yet soon enough he became engaged with the local, and very wealthy, society. Durant recalled one evening when he was reluctant to dine with some neighbours. Yet 'we walked in and everybody congregated around him, you know. And he was a hero. He had an audience and he couldn't leave – wanted to stay until three o'clock in the morning. After that he wanted to go out every night, because they accepted him as a great artist and a wonderful person.' It was in Pebble Beach, too, that he began seriously to consider what would be the most ambitious and grandiose role of his life.

16

The German tramp

Chaplin had previously been sent a newspaper clipping in which it was reported that Adolf Hitler had banned his films in Germany on the grounds that the actor looked so much like him. 'Just think,' Chaplin told his oldest son, 'he's the madman, I'm the comic. But it could have been the other way round.' The immediate military situation may also have helped to concentrate Chaplin's mind. In the early spring of 1938 the German army invaded Austria. In this period, then, he began to consider the possibility of playing the part of a comic dictator.

The resemblances between Chaplin and Hitler were indeed startling. They had been born within four days of each other in April 1889. They both had drunken fathers, and grew up to worship their mothers; they possessed a similar familial inheritance of madness and illegitimacy. They sported a similar moustache, Chaplin in film and Hitler in life. It was even said that Hitler had imitated the appearance of Chaplin's 'little fellow' as a way of inspiring love and loyalty; he may also have realised instinctively that the small moustache gave a central focus to the face. In fact Chaplin's first impression of Hitler was as 'a bad impersonation of me'. They both purported to represent the 'little man' struggling against the forces of modern society, and they also shared an uncanny gift of appealing to millions of people with an almost mesmeric magic.

Both men were superb actors, inspired by their feelings of inadequacy and self-pity. They were both immensely photogenic. Where Chaplin only played the Tramp, however, Hitler had for a while literally become one in Vienna at the age of twenty. They both worshipped, and identified with, the figures of Napoleon and of Christ. They both loved music and believed that they could write it. Hitler had told a friend that 'I shall compose the music and you will write it down'; this was exactly Chaplin's method.

They were both capable of furious and irrational rages as well as of abrupt changes in mood; they both suffered from bouts of paranoia. A young acquaintance of Chaplin, Dan James, wrote that 'of course he had in himself some of the qualities that Hitler had. He dominated his world. He created his world. And Chaplin's world was not a democracy either. Charlie was the dictator of all these things.' Innumerable reports suggest that he was a despot in his studio. David Raksin recalled that 'Chaplin demanded unquestioning obedience from his associates'. Hitler resembled Chaplin in his distortions of his personal history, in his sudden lethargy no less than in his frantic bouts of work. To his contemporaries Hitler always seemed to be playing a part. We might be inclined to say, therefore, that Chaplin was uniquely placed to take on the part of the Führer.

He began serious work on the project in the autumn of 1938. He played newsreels of Hitler over and over again, noticing every mannerism and every gesture. 'That guy's a great actor,' he said, 'why, he's the greatest actor of us all.' One of his assistants on the film recalled Chaplin shouting at the screen images of Hitler, 'Oh, you bastard, you son of a bitch, you swine. I know what's in your mind!' He would play the role as Adenoid Hynkel, the dictator of Tomainia.

A provisional script was copyrighted in November under the title of *The Dictator*; it was summarised as 'a story of a little fish in a shark-infested ocean', a clear reference to the role of the Jewish barber also to be played by Chaplin. When Paramount objected to this title, which they had already used, he changed it to *The Great Dictator*. The finished script was ready by September 1939, at a length of 300 pages; it was the first film for which Chaplin had prepared so carefully. He started filming at once. He was already nervous about the impact of the subject on public opinion and he imposed strict conditions of secrecy on the production of what was known only as 'Project 6'. He had already decided that Rollie Totheroh, his cameraman of long standing, would not be capable of mastering a sound picture; so he was relegated in status as assistant cameraman to Karl Struss. Struss recalled that Chaplin 'had no knowledge of camera direction, his films were completely "theatre". It was very routine work with him; you'd just set up the camera and let it go, and he and the other actors would play in front of it'.

Chaplin was disconcerted by the silence on the set necessary for a sound film. He was accustomed to the faint whine, and regular clicks, of the old equipment, to the rhythm of which he timed his performance. He missed the laughter of the stagehands. He was also discomfited by the number of people on the set. 'Who are these people?' he would ask. He was told that the studio was now required by law to hire them. 'But we don't need them! What's a make-up man? I've been putting this on my face long before he was born!' A scheduler for the day's filming noted that 'this schedule is subject to revision at any time due to C.C.'s possible dissatisfaction with what has been shot. Or, as a matter of fact, for any other reason.'

It was noticed that when he first appeared on set in his military uniform, as the dictator, he was noticeably more curt and abrupt than usual; by putting on the costume, he had become the character. He improvised Hynkel's speeches by creating an inspired gibberish that sounded exactly like German but was in fact nonsense. 'Just keep the cameras rolling,' he would say as he launched into an invective of raucous gutturals. It had been an old party trick of his to recreate the sound and cadence of various languages without making any sense.

One of his assistants recalled that 'the temperatures were over one hundred, but he would go on interminably, it seemed, and then in between he amused the extras by doing scenes from *Sherlock Holmes* or demonstrating pratfalls. At the end of the day he would be deadly gray, sweating, exhausted, with a towel wrapped around his neck'. In the autumn of 1939 he filmed the scenes in the Jewish ghetto, although at one point a large door slammed shut and crushed his middle finger; when he and Paulette Goddard rushed to Hollywood Hospital they were studiously ignored. 'When I saw you both coming in in make-up,' the doctor eventually explained, 'I thought it was a couple of Hollywood jokers having a little fun at our expense.'

Yet the events of the world kept on breaking through. The *New York Times* reported, after the Germans had invaded Poland at the beginning of September 1939, that 'there are indications that he will postpone *The Great Dictator* until the future can be appraised with more assuredness'. It was unlikely, however, that Chaplin would willingly forgo the completion of the project. In the winter of the year, and in the early months of 1940, he shot the scenes set in the dictator's palace as well as the outdoor battle sequences. It was all coming together.

From April to June he shot the final and climactic speech, more or less delivered by Chaplin himself in the guise of the barber, in the very period when the Germans conquered Belgium and invaded France. It was reported that several executives at United Artists predicted that, in these unhappy circumstances, the film would be a disaster. Yet Chaplin persevered and issued a statement that 'the report I have now withdrawn the film is entirely without foundation. I am cutting it now and as soon as it can be synchronised, it will be released. More than ever now the world needs to laugh.' Yet still he was not happy with the completed project. In September 1940, just a month before the premiere, he ordered that the sets of the ghetto be reconstructed and the actors rehired. He could do better. He had wanted to write the music for the film but, at the close, he was too exhausted to attempt it. The production had lasted for 559 days and cost over $2 million, the largest amount Chaplin ever spent on a picture.

In his role as the unnamed Jewish barber he is much more subdued and gentle than Charlie had ever been, all of his wild energy going into the part of the dictator Hynkel; it might even be said that Hynkel represents the anarchic and demonic side of the Little Tramp. He chose an American comic actor, Jack Oakie, to play Benito Mussolini, or Benzino Napaloni as he is called in the film. 'Look,' Oakie said, 'I'm a Scotch–Irish boy. What you want to look for is an Italian actor.'

'What's funny about an Italian playing Mussolini?'

And of course his heroine was Paulette Goddard, just as he had promised her. Her role was once more that of a gamine, a bold and adventurous girl of the ghetto who puts up her own resistance to the German soldiery. He asked Goddard to arrive on the set at 8.30 each morning, so that he could style her hair. He liked cutting the hair of his wives and of other women.

Goddard herself was not happy with Chaplin's method of direction, which amounted to bullying and humiliation on the set. His lectures to her on the art of acting were a direct affront to her pride. On one occasion Chaplin told his oldest son that 'your stepmother worked very hard today and I had to tell her a few things about acting'. She lay down on the sofa and cried.

The film's premiere took place in New York on 15 October 1940. The reviewer of the *New York Times* noted that 'no event in the history of the screen has ever been anticipated with more hopeful excitement than the premiere of this film, no picture ever made has promised more momentous consequences'. In the press-book for the film it was announced that 'here is the picture that has never before been equaled in advance interest and entertainment importance. Here is the picture that is actually a national event.'

All this was in part hyperbole but at the time it was unprecedented and astonishing that the most loved comedian in the world was ready to parody the most hated of its leaders. In the event it was a greater success with the public than with the critics, with particular acclaim coming from England even then suffering from the first experience of the Blitz. The film earned more money than any previous Chaplin film. Bernard Shaw wrote of it that 'Chaplin is more than a genius. He is an institution, the idol of millions of all races and creeds, the champion of the pathetic and oppressed. At a time when the world is sore and sick at heart, the little man with the funny moustache is something of a saviour.' Thomas Mann was less enthusiastic. He told a friend that 'we have seen Chaplin's somewhat weak, but in parts still very funny, travesty on dictators'.

In this first full sound and dialogue film he ever made, Chaplin was in a sense already old-fashioned. He reverts to slapstick at crucial moments of the film, a style critically at odds with its content. The German storm troopers, for example, appear as latter-day Keystone Cops. The full truth of German policy was of course not known to him, and he said once that 'had I known of the actual horrors of the German concentration camps I could not have made *The Great Dictator*'.

Yet the old comedy still does not fit the new situation. It teeters between the brilliant and the silly, with some rather poor farce. At times it verges upon the facetious and the verbal jokes are often lame. Nevertheless Chaplin's visual humour is as sharp as ever. The most arresting scenes in the film are performed entirely without words. Hynkel accomplishes a wonderful dance with a floating globe to the music of the prelude to the first act of Wagner's *Lohengrin*; this balletic triumph is followed by a scene in which the little barber shaves a customer to Brahms's Hungarian Dance No. 5. Both sequences are a tribute to Chaplin's true cinematic genius that survives his specious and somewhat sentimental return to farce.

His oration at the end, in which Chaplin takes off his mask and speaks for himself, was perhaps an artistic mistake; he declares, for example, that 'the hate of men will pass, and dictators die, and the power they took from the people will return to the people'. No film should end with a magniloquent rehearsal of what were essentially conventional sentiments.

On one occasion Chaplin and Buster Keaton were drinking beer in Keaton's kitchen. 'What I want,' Chaplin said, 'is that every child should have enough to eat, shoes on his feet and a roof over his head!'

'But Charlie,' Keaton replied, 'do you know anyone who doesn't want that?'

That is perhaps the best response to the closing speech of *The Great Dictator*.

Chaplin received the award for Best Actor from the New York critics for his performance, but he refused to accept it. He considered that his acting was only a small part of his achievement in *The Great Dictator*, and his publicity agent remarked that 'many hurtful things happened to Chaplin all through his life, many more than he deserved. But I doubt that any caused him more pain than to be regarded as a mere actor.' He had in the past turned down other awards; he sent back one of them with the note that 'I don't think you are qualified to judge my work.'

It is reported that Hitler himself saw *The Great Dictator*. An official from the film division of the German Ministry of Culture told Chaplin, after the war, that the Führer 'insisted on seeing the film – alone. The next night he saw the film again, and once more alone.' The American critics had not favoured the final speech, and disliked in particular Chaplin's call to 'Soldiers! Don't give yourselves to these brutes . . . who drill you, diet you, treat you like cattle and use you as cannon fodder.' He is supposed to be addressing German soldiers, but of course the message might be given a more general meaning. At a time of isolationism it was considered to be unnecessarily provocative and one syndicated columnist, Ed Sullivan, accused Chaplin of 'pointing the finger of Communism' in order to inflame his audience. Sullivan was not necessarily mistaken in his judgement. In England the Communist Party reprinted the speech as a pamphlet. The film critic of the *Daily Worker*, the Communist daily newspaper, described it as 'an eloquent plea for peace' and an assault upon 'the Roosevelts and Churchills and all the little Hitlers of the world' who promoted war.

Chaplin travelled to New York for the premiere of the film; he rented an apartment overlooking the East River and began contemplating his projects for the future. He was reported to be considering a picture about a refugee in New York or, alternatively, a film about a drunkard who falls in love with a chorus girl. Both of these ideas eventually emerged in very different forms.

When he returned to Hollywood Paulette Goddard had departed. They would not divorce for another two years but this was the final separation. She had endured enough of his attempts to control her, and had decided to make a career for herself outside the range of his supervision and criticism. 'Well, your stepmother and I,' Chaplin told his sons, 'don't see eye to eye any more.'

In this period Chaplin became noticeably more morose and depressed. He confided to his sons that he had always wanted to be a concert violinist, and lamented to others that all of his pictures had failed in one sense or another. He gave an interview at the time in which the journalist noticed his smile. It seems intimate and self-deprecatory but 'when you sit to one side and see it bestowed on someone else, the lips look mechanically creased, and the eyes seem absent, almost unseeing'. One of Chaplin's worst domestic disasters would soon follow.

17

Let us work and fight

Chaplin did not maintain his single life for very long, and saw a number of women in the period immediately after Paulette Goddard's departure. One of them in particular captured his attention. Joan Barry, now the age of twenty-two, had arrived in Hollywood from Brooklyn three years previously with the intention of becoming a film actress. This was not an unusual ambition for young women of more than usual good looks, but Barry had the good fortune to become acquainted – if that is the phrase – with John Paul Getty. Getty in turn introduced her to some of his friends and, by indirect means, she was somehow invited to one of Chaplin's large tennis parties. One thing led to another, as such things do, and before long they had become lovers.

Chaplin stated later that she had pursued him avidly and that he was in a sense an unwilling or at least innocent victim of her ambitions. Yet he was, in 1941, fifty-two years old and was no ingénue. He could have withstood her advances if he had been inclined to do so. Instead he persuaded himself that she had some talent as an actress and arranged a screen test for her. He had recently purchased the film rights for a play, *Shadow and Substance*, in which he now envisaged her as the heroine. Towards the end of June 1941, Joan Barry was put under contract. 'I can tell that you have a great deal of talent,' he had told her, 'just by speaking to you.' He arranged for her to attend classes at a school of acting.

By her own account it was only then that she agreed to have sexual relations with him. Before that time their familiarity had been restricted to his 'pawing and mauling' which she resisted. Their moment of intimacy occurred at Chaplin's house where according to Barry his 'success in this regard was due to his verbal persuasiveness'; she added that 'he is very proud of his success with women along these lines'.

On one occasion the two of them embarked upon a weekend vacation to Catalina Island, on Chaplin's yacht, in the course of which she had decided that she loved him. Chaplin had previously made protestations of love to her. He was intent now upon writing a film script of *Shadow and Substance*, but his concentration was broken. In *My Autobiography* he describes how Barry would drive to his house in her Cadillac, drunk, at all hours of the night; he would call his chauffeur to drive her home. One night she smashed her car in his driveway. Eventually he refused to open the door to her, at which point she began breaking the windows.

He discovered in this period that she had not in fact been attending the acting classes for which he was paying and, when he confronted her, she retaliated by saying that she had no intention of becoming an actress. She just wanted $5,000 to travel back with her mother to New York. When the money was paid, she would tear up the contract. Chaplin, now believing that she was unstable to the point of being dangerous, assented. She told a quite different story. She had discovered that she was pregnant, and Chaplin had given her the name of a doctor in New York who could perform what was then a criminal abortion. That was why she had travelled to the city. Once there, however, she decided against the procedure.

She returned to Hollywood some weeks later to be confronted by Chaplin; she confessed to him that she was still pregnant. She recalled him shouting at her that 'For God's sake, you've got to do something about it!' So he called on his associate, Tim Durant, to arrange an abortion in Los Angeles. She told an interviewer that 'I really wanted to go ahead and have the baby, and here were

Chaplin and Durant trying to high-pressure me into having an operation.' Eventually they succeeded in persuading her.

Chaplin's political beliefs, as intimated in *The Great Dictator*, now began to emerge more fully formed in public. In the spring of 1942 he was asked to speak in San Francisco on behalf of the American Committee for Russian War Relief; he had a nervous fear of speaking in front of large audiences but on this occasion his indignation seems to have conquered his apprehension. He began by addressing the 9,000 or so assembled as 'Comrades!', at which unlikely greeting the audience erupted into laughter. This was the period of the Anglo-Soviet Treaty that had established a military and political alliance between the British Empire and the Soviet Union.

When the laughter had subsided he added that 'I *mean* comrades. I assume there are many Russians here tonight, and the way your countrymen are fighting and dying at this very moment, it is an honour and privilege to call you comrades.' He included what seemed to be a jibe against his compatriots when he declared that 'I am told that the Allies have two million soldiers languishing in the north of Ireland, while the Russians alone are facing about two hundred divisions of Nazis'. He ended by exhorting his audience to send 10,000 telegrams to President Roosevelt with the demand for a 'second front' in Europe against the Germans, in the western half of that continent, thus diverting Hitler's push against the Soviet Union.

In another speech on behalf of the same cause, in Los Angeles, his contribution was followed by members of the audience singing a tribute to the 'victorious banners of the glorious Soviet army'. He was beginning to enjoy his role as a public spokesman; it fed both his vanity and his histrionic skills.

He was asked two months later to address by radio-telephone a rally of trade unionists in Madison Square Garden, New York.

It was reported that 'the great crowd, previously warned not to interrupt with applause, hushed and strained for every word'. Once more he called for a second front and declared that the Allies must aim for victory by the spring of 1943. He exhorted 'You in the factories, you in the fields, you citizens of the world, let us work and fight towards that end.' He had once more summoned up the spirit of his final speech in *The Great Dictator*, and it is possible that he was in the public arena simply following up the consequences of his film role. He was, in other words, still acting. Douglas Fairbanks Junior believed that the speech relayed to Madison Square Garden was 'a tragedy of errors and a damn shame'.

In the autumn of the year he accepted an invitation to speak at a rally in Carnegie Hall, New York, in an 'Artists' Front to Win the War' together with such luminaries as Orson Welles and Pearl Buck. In the course of his speech he dismissed fears that, after the war, the Communist system would prevail everywhere. 'I can,' he said, 'live on $25,000 a year.' That was, on the face of it, unlikely.

He wrote an address for a 'Salute to our Soviet Ally' held in Chicago, and then spoke at an 'Arts for Russia' dinner in New York, in the course of which he told the other guests that 'the Russian purges' were 'a wonderful thing' and added that 'in these purges the Communists did away with their Quislings and Lavals . . . the only people who object to Communism and who use it as a bugaboo are the Nazi agents in this country'. His oldest son recalled that in this period he was not so welcome in some quarters as he once had been. The country-house weekends with rich and famous Americans came to an end.

He delivered a radio speech to be broadcast in Russia, and recorded another speech for an English audience in the course of which he said that 'I remember the Lambeth streets, the New Cut and the Lambeth Walk, Vauxhall Road. They were hard streets, and one couldn't say they were paved with gold. Nevertheless the people who lived there are made of pretty good metal.'

At the end of 1942 a syndicated columnist, Westwood Pegler, commented that 'Chaplin lately has said that he was pro-Communist which means only that he is anti-American.' Pegler accused him of concealing his political opinions until he had made enough money to protect his business interests. In a remark that would find an echo in later years the journalist wrote that 'in common, I am sure, with many other Americans, I would like to know why Charlie Chaplin has been allowed to stay in the United States about forty years without becoming a citizen'.

Chaplin always claimed that he was not a Communist, even though he expressed his admiration for the Stalinist regime. In 1943 he once more exuberantly applauded the Soviet system as a 'brave new world' that lent 'hope and aspiration to the common man'. Its aspiration for justice and liberty 'grows more glorious year by year. Now that the agony of birth is at an end, may the beauty of its growth endure forever.'

These words may ring hollow at the beginning of the twenty-first century but, at the time, the sentiments were shared by many. Chaplin had friends and acquaintances in Hollywood who were avowed radicals, among them the writers Donald Ogden Stewart and Clifford Odets; he had also formed friendships with left-wing exiles from Europe, such as Bertolt Brecht and Fritz Lang, who formed an angry and sometimes bitter émigré community. Hollywood itself became a refuge for many Jewish artists and writers fleeing from Hitler's persecution. Chaplin was in particular well acquainted with Hanns Eisler, a composer who was later suspected of being a Soviet agent; his friendship with Eisler would eventually be held against him.

It is difficult to believe, however, that Chaplin had either the rigour or the commitment to become a Communist. He made, and continued to make, a great deal of money out of the stock market; to many he seemed to be the epitome of the successful self-made man. His friends considered him, in the phrases of the time, to be a 'parlour pink' or a 'limousine liberal' ready to assume socialist convictions without any attempt to carry them out in practice.

Yet he did possess an angry instinct against injustice and oppression; all his life he fought against authoritarian control and domination. He said once that 'I've known humiliation. And humiliation is a thing you never forget.' That was the lesson of his childhood. It would be better to say that he was a libertarian with tendencies towards anarchism. He had demanded, and gained, freedom for himself. He refused to be told what day of the week it was, for example, and never wore a watch. That passionate individualism was the foundation of his political sentiments.

There may be of course an even simpler explanation since, as Tim Durant said, 'He is a ham at heart – he admits that. He wants to startle people and interest people.'

At the end of 1942 Joan Barry re-entered Chaplin's life, although in truth she had never really gone away. Various and diverse reports can be found on the nature and course of their mercurial relationship. She had been in New York when Chaplin addressed the rally in Carnegie Hall, and it is likely that he paid for her to travel there by train from California; she gave evidence later that the two had then engaged in sexual intercourse. There may have been another abortion. There may have been more drunken scenes inside, and outside, the house on Summit Drive. Yet the complicated and in some ways mysterious saga serves only to emphasise the erratic, whimsical and imperious way in which Chaplin conducted his private life.

On the night of 23 December 1942, Barry arrived unexpectedly at Summit Drive. Chaplin either refused to see her or told her to wait. She then climbed a ladder and entered the house; she brought out a gun and, while pointing it at him, threatened to commit suicide. At this moment Chaplin's two sons arrived, at abut 2.30 in the morning, and found the ladder propped up against their father's bedroom window. On the grass were a pair of women's shoes, a purse, and a pair of silk stockings. Something was wrong.

When they rushed into the house, Chaplin intercepted them and asked them what they were doing. It seems to have slipped his mind that they lived there. He told them to go to their rooms. He then returned to Barry, who still held the gun; she and he talked for an hour and a half before going to bed together. She had placed the weapon on a bedside table, and Chaplin later joked that he had never before had sex with a loaded gun at his head. 'Well,' he said, according to Barry, 'this is a new twist.'

Barry returned a week later, and remained with Chaplin for an hour or so. He then offered to drive her home, but on the journey they argued once more; Chaplin took her to the local police station and left her there. Once more she was becoming a serious problem for him. On the following night a guard found her wandering through the garden of Summit Drive with a gun in her hand; he confiscated the weapon but, on the excuse of wanting to use the lavatory, she escaped through a downstairs window.

She made her way to the house of a friend who telephoned the Beverly Hills police, and the offices of the *Los Angeles Herald Examiner*, with the news that Barry was threatening to commit suicide after being 'dumped' by Charles Chaplin. A few hours later Barry was found in the front seat of a car, wearing pyjamas, with her lips smeared with iodine. Another report suggests that she had taken a large dose of barbiturates. A doctor was called. When he diagnosed a 'simulated suicide attempt', she was charged with vagrancy. On the following day she was sentenced to ninety days in prison, suspended on condition that she left Los Angeles for a period of two years.

She returned sooner than expected, however, and in early May

1943 she drove back to Summit Drive in order to confront Chaplin with the news that she was once more pregnant. She got into the house by the back door and mounted the stairs to his bedroom; throwing open the door, she discovered a naked woman in his bed, while he sat fully clothed at the end of it.

Barry's reaction to the unexpected sight of the young woman was one of hysterics. She ran downstairs. Chaplin followed her, asking her to wait by the swimming pool until he could talk to her. She waited for twenty minutes and, dismayed by his long absence, broke an ashtray and tried unsuccessfully to slash her wrists. Chaplin's butler than drove her back to her hotel.

She now began to attack Chaplin by other means. On the following morning she went to the house of Hedda Hopper, a notorious columnist who specialised in gossip about the film industry and its stars. She informed Hopper that she had been signed up by Chaplin to become a film actress before he seduced her. She was now pregnant with his child, and Chaplin would have nothing whatever to do with her. Hopper sent her to her own physician, who confirmed the fact that she was pregnant. This had all the makings of a sensational story. But Hopper needed time to verify and confirm the details.

The naked girl in the bed was Oona O'Neill, daughter of the American playwright Eugene O'Neill. Chaplin had met her in 1942. She was then seventeen and had been suggested to him as a possible candidate for the part of Bridget in *Shadow and Substance*; this was the role he had originally envisaged for Joan Barry. Oona O'Neill had always enjoyed a privileged life. After attending a number of private schools she soon became a New York 'face' and celebrity; the gossip columnists named her as 'the toast of café society' and in the spring of 1942 she was named as Debutante of the Year. At this point she decided that she would turn down a place at Vassar and become a screen actress.

This was the opportunity for O'Neill's film agent, Minna Wallis, to contact Chaplin. He visited the agent's house, and was at once struck by the beauty and self-possession of the young actress. The sequence of events is not entirely clear. It has been reported that, a few days after this meeting, Oona O'Neill turned up outside the gates of the Chaplin studio where Alf Reeves and Rollie Totheroh were not particularly happy about the appearance of another girl in Chaplin's life.

Minna Wallis, however, had made another call to Chaplin with the news that the Fox studio had become interested in her pretty client; he was at once roused to action and immediately put her under contract. He decided that he should give her acting lessons himself which, of course, meant that they spent much time together at Summit Drive. Soon enough Oona O'Neill had moved into the house. After the events of the recent past, he might have been more hesitant and uncertain than before. The difference in age between them was some thirty-six years. Yet his instant attraction to her was more powerful than any considerations of common sense.

Chaplin's sons seem to have been immediately reconciled to the presence of this new girl in their lives. Charles recalled that 'she worshipped him, drinking in every word he spoke, whether it was about his latest script, the weather or some bit of philosophy'.

Joan Barry made a further attempt to confront Chaplin. He refused to see her and, as she waited in her car, Chaplin whispered to Tim Durant that 'I'm afraid she will shoot me.' He then plucked up courage and came to the door shouting 'You dirty little black-mailer. Get the hell out of here. I mean it this time . . . if you don't get off, you'll be put in jail.' His butler later commented that 'she looked like a little girl of sixteen . . . I don't like to see people talk like that to anybody, no matter how bad they are.'

The police were called and Barry was sentenced to thirty days' detention for violating the terms of her probation. She was placed on suicide watch and, while in the prison hospital, it was confirmed that she was five months pregnant.

In the middle of May Chaplin decided to announce his engagement to Oona O'Neill. She had just turned eighteen, and so the union was at last legitimate. Oona herself wrote to her mother that 'if I don't marry Charles . . . I'll never marry anyone. This is going to be the love of my life.'

Joan Barry was still under the illusion that Chaplin truly loved her, however, and after her eventual discharge from prison she telephoned him once more. It was the beginning of June. He agreed to talk to her again. Chaplin tried to cajole her into saying nothing further. 'You've got to protect me, Joan,' she reported him as saying to her, 'I've got to have peace. Joan, if you bring this into court you know what it will be. The newspapers will be after you, your picture will be taken.' He told her that 'even if he was proven to be the father, that he would blacken my name so that won't be the issue involved at all'.

The affair would not be so quickly over. A gossip column, at the beginning of June, intimated that 'Joan's mother is saying it would be nice – with baby on the way – if Joan and Chaplin would wed.' On the following day the mother herself, Gertrude Barry, filed a suit on behalf of the unborn child naming Chaplin as the father; she asked for $2,500 a month for the support of the baby, and $10,000 for prenatal costs. Chaplin denied paternity, and refused to make a quick settlement. The law now made its slow way. In the course of their investigations the district attorneys became aware of the possible charge that Chaplin had financed two illegal abortions. The FBI now became involved in the case, with a memo to its director, J. Edgar Hoover, on 'Information Concerning Charles Chaplin'. If Chaplin had paid for Barry's train tickets to New York, and they had been intimate there, he could face a charge under the Mann Act for transporting a 'sex victim' across state lines.

Chaplin now took refuge at the house of some friends in western Los Angeles, where Oona O'Neill often stayed with him. Her closest friend, Carol Matthau, recalled that 'Oona felt something she had always wanted to feel, but had never felt before now – safe. Not only was he older and a great man, he protected her and she knew he would for the rest of their lives.' Yet Carol Matthau also conceded that in exchange her friend 'was to allow parts of herself to grow dormant . . . Part of her always had to be a little girl. Charlie's little girl. She always had to be The One.' Before meeting Chaplin, Oona O'Neill had been spirited and rebellious; it was not clear that she would be able to retain those qualities for very long.

They married on 16 June 1943, six weeks after Joan Barry had declared that she was bearing his baby. They left Hollywood very early in the morning and arrived at Santa Barbara just as the courthouse was about to open. This was to be his fourth marriage, if we include one with Paulette Goddard, even though the earlier unions had ended so disastrously. When Chaplin went to sign his name in the register, his hand shook so violently that he could hardly hold the pen.

Oona and Chaplin remained in Santa Barbara for the following six weeks where it seems that, miraculously, they were not followed by the press. They had leased a house, where they remained during the day, and in the evening took quiet walks into the countryside; they were careful according to Chaplin, 'not to be seen or recognised'. In a period that should have been characterised by marital bliss, Chaplin fell into a depression; he feared that the American public would now turn against him, and that his film career would be over.

Yet after this interval they soon settled down to life at Summit Drive, where Oona Chaplin fulfilled all of her new husband's expectations; she began typing the script of a projected film and generally ensured that his life proceeded calmly. A mutual friend, Florence Wagner, noted that 'her dressing-table mirror is lined with snapshots of him and apparently, at last, there is happiness in that house'. In a letter to a friend, written in the summer of this year, Oona Chaplin wrote that 'I am so happy now – Charlie's a wonderful man.' That happiness, however, was not to endure without severe trial for both of them.

18

Proceed with the butchery

On hearing the news of Chaplin's marriage to Oona O'Neill, Joan Barry went into a dangerous state of hysteria. A photograph of the time shows her distraught to the point of madness. She now sought revenge. It seems that, in advance of the imminent trial for immorality, Chaplin was trying to find witnesses who would declare that they had also been intimate with Barry, thus casting doubt upon his supposed fatherhood of the expected child; his enormous financial resources must surely have helped in that search. At the beginning of October 1943, Joan Barry gave birth to a baby girl.

In February of the following year, Chaplin was charged with violating the Mann Act by transporting Joan Barry across state lines for immoral purposes and for conspiring with the Los Angeles police to have her imprisoned on charges of vagrancy; Chaplin was indicted on all counts by the federal grand jury. If he were found guilty as charged, he might face a prison sentence of twenty years. Yet he had deep faith in his own abilities to persevere and to overcome all impediments. That confidence came directly from his troubled childhood.

The trial opened on 21 March. Hundreds of people lined the hallways of the courthouse to catch a glimpse of Chaplin on his arrival, and press photographers were allowed into the area where his fingerprints were taken. It was all good theatre and, on one level at least, he might possibly have enjoyed it. On another occasion in court, he joked with the reporters by putting a handkerchief over his head. Yet of course his freedom was in jeopardy. His lawyer, Jerry Giesler, asked the jury whether it was likely that his client would pay Barry to travel 3,000 miles to New York when she 'would have given her body to him at any time or place'; he added that 'there was no more evidence of Mann Act violation than there is evidence of murder'.

Barry herself gave evidence and repeated her claim of intimacy in New York; she was followed on to the stand by various travel agents, hotel employees and railroad staff. John Paul Getty also gave evidence to the effect that Barry had visited him in Tulsa after she had left New York, thus raising once more the subject of her behaviour with other men.

The last witness was Chaplin who denied Barry's claims. In a subsequent memoir Giesler recalled that Chaplin 'was the best witness I've ever seen in a law court. He was effective, even when he wasn't being cross-examined, but was merely sitting there, lonely and forlorn, at a far end of the counsel table. He is so small that only the toes of his shoes touched the floor.' As Virginia Cherrill had once said, he was always acting; he was always 'on'.

On 4 April, to screams and tumult in the courtroom, Chaplin was acquitted of all charges. One of the jurors told him with a smile that 'It's all right, Charlie. It's still a free country.' When Oona Chaplin heard the news over the radio, she fainted. Yet the damage had been done to Chaplin's reputation and Giesler himself said that 'the trial of Charlie Chaplin carried with it the heaviest weight of public loathing for a client I've ever had anything to do with'.

Yet Chaplin still awaited the ordeal of a paternity case at the end of the year. There was in fact not much to be added to the testimony of the previous trial, except evidence in Chaplin's favour. As a result of blood tests three doctors agreed that Chaplin could not possibly be the father of Joan Barry's baby. At this point Barry's lawyer, Joseph Scott, decided upon an ad hominem attack in order to sway the jury. He denounced Chaplin as a 'grey-haired old buzzard', 'a little runt of a Svengali', a 'debaucher' and 'lecherous hound' who 'lies like a cheap cockney cad'. Chaplin, now incensed, turned to the judge. 'Your honour,' he said, 'I've committed no crime. I'm only human. But this man is trying to make a monster out of me.' Scott had not finished his attack. He told the jury that 'there has been no one to stop Chaplin in his lecherous conduct all these years – except you. Wives and mothers all over the country are watching to see you stop him dead in his tracks. You'll sleep well the night you give this baby a name – the night you show him the law means him as well as the bums on Skid Row.' The attack affected Chaplin very deeply, eliciting once again the humiliation and shame he had experienced as a child.

This unwarranted appeal to the emotions of the jurors did not altogether work, however, since the case ended in deadlock. A further trial was ordered for the spring of the following year, but Chaplin declined to appear as a witness. On this occasion, despite the evidence of the doctors that he was not the father of the child, he was deemed to be responsible by a majority of ten. His reputation in the United States fell into a decline from which it never recovered until his final years.

The judge awarded the infant girl, Carol Ann, the sum of $75 a week; she could also be given the name of Chaplin. Joan Barry never really profited from the verdict in her favour. She married again but, after separating from this husband, she drifted through her life until in 1953 she was found wandering in a confused state; she was holding a pair of baby's sandals and a child's ring, whispering 'This is magic.' She was admitted to a mental hospital and, after her release, disappeared from all records. The little daughter was brought up by relatives and continued to receive Chaplin's payments.

Between the two trials for paternity, Chaplin was intent on finishing the script for a film that had provisionally been entitled *The Lady Killer*. Orson Welles had suggested to him three years before that the career of a notorious killer of eleven women, Henri Désiré Landru, might prove to make an interesting film. Chaplin was intrigued by the idea, no doubt provoked by his own difficult relations with females at the time. Welles later claimed that he had himself written a script for the projected film, and it is certainly possible that Chaplin lifted ideas and themes from him.

Chaplin had always been fascinated by the violent and the macabre; his own favourite reading at home was the magazine *True Detective*, well known for its lurid sensationalism. The case of Landru had all of the appropriate elements, since he had dismembered the bodies of his victims before burning them. Chaplin was now determined to turn this criminal career into comedy, and even farce, in a film that was entitled *Monsieur Verdoux*.

He had worked intermittently on the script for the last two years, during bouts of what might be called legal and social persecution; much of the bitterness and anger he felt was now redirected into Verdoux's cynicism towards the conventional pieties of modern society. Some of Chaplin's early notes for the film testify to his state of mind; he wrote, for example, that 'when all the world turns against a man he becomes holy . . . where there are no facts, sentiments prevail . . . a reputation is the concern of cooks and butlers'. In one of the last scenes of the film Monsieur Verdoux is savagely attacked in the courtroom in the same manner as Joseph Scott had once excoriated Chaplin himself. A strain of deep misogyny can also be detected throughout the film, in which the women are largely characterised as harsh, loud or foolish. Yet Verdoux is animated not so much by hatred of women as by love of his own self.

Chaplin began filming *Monsieur Verdoux* on 21 May 1946, and finished twelve weeks later; this in itself was a record of brevity. There had been occasions in the past when he had spent the same amount of time in shooting a single scene. He had a clear conception of the story, however, and of his own role as the dapper if somewhat precious mass murderer. He spent six weeks growing a real moustache for the part; a false one would of course have conjured up memories of Charlie. When at the premiere of the film in New York some children came after him calling out 'Charlie! Charlie!' he told them that 'This is the new Charlie.' Yet the Little Tramp's individualism, and his indifference to the moral conventions of the world, are shared by Verdoux himself to a murderous degree. This is where we may find the identity of Chaplin himself.

He also hired a strong supporting cast, principal among them the American comedienne Martha Raye whose raucous laugh and wild behaviour manage to upstage Chaplin's own performance. She admitted that on her first day she was 'sick with fear' at the thought of working with him; yet she cheered up and he patiently taught her how to smoke, and to walk, for the part. 'I learned so much from Charlie,' she said. 'We became friendly but if he said, jump . . . I jumped.' He told her not to wear earrings because they diverted attention from her uniquely comic facial expressions; he also designed her clothes and her hair. Raye also noticed that he would break from one scene and start another, according to his mood of the moment.

He had hired an assistant director, Robert Florey, who was in practice assigned the role of director without receiving the title. Florey recalled the process of filming in an essay written some years later. He noted that Chaplin was resolutely old-fashioned in his film techniques. Chaplin liked the camera to be immobile, with himself preferably at the centre of the composition. He was not interested in close-up shots of the other performers because 'people come to see me'. Any attempt at another camera angle or change of focus was dismissed by him as 'Hollywood chi-chi'; he was continually angry at the cameraman for what he called his 'technical tricks'. He also seemed quite happy to retain certain inconsistencies and aberrations pointed out to him by the 'continuity' team, on the principle that the audience's attention would be entirely drawn to him. He asked a colleague his opinion of four different takes of the same scene. The colleague commended the first and fourth. What was wrong with the third?

'Well, you can see the electrician.' The camera had momentarily strayed to show an electrician holding a light.

'What are you watching him for? You're supposed to be watching me.'

Florey jotted down at the time his stream of remarks against an unfortunate colleague on the set. 'No, no, no, shut up you silly bastard, for Christ's sake, we cut to Annabella, you don't understand anything about motion pictures. I know what I am doing, yeah, that's what I cut to, I have been in this business for twenty – for thirty years. You don't think I am gaga? Oh shut up . . . Christ.' Florey observed that 'with Chaplin things just broke up or faded away, like a storm in late summer'. He concluded, like many observers, that Chaplin had 'two distinct personalities'. One was the comic genius and social charmer, while the other was 'the tyrannical, wounding, authoritarian, mean, despotic man imbued with himself'.

The actor who played the part of the prefect of police in search of Verdoux, Bernard Nedell, recalled that 'the cast loved him' and that he had 'that curious mixture of a hot temper and very great patience'. He recalled one occasion when Chaplin, physically exhausted and almost sick from overwork, went endlessly through one scene with an actress until she had achieved the effect he desired.

The premiere of *Monsieur Verdoux* was held at the Broadway Theatre, New York, in the spring of 1947. It was the first time he had encountered his public since the trials and tribulations of the previous three years, and it was reported that scattered hissing and booing broke out at the close of the film. Chaplin had never before endured such an experience. It was not a good omen.

In the final scenes, before going to his death on the guillotine, Verdoux effectively impugns the capitalist and military system for committing crimes much greater than his own. He remarks that 'wars, conflict, it's all business. One murder makes a villain; millions a hero. Numbers sanctify.' It is possible that Chaplin believed that the audience would sympathise with a mass murderer, or at least accept the man's analysis of the hypocrisy of society, but he misjudged the effect of the narrative. Verdoux made an unlikely hero. A producer sent a telegram to the gossip columnist, Hedda Hopper, with the words that he had witnessed an historic event. 'I have seen the last film of Chaplin.'

The film met no greater success with its first critics than with its first audiences. Howard Barnes, in the *New York Herald Tribune*, commented that 'Charles Chaplin has composed what he likes to term "a comedy of murders" with a woeful lack of humour, melo-drama or dramatic taste.' The reviewer for the *New Yorker* berated Chaplin for trying to exonerate Verdoux's murders 'on the ground that they were justified by the twisted economic shape of the modern world'. Yet there can be no doubt that the film was coldly received as a direct result of his unhappy public reputation in the period. Oona Chaplin wrote to a close friend that the film 'got a lot of bad – really bad – reviews – even the good ones were not very good – this was a great blow to Charlie – and to me naturally . . . Poor Charlie is so depressed and low – this has never happened to him before – it is really a horrible strain.'

Chaplin held a press conference in the ballroom of the hotel at which he was staying on 14 April, three days after the opening. One of the publicity staff at United Artists sent out a memorandum that 'Chaplin today requested mass meeting of the press . . . I am setting up such a mass meeting for Monday April 14. Chaplin expects this will be controversial and understands we can do nothing to protect him or [the] picture once he submits to mass questioning.'

The press conference was described by Orson Welles as 'the worst lynching by critics you ever heard'. A radio reporter who recorded the entire event observed that 'the ballroom was literally filled to the rafters. Every seat on the floor was taken. People were standing in the doorways, and on the seats encircling the balcony.' 'Thank you, ladies and gentlemen of the press,' Chaplin began. 'I am not going to waste your time. I should say – proceed with the butchery. If there's any question anybody wants to ask, I'm here, fire away at this old grey head.'

And so the interrogation began, of which these extracts will give the flavour.

'*Question*: There have been several stories in the past accusing you more or less of being a fellow traveller, a Communist sympathiser. Could you define your present beliefs, sir?

'*Chaplin*: Well, I think that is very difficult to do these days, to define anything politically . . . I have no political persuasions whatever. I've never belonged to any political party in my life, and I have never voted in my life. Does that answer your question?

'*Question*: Could you answer a direct question? Are you a Communist?

'*Chaplin*: I am not a Communist.

'*Question*: A Communist sympathiser was the question.

'*Chaplin*: A Communist sympathiser? That has to be qualified again . . . during the war I sympathised very much with Russia because I believe that she was holding the front.'

He was then asked why he had decried patriotism or nationalism and had declared himself to be a 'citizen of the world'; he was told that this was considered to be an insult to the American soldiers who had recently fought in the war.

'*Chaplin*: Now whether you say that you object to me for not having patriotism is a qualified thing. I've been that way ever since I have been a young child. I can't help it. I've travelled all over the world, and my patriotism doesn't rest with one class. It rests with the whole world.'

And so it went on.

'*Question*: Mr Chaplin, according to a report from Hollywood, you are a personal friend of Hanns Eisler, the composer?

'*Chaplin*: I am. I am very proud of the fact.

'*Question*: Are you aware of the fact that his brother is the Soviet agent, so attested by—

'*Chaplin*: I know nothing about his brother!

'*Question*: Do you think that Mr Eisler is a Communist?

'*Chaplin*: I don't know anything about that. I don't know whether he is a Communist or not. I know he is a fine artist and a great musician and a very sympathetic friend.

'*Question*: Would it make any difference to you if he were a Communist?

'*Chaplin*: No, it wouldn't.

'*Question*: A Soviet agent, as he's been accused of being.

'*Chaplin*: I don't know what you know of. A Soviet agent? I don't know – I don't – amplify that. Do you mean a spy?

'*Question*: Yes.

'*Chaplin*: It certainly would. If he were a spy, that would make a great deal of difference.'

The interrogation then turned to the film itself.

'*Question*: What was your reaction to the reviews – the press reviews – in New York on the picture?

'*Chaplin*: Well, the one optimistic note is that they were mixed.

'*Question*: I say you have stopped being such a good comedian since your pictures have been bringing messages – so called.

'*Chaplin*: Oh you have. That's your privilege. I mean – I do something and I throw it, as we say, to the wolves. That's your privilege.'

If he had hoped to confront and quell his critics, he had failed in the attempt. His equivocations about his possible Communist sympathies, and the political allegiances of Hanns Eisler, did not help his position.

The takings at the box office of the Broadway Theatre were so poor that the manager closed down the film after five weeks. Chaplin immediately withdrew it from circulation, only to re-introduce it in the early autumn with the slogan 'Chaplin changes! Can you?' The public did not in fact rise to the challenge. For the first time in Chaplin's career, one of his films had lost money. Chaplin, however, remained defiant and proclaimed the virtues of the film. At a later date he restrained his enthusiasm a little. He said in an interview that 'there was some clever dialogue in *Monsieur Verdoux* but now I think it was too cerebral and should have had more business. If you have a bit of a message it's better to put it over through business than through words – better for me, anyhow.' It is perhaps regrettable that in his last films he did not take his own advice.

Nevertheless *Monsieur Verdoux* is in fact much more accomplished and entertaining than its early reception might suggest. It has many moments of high drama and Chaplin's part offers him the opportunity for subtle and ingenious comedy; he perfectly enacts Verdoux's air of fastidious disdain. It is a fable, or a satire, in the manner of Swift. It is in certain respects too explicit and too overt, with a prevailing expository tone, but it has scenes of genuine power. In one of them Verdoux changes his mind about killing a prostitute. 'Life is beyond reason,' he tells her. 'Fulfil your destiny.' 'My destiny!'

His energy was such that in this period he found the time and patience to work with a small theatrical company called the Circle Theatre; it had been founded by Jerry Epstein, a friend of his youngest son, and Sydney Chaplin himself played many of the leading roles. Chaplin came to the performances and, soon enough, took on a more active role as an adviser and then a producer. A friend of his, Lillian Ross, left a verbatim record of his conversations with the young actors. 'You must not act. You must give the audience the impression that you've just read the script. It's phoney now. We don't talk that way. Just state it . . . Give the audience the feeling that they're looking through the keyhole.' He told them later to keep the action simple and that 'too many gestures are creeping in . . . Good exits and entrances. That's all theatre is. And punctuation. That's all it is.'

One of the members of the Circle, Julian Ludwig, recalled that on one occasion Chaplin remembered every word and every stage direction from the play *Sherlock Holmes*, in which he had acted forty-four years before. His memory, however, was less perfect in more immediate matters. Ludwig said that 'Mr Chaplin couldn't remember his own phone number, he couldn't remember names.'

In this year, 1947, Chaplin came under direct and sustained attack from the American government. Two months after the hostile press conference in New York, a congressman demanded Chaplin's deportation on the ground that he was 'detrimental to the moral fabric of America'. In July Chaplin learned that he was being investigated by the House Un-American Activities Committee, and responded by writing that 'I suggest you view carefully my latest production, *Monsieur Verdoux*. It is against war and the futile slaughter of our youth. I trust you will not find its humane message distasteful. While you are preparing your engraved subpoena I will give you a hint on where I stand. I am not a Communist. I am a peace-monger.' There the matter rested. He told his son that 'they don't call me because they have nothing on me'.

Yet it was a highly dangerous moment. The committee, under the chairmanship of Joseph McCarthy, had vigorously pursued anyone whom they considered to be disloyal or subversive, resulting for most of the victims in ostracism or unemployment. In 1947 the committee had turned its attention to supposed Communists working in the film industry; as a result of their investigations 300 employees were blacklisted or boycotted by the studios, and only thirty of them ever worked again in Hollywood. It was a desperate time, even for Chaplin.

In the spring of 1948 an official from the Immigration and Nationalisation Service came to Summit Drive with an FBI officer and a stenographer; Chaplin had planned a short visit to London and had applied for a re-entry certificate. The official began to question Chaplin about his association with various Communists or Communist organisations, but Chaplin was studiously vague in his responses. 'Oh I am sure I am not a member of anything . . . I think yes, maybe, yes . . . I think I have to belong to an Actors' Guild in order to work . . . I think I met him once.' Of his close friendship with Hanns Eisler he said only that 'I met him socially, through other people.' When asked if he had ever entertained members of the Soviet embassy he replied that 'I don't recall. You see, we get a lot of people.'

'*Question*: Have you ever made any donations to the Communist Party?

'*Answer*: I am sure, never, not to my – I am sure.'

The official from the INS said that he would grant him a re-entry certificate if Chaplin would sign the stenographer's report of the interview. Chaplin's lawyer, who was present at the proceedings, advised him not to do so; he may have suspected that his client had not been telling the whole truth and might later be accused of perjury. Chaplin followed his advice, refused to sign, and cancelled his proposed journey to London.

19

No return

He was angered and frustrated by the humiliations that he had been obliged to endure. In an article for the English newspaper *Reynolds News*, he wrote at the end of 1947 that 'I have made up my mind to declare war, once and for all, on Hollywood and its inhabitants . . . I, Charlie Chaplin, declare that Hollywood is dying'; he also wrote that 'before long, I shall perhaps leave the United States'. At the beginning of the following year he began preparations for the last film that he would ever make in his adopted country.

In the autumn of 1948 the records of his studio refer to a project known as *Footlights*; yet at this stage it was a novel rather than a film. Chaplin was dictating passages of it into a Dictaphone that his secretary would then transcribe. At the same time he was trying out various stray melodies on his piano that might help to invoke the spirit of London immediately before the First World War. Once more he was returning to the past, and to the life that he and his mother had known. For many months he remained at Summit Drive, drawing inspiration from his memories of the world of the music hall. By the autumn of 1950, a script had emerged with the title of *Limelight*.

The original prose narrative was some 100,000 words in length. It was in part autobiographical with the depiction of the central character, the clown Calvero, who had once longed to be a romantic actor but 'he was too small and his diction was too uncultured'. He was bound instead for the late Victorian music-hall stage, upon which he became a principal comedian with top billing. On the first page of the manuscript Chaplin wrote that Calvero despised comedy because it required some kind of intimacy with the audience which he never felt. Calvero was analytical, introspective, understanding himself by perceiving others.

Other passages from the novel never reached the film script. Chaplin wrote that Calvero had taken revenge on bourgeois society as a resut of his experience of poverty as a child, that he was highly strung and nervous, emotional and egotistical. In the film itself an old poster hanging in Calvero's small flat bears the inscription 'Calvero, Tramp Comedian'. Over the mantelpiece hangs a photograph of Chaplin himself from the 1920s. The audience is invited to see Chaplin's own story in Calvero's downfall and loss of popularity.

Other memories and fantasies abound. Calvero, like Mr Charles Chaplin, follows a trajectory from success to failure upon the music-hall stage; he eventually drinks himself to death. Like Chaplin's father, too, Calvero was unfortunate in marriage; his wife, Eva, was unfaithful to him with the promptings of a sexual desire that 'was insatiable and verged on being pathological'. It may be possible to glimpse here something of the relationship between Hannah Chaplin and her husband.

Yet in *Limelight* Calvero himself is redeemed by the love of a young ballet dancer, Terry Ambrose, whom he has saved from an attempt at suicide; Terry's older sister had been a London prostitute who financed the young girl's training as a dancer and in this vignette, too, we may glimpse Chaplin's abiding preoccupation with his mother. In the rapport between Calvero and Terry there is also some intimation of the relationship between Chaplin and his young wife. The actress whom he chose for the part bore a strong resemblance to Oona Chaplin. The film is filled with so many allusions and duplications that it becomes an echo-chamber of Chaplin's own memories or desires.

An advertisement had been placed in the press. 'Wanted: young girl to play leading lady to a comedian generally recognised as the world's greatest.' For seven months at the beginning of 1951 he interviewed and tested many aspiring actresses and eventually, after much deliberation, he chose a twenty-year-old Englishwoman by the name of Claire Bloom.

Claire Bloom recalled in her memoir, *Limelight and After*, that Chaplin discussed the plot of the film almost as soon as he met her and her mother at the airport in New York. He told her that the story 'took place in the London of his childhood'. It was clear that his earliest theatrical memories helped him to reimagine the dressing rooms, the agents' offices, the 'digs' and landladies of the Edwardian world. He also took evident pleasure in recreating the gas-lit atmosphere of the music hall that he had experienced as a child; the strident songs and the insinuating glances, the patter and the double entendre, the mock-heroic monologue and the over-colourful costume, are all part of *Limelight*. Yet Hannah Chaplin was never far away. When choosing costumes for Claire Bloom's film tests, Chaplin would point out that his mother wore such a dress or preferred such a shawl.

By this time he had become a much lonelier figure. In restaurants some customers would make loud and unfavourable comments about his perceived politics. Many old acquaintances no longer dared to visit him for fear of guilt by association, and he was shunned or rejected by many erstwhile friends. At a New Year's Eve party one of the guests spat in his face.

Once she had been given the part, and had flown out to Hollywood in September 1951, Claire Bloom was immediately placed under a strict routine to prepare herself for the role; she began with a workout at the gymnasium before attending five hours of rehearsals, followed by a ballet class. The shooting of the film began in November. As always, Chaplin was thoroughly in earnest over every detail of the production. He was the first on set, before nine o'clock, and the last to leave after six in the evening.

He told his sons that he expected *Limelight* to be his last, and greatest, film. That is perhaps why he decided to include the members of his family which had grown since his marriage to Oona. They lived comfortably and happily in Beverly Hills where she took on the role of mother and housewife with apparent gracefulness. The children came quickly; Geraldine was born in the summer of 1944, Michael in the spring of 1946, and Josephine in the spring of 1949. A fourth child, Victoria, was born just a few months before the filming of *Limelight* itself.

Geraldine, Michael and Josephine in fact appeared in its opening scene. Wheeler Dryden, his half-brother and Hannah Chaplin's illegitimate son, was given the two parts of clown and doctor. Oona Chaplin herself 'doubled' as Terry in two brief shots. His two older sons were also part of the cast. Sydney played the romantic hero, while Charles was given a minor role. Charles recalled that he and Sydney became the targets of their father's 'drive for perfection'. He bullied them relentlessly.

Sydney Chaplin noticed his father's excitement and extreme sensitivity while on the set. Chaplin's remarks to various members of the cast have been recorded. 'Come on, Syd, what the hell is the matter with you! . . . Jesus Christ, just act like a human being! . . . You're working for Charlie Chaplin now. No Shakespeare, please!' This last retort was directed at Claire Bloom.

He would become furious if any of the crew seemed tired or bored. On seeing one technician watching him with an uninterested expression he called out 'Quick, get that man's face out of here.' He also suffered from a certain amount of paranoia; if a problem occurred with a negative he was prone to blame it on a conspiracy among his 'enemies'. He believed one technician to be wearing an American Legion ring, symbol of an organisation opposed to him, but it turned out to be a college ring. Rollie Totheroh was still relegated to the role of assistant cameraman but, on the set, he showed no sign of resentment. He would sometimes go over to Chaplin and tell him to 'Keep your head up, sweetheart. Too many chins showing.'

In one scene Claire Bloom found it difficult to cry convincingly. Chaplin grew more and more irritated until he launched an angry tirade against her, whereupon she burst into tears. The camera crew had been forewarned and instantly captured the scene in a single take. He had forced her to cry real tears. A reporter from the *New York Times* asked Chaplin to characterise the film. 'It's a funny picture,' he answered quickly, 'I hope.'

Limelight is in many respects a self-conscious and over-determined film, stagey and loquacious in equal measure. Calvero is sometimes a little glib and portentous, while Terry is continually in tears. In one scene Calvero denounces the public as 'a monster without a head that never knows which way it's going to turn and can be prodded in any direction'. This seems to be a clear reference to Chaplin's own treatment at the hands of press and public. He also complains that, when a man is growing old, 'a feeling of sad dignity comes upon him, and that's fatal for a comic'. When Terry objects to their feigned marriage, for the sake of respectability, Calvero replies that 'I've had five marriages already. One more or less won't matter to me.' Chaplin himself seems to be aware that there may be too much philosophising; at one point Terry turns to Calvero and tells him that 'to hear you talk, no one would ever think you were a comedian'.

Chaplin relies heavily upon sentiment and nostalgia by playing himself, as it were, at the end of a great career. The film can in fact be best seen as a tribute to his own genius in what Calvero describes as 'the elegant melancholy of twilight'. The sad clown even manages to die on stage, which might be seen as the ultimate act of self-indulgence or perhaps of self-pity.

Yet we may speak of Chaplin here rather than of Calvero. The depth of his self-absorption is apparent at every level of the film. The photographs and posters in the lodgings are all images of his past career. When Terry tells him after many months of his self-imposed absence that she still loves him, he replies 'Of course you do. You always will.' His talk is essentially about himself, testifying to his own artistry and his own genius. He takes himself very seriously indeed, even when he pretends the opposite. Ultimately it is a highly dispiriting film.

Yet moments of distinction can be found within it. The portrait of Calvero's landlady, prurient and vulgar, is an exact one. One of the most appealing interludes in the film is the double act of Chaplin and Buster Keaton in a wild musical duet of broken strings and frantic chords. One of the assistants on the set noted that 'there was a certain jealousy between them because each of them wanted to have the better piece of the pie . . . each of them wanted to grab the attention of the audience'. So Chaplin would say to his colleague, 'Oh, Buster, it's too much, too much of that, I think, don't you think so?' Keaton said later that 'in truth it is *at work* that he is least funny, if I may say so'.

In the spring of 1952, just after the principal shooting of *Limelight* had been completed, he engineered a change in his financial affairs. He placed certain documents in a safety deposit box, to which he gave his wife a key. He transferred his stock in United Artists to her; he added her name to his bank accounts, and granted her power of attorney. He once more applied for a re-entry permit and, after a short delay, was granted one. He also settled all his claims with the Internal Revenue Service.

He was now intent upon travelling to London where the premiere of *Limelight* would take place. He could no longer rely upon a sympathetic reception in the United States, and at a press preview of the film in New York he sensed the coldness or hostility of the audience. He told his friends and colleagues that he was simply going on a vacation with his wife and children, but the fact that he had set in order his financial affairs suggests that he was leaving nothing to chance. He had at least a vague apprehension of being denied re-entry to the United States.

On 17 September, he and his young family sailed for England on the *Queen Elizabeth*. He had been only two days at sea when he was informed that his re-entry permit had been withdrawn; he could not return to the United States without being interrogated on his moral character and his political affiliations. The Attorney General of the United States told the press that Chaplin 'is in my judgement an unsavoury character' and accused him of 'making statements that would indicate a leering and sneering attitude' towards the country.

Chaplin's first response was one of defiance, and he stated his intention of returning to face any charges or accusations made against him. In this respect he might have been vindicated. The Federal Bureau of Investigation had for a number of years been probing his speeches and activities, but they had uncovered no evidence that was not based on hearsay and rumour. Yet he was terrified that the American authorities would strip him of his assets and posessions. That had always been his greatest fear – that his wealth would be taken from him. All his life he had expressed a horror of returning to the poverty he had known as a child. It is likely enough that he fell into a state of anxiety not far from panic.

Chaplin was greeted in London by a cheering crowd, although many believed that his reception was smaller than that granted to him in previous years. He wanted to show his young wife and children the immensity of London, and in particular those areas in which he had grown up. He wanted to take them to the source and spring of his imagination. From their suite at the Savoy they could see the newly built Waterloo Bridge but for Chaplin it was of no importance except that 'its road led over to my boyhood'. They wandered through the streets of Kennington and of Lambeth, but much of its charm had for him been destroyed by bombing or by recent development. Yet still he went back.

He was still a London, or cockney, figure. He and Claire Bloom decided one morning to take a walk through Covent Garden Market, where news of his presence quickly spread. The fruit-sellers and vegetable-sellers did not crowd around him, however; they stood in front of their stalls as he passed and saluted him. He was moved and delighted that they still believed him to be one of them. He was a man of the theatre, too, and in these London days he mixed with the variously celebrated figures of the West End. He and Oona flew to Paris for the French premiere of *Limelight*, in the course of which journey they visited Picasso's studio. The two artists had no language in common, and so Picasso simply showed him the paintings on which he was then working; Chaplin in turn executed for him a routine known as the 'Dance of the Rolls' from *The Gold Rush*. Picasso wrote later that 'his body isn't really him any more. Time has conquered him and turned him into another person. And now he's a lost soul – just another actor in search of his individuality and he won't be able to make anybody laugh.' This was a common response to him – Chaplin did not look anything like Charlie. He was a small, pink-faced and silver-haired gentleman who was obliged to smile and be cheerful.

It would be reasonable to suspect that he had other matters on his mind. His youngest son, Michael Chaplin, recalled that in London 'I'd see my father sitting, momentarily alone, in a big chair, staring ahead of him just like any other preoccupied guy looking for help.' On 17 November Oona travelled by plane from London to New York and then to Hollywood. She had come to rescue her husband's finances. In two days she managed to gain access to the safety deposit boxes and remove the assets stored there; she also sent $4 million to foreign accounts, closed down the house and arranged for the furniture to be shipped to Europe. In her absence Chaplin suffered what seemed to be a nervous collapse; he feared that her plane might crash or that she might be detained by the American authorities. He could not envisage life without her. He must also have been terrified that her journey might come to nothing, and that all of his money would be irretrievably lost.

She herself discovered that FBI agents had been questioning the staff at Summit Drive in the quest for evidence of Chaplin's 'moral turpitude'; they also interrogated his friends, lawyers and even his ex-wife, Lita Grey, but nothing was uncovered. It must have become quickly clear to all concerned that Chaplin would not be returning to California.

20

The shadows

Chaplin and his wife had decided to move to Switzerland. He had previously said that he did not appreciate mountainous countries, but Switzerland had certain virtues. Taxes, in particular, were very low. His affection for London was not strong enough to keep him there; England had a treaty of extradition with the United States which might be exercised against him.

By the beginning of 1953 they had moved into the Manoir de Ban in Corsier-sur-Vevey, a commune beside the left bank of Lake Geneva; the mansion had fifteen rooms, spaced over three floors, and an estate of thirty-seven acres complete with park, orchard and garden. The emphasis was upon seclusion. Chaplin had announced that 'I want to have six months of peace and quietness in this house. We will not go in for big parties and large receptions, but keep to ourselves.' Two or three months later he explained his decision to leave America on the grounds that 'since the end of the last war I have been the object of vicious propaganda by powerful reactionary groups'. In letters from Switzerland it is clear that he now despised and detested what was once his adopted country. He would say that the only thing he missed about America was the Hershey candy bar.

All was arranged with Chaplin's usual efficiency. The interior was decorated in a style that was somewhat lush and ornate, becoming known to the locals as 'Beverly Hills baroque'. A large drawing room on the first floor opened out on to a terrace from which could be seen the lake and the mountains beyond it; on the other side of the house stood a library and dining room. The second floor harboured two master bed-suites and two guest rooms. In the cellar were stored Chaplin's films and papers. The five children, with the youngest, Eugene, born in the summer of 1953, were ensconced on the third floor with two nannies, Kay Kay and Pinnie, to keep them in order. Three more children were to follow in subsequent years, thus creating what might be considered to be a good-sized and almost Victorian family. He was obliged to hire twelve servants to maintain the house; three gardeners were also needed to tend the park and garden. A swimming pool and tennis court were eventually installed.

The children went to a local school in Vevey, where their lessons were conducted in French; they soon spoke that language as well as they spoke English. Chaplin was in any case convinced that the discipline in French schools was infinitely superior to that of American schools. They were taught largely by Catholic nuns and priests and, when Geraldine Chaplin was discussing the perils of hell with her father, he replied that 'I am so happy you believe. I would give anything to believe. It makes life so much easier, but I can't. I would love to believe but I can't.'

He approved of discipline for his children, once remarking that 'they must be prepared for life by some form of hardship'. He told his children that 'education is the only defence'. They were forbidden to make any noise on the ground floor where their father might be working. If he heard them clattering down the stairs he would storm out in a tempest of rage. He was particularly incensed if anyone should open the door without knocking; his need for privacy was so great that he would shout abuse at the offender.

The family soon established a comfortable regimen, with dinner at 6.45 and bed at 9.00. The children joined their parents for lunch, and then for a brief period after dinner. Chaplin wrote to a friend that 'we are very comfortable and happy living in Switzerland' and added that 'the Swiss government are splendid people, stolid and reliable and have been most hospitable to me'. Of his wife he reported that 'fortunately for me, Oona is not social-minded and, as you know, is somewhat of a recluse . . . so everything works out very well'. She seems to have settled down into her role as mistress of the establishment, with occasional forays into the kitchen, although there are reports that she had already started to drink more than was customary.

According to a close family friend, Betty Tetrick, for Oona Chaplin 'Charlie came first. The children had to understand that. She tried to make his exile pleasant. She entertained him at dinner – she was always a witty conversationalist. And she always made sure she looked her best . . . And he had that terrible temper, and she had to defuse that.' The English actress, Margaret Rutherford, observed that her 'stillness and gentleness pervaded the room like pot-pourri. She rarely spoke, but you felt that she was there to protect her husband from any strain.' Another contemporary wrote that 'it was good to see them together, impossible to imagine them otherwise'. He called her 'the old woman', 'the old girl' or 'the missus'; she called him 'Charlie'.

His oldest son, on a visit to the mansion, found it altogether too quiet for his taste. He could endure it for four or five days at the most while his younger brother, Sydney, lasted for two weeks before returning to city life. Chaplin and his wife also made regular trips to London and Paris. They always booked into the Savoy Hotel in his home city; his doctor and tailor were also in London.

In the spring of 1954 he announced plans for a new film that would concern a king in exile. He said that in Switzerland there were plenty of kings in exile, from which he might draw inspiration, but perhaps the most important one was himself. At once he went into a flurry of preparations for which he needed the help of a competent stenographer. He chose Isobel Deluz, an Englishwoman married to a Swiss professor who had worked on film scripts before. Deluz recalled that for much of the time he was 'just brooding and mooching about, and then he was a neurotic terror. I was just beaten down by his tantrums – his first-rate clowning, his second-rate manners and his sixth-rate philosophy'.

She was obliged to follow him wherever he wandered, taking down his thoughts and ideas; she said that 'he never just dictated a letter to me . . . he acted every word'. There were occasions when 'he would begin to prance around, talking at the top of his voice, repeating the same sentence over and over again . . . or he would gesticulate madly, his mouth forming noiseless words'.

His moods at Vevey veered wildly in all directions. When he wished to have a swimming pool and tennis court built in the grounds, he quarrelled with the architect and the contractor. 'I've been building swimming pools for thirty years,' he told them. He insisted that they were stealing from him and declared that he would not pay them. The Swiss workmen would down tools and watch these arguments; according to Deluz, 'they would stand behind Chaplin, grin and wink at each other, point a finger to their foreheads, raise their eyes to the heavens'. When he ruined the red asphalt of the tennis court by playing upon it too soon, he fell into a rage and covered it with concrete. He ordered granite slabs for the 'deck' of his swimming pool but, when they were delivered, he demanded that the 'tombstones' be removed at once. Finally he accused Deluz of being engaged in a conspiracy with the contractor, at which point she shouted at him and left his employ. She sued him for three months of back pay.

The citizens of Vevey had at first welcomed Chaplin; after his arrival they arranged a candlelit dinner for him and presented him with a gold Swiss watch. They even asked him to participate in the harvest celebration in the local vineyards. But soon enough he picked a quarrel with the authorities of the town by objecting to the noise from a rifle range in a ravine close to his home. It

233

was an ancient tradition for the Swiss to take out their weapons as part of a citizen army; Chaplin complained that the sound of rifle shots prevented him from working. The members of the local council tried to conciliate their famous guest by introducing sound-proofing, but still he was not satisfied and filed a suit against them. When he discovered that men from other communes were allowed to use the range, he suggested that the local councillors were being bribed. The authorities replied that 'the commune of Vevey makes no profit in putting the range at the disposal of other communes'. A compromise was eventually reached whereby Chaplin would pay some of the costs of renovation. He was exasperated by smells as well as by noise. He began to complain of the odour of sewer gas in his property and, when the plumbers could find no evidence for it, he asked the local authorities to dig up the roads and inspect the pipes.

It is hard to say whether the Chaplin family was a happy one. He would administer spankings to his children for any infraction of his rules. Geraldine Chaplin recalled that 'we got the full routine, on the bum, over your father's knee'. They were only permitted to see Chaplin films, and television was not allowed. Betty Tetrick revealed that Oona Chaplin's favourite child was Michael and that as a result Chaplin became jealous; she added that 'he wasn't very nice to Michael and often he was a sad little boy'. One visitor to the house recalled that the children were 'scared shitless' of their father and that he 'corrected them all the time. Hence they gave him a wide berth and did not speak to him if they could help it.'

In a memoir, *I Couldn't Smoke the Grass on My Father's Lawn*, Michael Chaplin wrote that 'he was, and is, to put it mildly, a bit of a handful as a father'. He added that 'I never argued with the old man. I never dared to. In any case, it's useless to argue with my father. He is too stern, too inflexible, too overpowering.'

The family attended each October a circus owned by the Knie

Brothers, Rolf and Fredy, that was put up near Lausanne. Chaplin had a great fondness for clowns, naturally enough, and the Knie clowns showed great affection for him. A dancing elephant, on one occasion, came out with Charlie's shoes and coat as well as a bowler hat and cane. The crowd, recognising Chaplin in the audience, called out 'Charlot! Charlot!' until Chapin stepped into the ring and presented the elephant with a loaf of bread; the elephant accepted it and bowed, to which gesture Chaplin bowed back. The Chaplins and the Knie brothers remained friends for the next twenty years.

A few other vignettes of his life at Vevey may be recorded here. He contracted eczema and was obliged to wear white gloves; he received several allergy tests and it was finally resolved that he was allergic to film. This paradoxical diagnosis led Chaplin to believe that the cause lay in his early use of nitrate film. His lawn was plagued by crows and so he devised a form of mirror that he would shine in their eyes. He had a hatred of flies, also, and kept a swatter with him when he had lunch on the verandah. To the delight of his children he would sometimes go behind the sofa and pretend that he was walking down some steps into the basement; before their eyes he grew smaller, and smaller, and smaller. 'Sweet' was one of his favourite words. 'Oh you're so *sweet*' or 'It's so *sweet*' were the phrases he tended to use. Another common phrase was 'modesty forbids'.

In the first two or three years at Vevey he was working on the proposed film on an exiled king. By the autumn of 1955 the script was nearing completion, and he began filming in the late spring or early summer of the following year. He chose as his leading lady Dawn Addams, whom he greatly admired; he told her at one point that 'I won't make the picture without you.' His one principal piece of advice to her was to keep her head still, telling her to 'remember to be definite. Moving your head is indefinite. Only make a move when it means something.' He chose his young son,

Michael Chaplin, to play the role of an unhappy victim of America's 'Red Scare' that even then was growing to fresh heights. He was in fact intent upon mocking all aspects of American life, from its television advertisements to its popular dances, from its snobbery to its hypocrisy. Michael Chaplin said later on the new experience of working with his father that 'I was happy to have this relationship with him, which I never had before.'

The filming took place at Shepperton Studios outside London, and the family ensconced itself at the Great Fosters Hotel in Egham. It was a sombre if stately house where the Chaplins made themselves as comfortable as possible; there was only one communal room for television, however, and they had to sit down and watch whatever the majority of guests had chosen.

The production was to last for nine weeks, with one week for location work. Shepperton Studios was an unfamiliar environment for Chaplin, who had previously worked only in American studios, and his discomfort was compounded by the multitude of English union rules and regulations that governed working practices. 'If you want a chair moved,' he was told, 'ask a prop person to move it.' Work stopped when the tea-trolley came around at three thirty. A cameraman was fiddling with the lights. 'I have to give a performance,' Chaplin shouted, 'I don't give a goddam about your artistic effects! . . . Besides they're coming to see Charlie Chaplin, not your goddam lighting!' Oona Chaplin always travelled with him and would sit, working on her embroidery, at the side of the set. Chaplin left England in July, as soon as the film was completed; for tax reasons, he could remain no longer.

The film was released in England in the early autumn of 1957 to a generally warm welcome. There was no grand premiere for the simple reason that the Chaplins had returned to Vevey. It was his eighty-first film, but there was for him no sense of an ending. He told one friend that 'It's good, it's my best picture, it's entertainment, don't you think?'

A King in New York concerns the tribulations of an exiled European monarch in that city; it is part farce and part satire, but never seems quite sure in which of those directions it is going. The exiled King Shahdov is clearly a version of Chaplin himself. He is fingerprinted at the airport, with the photographers all around him, just as Chaplin was photographed at his trial thirteen years before. The film is on one level a spirited response to the hatred and humiliation that he had endured in that earlier period. It is sometimes crude, but it is also often lively and vigorous; at its best, it provides charming comedy.

In the *Evening Standard* John Osborne wrote that 'for such a big, easy target, a great deal of it goes fairly wide. What makes the spectacle of misused energy continually interesting is once again the technique of a unique comic actor'; in *The Observer* Kenneth Tynan made the similar point that 'in every shot Chaplin speaks his mind. It is not a very subtle mind, but its naked outspokenness is something rare.' In those two comments something of the strength, and much of the weakness, of the film can be found.

When asked about the generally negative presentation of the United States Chaplin replied that 'if you give both sides it becomes bloody dull'. When the film had its premiere in Paris, he barred any critics or reporters from the United States. That, however, did not prevent some of them from seeing it. The *New Yorker* reported that it was 'maybe the worst film ever made by a celebrated film artist'; Oona Chaplin promptly cancelled her subscription to the magazine. It was not shown in America for another sixteen years. In later life Chaplin wrote that he was 'disappointed' and 'a little uneasy' with the film.

For some of the music of *A King in New York* he had hired a pianist, Eric James, who eventually became his musical associate. In a memoir, *Making Music with Charlie Chaplin*, James records their sometimes troubled association. He had to endure 'the arguments and bullying that happened so frequently' and that were an aspect of Chaplin's 'fiery temperament'; when James made a suggestion Chaplin might shout, 'Don't tell me what to do!' The pianist soon came to realise that 'in other directions he was no better than any other man and probably a good deal worse than some'. He noticed, in particular, his meanness in matters of money.

Chaplin still made regular journeys to London, where he would revisit the haunts of his youth; he would return to the Three Stags public house, for example, where he had last seen his father alive. On one occasion he went with Oona and a friend to Southend; this was the resort where his mother had taken him and Sydney for an impromptu day out. He bought cockles from a stand, just as he had once done as a child. He was spotted one day staring into a butcher's shop window off the Old Kent Road; a man walked over to him and stood next to him. 'Excuse me. Are you Charlie Chaplin?' "Shush, don't give me away.' On another occasion he was seen to trip up and fall on the pavement outside Kennington underground station. He loved the Christmas pantomimes in the London theatres. He peered through the windows of restaurants to look at the diners. He would get on a London bus and gaze at the crowds.

Yet there were times when the crowd looked back at him. He was spotted walking along the Embankment and some people called out 'Charlie Chaplin! Charlie Chaplin!' Chaplin became nervous and told his companion, 'Let's get out of here.' A tourist boat was just about to leave its mooring, and Chaplin hopped on with his friend. Just as they reached Greenwich another boat came up. The passengers were lining the deck shouting out 'Charlie Chaplin! Charlie Chaplin!' They had followed him from the Embankment pier.

He also enjoyed holidays elsewhere. He journeyed to Kenya with his family, where he went on a safari. He often visited Ireland in the spring, where he liked to fish. At the beginning of 1960 he and the family ventured upon a world tour which took them from Alaska to Japan, Bali and Hong Kong before returning by way of India and the Middle East. Michael Chaplin recalled that, in the course of the tour, 'if we went into a store, it was a production. If we went to a restaurant we were on show like a pack of zoo characters.'

In June 1962 Chaplin received an honorary doctorate from Oxford University, which he gratefully accepted. An Oxford don by the name of Hugh Trevor-Roper objected to the decision on the grounds that 'we might as well be honouring a circus clown'. At the ceremony Chaplin delivered a short speech in which he adverted to this controversy. He confessed that he was not a man of letters but he felt himself qualified to speak on matters of beauty rather than knowledge or morality. Beauty could be found in various places, in a garbage can or in a rose. 'Or even,' he added, 'even in the antics of a clown.' He was greeted with loud applause.

This was the period in which Chaplin began to write his autobiography. He used to read out passages to his guests at Vevey. One of them, Lillian Ross, recalled that 'I sat with him on his terrace as he read parts of his book manuscript to me, the tortoiseshell glasses a bit down on his nose, his reading dramatic to the point of melodrama, his devotion to his subject unselfconscious and complete.' He asked Truman Capote to read the manuscript and, when the American writer suggested changes and additions, Chaplin lost his temper. 'Get the fuck out of here,' Capote remembers him saying, 'I wanted you to read it. I wanted you to enjoy it. I don't need your opinion.' He never spoke to Capote again.

My Autobiography was published in the autumn of 1964, and was soon selling well all over the world. It was of course a self-serving account replete with inaccuracies and evasions. He had never really spoken the truth about his life, and it would have been unwise to expect him to start at the age of seventy-five. It was perhaps more notable for its omissions than its conclusions; Chaplin's political record was conveniently sanitised, and he failed to mention many people who had been instrumental in his success. He never really discussed his work in film, except as a matter of profit and loss, while the last third of the book often resembles a social diary rather than a considered self-appraisement.

Nevertheless it does have passages of genuine power and pathos, particularly in Chaplin's evocation of his London childhood. It received a mixed response. Some critics believed that Chaplin had concealed 'his vociferous left-wing politics'; his marriages and affairs 'are passed over, almost pushed aside'. Yet no man needs to become witness for his own prosecution. Another reviewer remarked, in Chaplin's defence, that 'the persecution of Chaplin in the name of American patriotism is a scandal this era is saddled with forever'.

There was to be one last film, his eighty second. At a press conference in London, on 1 November 1965, he announced that he was about to begin production of *A Countess from Hong Kong* that would include in its cast Marlon Brando and Sophia Loren. A journalist present on the occasion described him as 'bright-eyed, clear-voiced, quick-talking, he is, if not exactly youthful, fairly ageless'.

The filming, begun at the start of the following year at Pinewood Studios in Buckinghamshire, encountered problems. Chaplin had never before directed established stars, and in particular found it difficult to deal with Brando; Chaplin as director was also Chaplin as dictator, as we have seen, and the actor did not take kindly to Chaplin's desire to control his performance. An observer on the set wrote that 'the action did not proceed smoothly. Brando, sullen, kept saying "All right, all right." He did not seem to be listening as Chaplin instructed him again.' The actor went through the prearranged movements without any real enthusiasm. An actress from the days of silent cinema, Gloria Swanson, visited the set where she confided that 'you can see why actors find him difficult. This is a simple scene, and he's making much ado about nothing.' Sophia Loren, however, willingly accepted his close tuition.

Brando wrote later in a memoir that 'Chaplin was a fearsomely cruel man . . . probably the most sadistic man I'd ever met.' He was also an 'egotistical tyrant' and a 'penny-pincher' who 'harassed people who were late, and scolded them unmercifully to work faster'. Immediately after the filming was over, in the spring of 1966, Chaplin told a reporter that 'it's all such fun, every minute I'm proving something to myself. I don't know what it is . . . but I'm proving that I can do it. I've always been enthusiastic about work. Sometimes I've been more enthusiastic than the work deserved, I suppose.'

In the autumn of that year he slipped on the pavement outside Pinewood Studios and broke his ankle. For the next seven weeks he was obliged to hobble around in a cast, with the aid of a crutch, or to use a wheelchair; this was not designed to raise his spirits, and indeed he became morose. He carried on working but, when the cast came off at the end of November, he never had as much energy or mobility as before. He may also have suffered a minor stroke. It was the first sign of frailty and, as a result, his wife's care became ever more insistent.

A Countess from Hong Kong opened at the beginning of 1967 to generally cool or hostile reviews. It was considered to be slow and old-fashioned. It concerned a countess, apparently doomed to become an expensive prostitute, who stows away in the cabin of a millionaire on his way back to New York. The consequences are predictable enough, with love at the end of the story, but romantic comedies of the light and gentle type had gone out of style. It is charming, with Chaplinesque touches, but charm on this occasion was not enough. The film was not helped by Brando's performance that was generally regarded as 'wooden'; he had perhaps been too much out of sympathy with his director to overexert himself in the role. He is vaguely menacing, and laboured, throughout the film. Yet compensation can be found in the smaller roles of Patrick Cargill and Margaret Rutherford who deployed their English manner to great effect.

Chaplin told one journalist that 'what shocked me about the English reviews of the *Countess* was the fact that they were unanimous. And they seemed so personal, an attack upon me. All they were interested in was "Chaplin has a flop".' Brando telephoned Loren to say that 'the critics just destroyed all of us'. The American reviewers were no kinder. Bosley Crowther, in the *New York Times*, lamented 'this fiasco, which is one of the most humiliating and unnecessary I have ever known to happen in films'. When Crowther's words were read out to him by an assistant, Chaplin 'listened stoically with his arms folded across his chest – his expression never changed. He made no comment. When I finished, he left the room.'

The shades of death were now reaching closer to him. Sydney Chaplin, his older brother, had died on 16 April 1965, which was of course Chaplin's birthday. His principal cameraman for many years, Rollie Totheroh, died in the summer of 1967. Then, in the following year, his oldest child died; Charles suffered from a fatal thrombosis, possibly induced by alcoholism. In these circumstances Chaplin was comforted by his devoted wife. He could not bear her to be away from his side, not even for a moment. Ian Fleming, after a visit to Vevey, remarked that it was 'wonderful to see two people bask unaffectedly in each other's love'. They had a delight in one another's company that seemed sometimes to be at the cost of excluding their children. They held hands constantly; she might stroke his hair, or pet him.

Yet there is another aspect to this story of marital bliss. Some people observed a certain nervousness, or tension, within Oona that she began to assuage with drink. Chaplin's business manager,

Rachel Ford, explained that 'she always drank secretly. Charlie knew. She tried to shut herself away when they had a row – locked herself in for days at a time and drank . . . I used to come in to sort out some business and he was in a terrible rage and she'd run into her room and lock the door. And he'd try to get her out, and it was all hell.'

He said in 1967 that 'at my age I don't want to wish days away. I want to live every minute.' In this, his seventy-eighth year, he attacked his birthday cake in mock ferocity; there is a photograph of him bearing down on the cake with a large knife. He still worked on and, in this year, he began preparations for another film.

He was working on a script he called *The Freak*. It was the story of a winged girl who in Chile is worshipped, as an angel descended from heaven, but who is then kidnapped and sent to London where she suffers many misadventures. He had designed the part of the girl for his daughter, Victoria, but the idea came to nothing. Some tests were done at Shepperton Studios, and some storyboards were created, but nothing more. Victoria Chaplin said that 'I was dying to do *The Freak*, but I could feel this holding back about the film. I remember my mother telling me at Christmas, in 1969, privately in the pantry of the house, "Well, actually, I don't want him to do it. If he goes through the ordeal it will kill him . . . I can have him alive or have him die making the film."' So the project was cancelled. Chaplin did not notice, or was not told; he continued intermittently working on the idea for another five years.

Yet his putative heroine had left him. Victoria Chaplin eloped to Paris with a young French actor, Jean-Baptiste Thiérrée, and in 1971 they created their own circus that became known as Le Cirque Imaginaire. Chaplin complained to his musical adviser, Eric James, that 'I loved her as I do all my other children and I gave her everything she wanted. Why should she repay me in this way?' James suggested that he might try to help her in a difficult period. In response 'Charlie jumped to his feet and, literally quivering with rage, shouted "Help her! Help her! She will never, and I mean never, set foot in this house again!"'

Eric James was at Vevey to help Chaplin prepare a new score for the reissue of *The Circus*. Chaplin had been responsible, over the course of his career, for more than eighty musical compositions. Yet his strain of inventiveness was beginning to fail and, in his memoir, James recalled that 'I was able to suggest melodies and ideas that were agreeable to him.' James remembered other details of life at Vevey. He recollected how Chaplin 'felt the cold very much' and demanded a log fire in any room he was using; how he often talked of his early life and expressed a deep fear of returning to the same penury; how he began taking short naps after lunch; how he liked simple food at home but in restaurants preferred more exotic fare such as caviar and roast partridge; how he would like to hear James play the music-hall songs of his childhood; how on occasions he would even perform those songs in the manner of Vesta Tilley or Marie Lloyd; how he hated Christmas.

In the early spring of 1972 Chaplin was rewarded with a five-pointed terrazzo and brass star as part of the Walk of Fame on Hollywood Boulevard, yet this was only a prelude to a much grander reunion. He was coming back to Hollywood after an absence of twenty years. It was not simply a sentimental journey. He had just signed a munificent distribution deal, for the release of some of his earlier pictures, and it was believed that journeys to New York and Los Angeles would be the best kind of publicity tour.

He arrived in New York on 3 April 1972, but he had been tense during the flight, aware that hostility towards him might still emerge among the journalists who were waiting for him at the airport. He seems even to have feared being shot and he vowed that, if he saw any pickets against him, he would return at once to Switzerland. Yet the welcome was spontaneous and friendly. Time seemed to have healed the breach as well as the subsequent resentment and suspicion.

He attended a dinner party at a town house in Manhattan, where he was obliged to shake the hand of every guest; he was so exhausted that he even shook the hand of his wife and of the waiter who brought him a glass of wine. At a screening of *The Idle Class* at the Philharmonic Hall on the following evening the audience rose at the end in a standing ovation with calls for 'Charlie! Charlie!' He told the assembly that 'I'm being born again. It's easy for you but it's very difficult for me to speak tonight, because I feel very emotional.'

He talked about the occasion with a reporter from *Life* magazine. 'My God,' he said, 'the affection of the people. So sweet.' Then he added that they were 'like children, after they've been slapped down, and they're sorry they've done something'. But the mood of resentment passed. 'Thought I was going to blubber like a big kid. I cannot cope with emotions any more.' He was more reflective still. 'What was real was afterwards, here in the hotel, after everybody had left and gone home and I felt as Hamlet felt. "So now I am alone." It sort of jumped me back into the beginning of my career. Very vivid. I had the same sort of depression inside me.' He may have recalled an evening in the spring of 1913 when, at a performance of Wagner's *Tannhäuser* in New York, he had burst into tears. He was asked if he felt any bitterness for his treatment in the 1950s. 'No, no, I don't feel anything at all.'

He flew with Oona to the West Coast and, on arriving in Los Angeles, he told those waiting to greet him that 'it's good to be back in New York'. There were times when he was no longer alert and lucid. He had come to attend the Oscar prize-giving ceremony, at the end of which a celebration of Chaplin's life and career was screened. When the screening was over the footlights went up to reveal Chaplin alone upon the stage, whereupon he was greeted with an unprecedented ovation. The cheering and applause lasted several minutes. He was presented with an especial Oscar 'for the incalculable effect he has had in making motion pictures the art form of this century'. Another standing ovation followed, and he seemed to be moved almost to tears. He waved his hand, and blew a kiss to the audience. 'Words seem so futile,' he said at last, 'so feeble.'

He was now very tired and, after returning to Vevey, he suffered a bad fall and injured a central vertebra in his back. He did not often leave the house now, and could not walk far without assistance; he also suffered from gout. He did not care to receive visitors often but one dinner guest recalled that he kept his eyes upon the plate and ate very slowly. He read and reread *Oliver Twist*, perhaps as a reminder of an older London. In his last years Oona would take him round the grounds of the house in a wheelchair.

He had the persistent fear that he would not be remembered. When he was not recognised, in earlier years, he had grown uneasy and even angry. He had always to be seen and known. Now in his last years he was sometimes overwhelmed by a more general sense of oblivion. In 1974 he collaborated with the writer Francis Wyndham on a photographic memoir entitled *My Life in Pictures*. Wyndham recalled that Chaplin required the warm light of his wife's care. 'He would not let her out of his sight. If she moved or looked as though she might be going out of the room he became frightened.' The strain upon Oona may be imagined.

In the spring of 1975 he made the journey to London, where he was to be knighted by the queen. He had once said that 'Mr Chaplin' was his name and he was proud of it; but he took considerable pleasure in becoming Sir Charles Chaplin. He had wanted to walk the thirty feet towards the queen, but had to be pushed in a wheelchair by an equerry. In the summer he returned to London, and to his familiar fifth-floor suite in the Savoy, but he fell on his back and had to be returned to Switzerland in the care of a twenty-four-hour nurse.

Throughout that year, and the next, Chaplin's condition worsened, and he found it difficult to communicate; there were times when he lapsed into somnolence, and on one occasion could not remember the name of the mother of his two eldest children, Lita Grey. In June 1976, however, he was reported as saying that 'to work is to live – and I love to live'. Oona recalled that she was woken at four in the morning by Chaplin talking to himself about his films, saying 'and they are *beautiful*, and I'll never make them again'.

He suffered a stroke soon afterwards that left him partially paralysed. He found it difficult to recognise people whom he had once known well. The film director Peter Bogdanovich contemplated a documentary on Chaplin's life but one of his associates recalled that when they arrived at Vevey, 'we discovered that Chaplin was no longer Chaplin. He had almost completely lost his memory, he was a body almost without a mind. He could hardly answer the questions; we heard only monosyllables, barely intelligible non sequiturs.' His youngest son, Christopher, recalled that 'my father became uncommunicative in his last year or so . . . my most vivid memory of him in that last year was that I used to sit across from him at the dinner table and sometimes he would just stare right at me. He had the most piercing blue eyes. I often wondered what he was thinking.'

The strain of caring for him continually was compounded by the fact that slowly he withdrew into himself; Michael Chaplin recalled that he was 'vanishing away, slowly drifting away'. He seemed in the end to be at peace, but in effect he had withdrawn into a vast and silent sphere of self-regard. His wife would wheel him down to the shore of the lake and then along its bank. In the last months of his life their butler would drive them down to the shore, and they would sit looking out at the water. He was still brought to the table for meals, and Oona Chaplin would help him to eat. She would then wheel him in front of the television, where he would watch news programmes and old films.

Only in the last three weeks of his life was he confined to his bedroom, where he needed oxygen to breathe comfortably. He died in his sleep before dawn on the morning of 25 December 1977. He had always hated Christmas. He was buried at the cemetery in Vevey two days later. So departed a great cockney visionary who was, for some years, the most famous man on earth.

Bibliography

Anthony, Barry: *Chaplin's Music Hall* (London, 2012)

Asplund, Uno: *Chaplin's Films* (Newton Abbot, 1973)

Bengtson, John: *Silent Traces* (Santa Monica, 2006)

Bessy, Maurice: *Charlie Chaplin* (London, 1985)

Bloom, Claire: *Limelight and After* (London, 1982)

Bowman, W. D.: *Charlie Chaplin* (London, 1931)

Brown, Pam: *Charlie Chaplin* (Watford, 1991)

Brownlow, Kevin: *The Parade's Gone By* (London, 1968)

Brownlow, Kevin: *The Search for Charlie Chaplin* (London, 2010)

Chaplin, Charles: *My Trip Abroad* (New York, 1922)

Chaplin, Charles: *My Autobiography* (London, 1964)

Chaplin, Charles: *My Life in Pictures* (London, 1974)

Chaplin, Charles: *My Father, Charlie Chaplin* (New York, 1960)

Chaplin, Lita Grey: *My Life with Chaplin* (New York, 1966)

Chaplin, Lita Grey and Vance, Jeffrey: *Wife of the Life of the Party* (London, 1998)

Chaplin, Michael: *I Couldn't Smoke the Grass on My Father's Lawn* (London, 1966)

Clausius, Claudia: *The Gentleman Is a Tramp* (New York, 1989)

Cooke, Alistair: *Six Men* (London, 1977)

Cotes, Peter and Niklaus, Thelma: *The Little Fellow* (London, 1951)

Delluc, Louis: *Charlie Chaplin* (London, 1922)

Epstein, Jerry: *Remembering Charlie* (New York, 1989)

Fleischman, Sid: *Sir Charlie* (New York, 2010)

Flom, E. L.: *Chaplin in the Sound Era* (London, 1997)

Geduld, H. M.: *Chapliniana* (Bloomington, 1987)

Geduld, H. M. (ed.): *Charlie Chaplin's Own Story* (Indiana, 1985)

Gehring, W. D.: *Charlie Chaplin: A Bio-Bibliography* (Westport, 1983)

Gifford, Denis: *Chaplin* (London, 1974)

Haining, Peter: *The Legend of Charlie Chaplin* (New Jersey, 1982)

Haining, Peter (ed.): *Charlie Chaplin: A Centenary Celebration* (London, 1989)

Hale, Georgia: *Charlie Chaplin* (London, 1999)

Harness, Kyp: *The Art of Charlie Chaplin* (London, 2008)

Hayes, Kevin J. (ed.): *Charlie Chaplin Interviews* (Jackson, 2005)

Hoyt, Edwin P.: *Sir Charlie* (London, 1977)

Huff, Theodore: *Charlie Chaplin* (New York, 1951)

Isaac, Frederick: *When the Moon Shone Bright on Charlie Chaplin* (Melksham, 1978)

Jacobs, David: *Chaplin, The Movies, and Charlie* (New York, 1975)

James, Eric: *Making Music with Charlie Chaplin* (Folkestone, 2000)

Kamin, Dan: *Charlie Chaplin's One-Man Show* (London, 1984)

Kamin, Dan: *The Comedy of Charlie Chaplin* (Plymouth, 2008)

Kamin, Dan (ed.): *Chaplin: The Dictator and The Tramp* (London, 2004)

Karney, Robyn and Cross, Robin: *The Life and Times of Charlie Chaplin* (London, 1992)

Kaushik, Manav: *Recollecting Charlie* (Gurgaon, 2009)

Kerr, Walter: *The Silent Clowns* (New York, 1975)

Kimber, John: *The Art of Charlie Chaplin* (Sheffield, 2000)

Larcher, Jérôme: *Charlie Chaplin* (Paris, 2011)

Louvish, Simon: *Chaplin: The Tramp's Odyssey* (London, 2009)

Lynn, Kenneth S.: *Charlie Chaplin and His Times* (London, 1998)

Lyons, Timothy J.: *Charles Chaplin* (Boston, 1979)

McCabe, John: *Charlie Chaplin* (London, 1978)

McCaffrey, Donald (ed.): *Focus on Chaplin* (New Jersey, 1971)

McDonald, G. D., Conway, Michel and Ricci, Mark (eds): *The Films of Charlie Chaplin* (Secaucus, 1965)

Maland, Charles J.: *Chaplin and American Culture* (Princeton, 1989)

Manvell, Roger: *Chaplin* (Boston, 1974)

Marriot, 'A. J.': *Chaplin, Stage by Stage* (Hitchin, 2005)

Mast, Gerald: *The Comic Mind* (New York, 1973)

Mellen, Joan: *Modern Times* (London, 2006)

Milton, Joyce: *Tramp* (New York, 1996)

Minney, R. J.: *Chaplin: The Immortal Tramp* (London, 1954)

Mitchell, Glenn (ed.): *The Chaplin Encyclopaedia* (London, 1997)

Neibaur, James L.: *Chaplin at Essanay* (London, 2008)

Okuda, Ted and Maska, David: *Charlie Chaplin at Keystone and Essanay* (New York, 2005)

Oleksy, Walter: *Laugh, Clown, Cry* (London, 1976)

Parkinson, A. F.: *Charlie Chaplin's South London* (London, 2008)

Payne, Robert: *The Great God Pan* (New York, 1952)

Quigly, Isabel: *Charlie Chaplin: Early Comedies* (London, 1968)

Reeves, May and Goll, Claire: *The Intimate Charlie Chaplin* (London, 2001)

Robinson, David: *Chaplin* (London, 1983)

Robinson, David: *Chaplin. His Life and Art* (London, 1985)

Ross, Lillian: *Moments with Chaplin* (New York, 1980)

Scheide, Frank and Mehran, Hooman (eds): *Chaplin's Limelight and the Music Hall Tradition* (London, 2006)

Schikel, Richard (ed.): *The Essential Chaplin* (Chicago, 2006)

Schroeder, Alan: *The Beauty of Silence* (New York, 1997)

Scovell, Jane: *Oona* (New York, 1998)

Seymour, Miranda: *Chaplin's Girl* (London, 2009)

Smith, Julian: *Chaplin* (London, 1984)

Smith, S. P.: *The Charlie Chaplin Walk* (Ammanford, 2010)

Sobel, Raoul and Francis, David: *Chaplin: Genesis of a Clown* (London, 1977)

Bibliography

Turk, Ruth: *Charlie Chaplin* (Minneapolis, 2000)
Tyler, Parker: *Chaplin: Last of the Clowns* (New York, 1972)
Von Ulm, Gerith: *Charlie Chaplin: King of Tragedy* (Idaho, 1940)
Vance, Jeffrey: *Chaplin* (New York, 2003)
Weissman, Stephen: *Chaplin: A Life* (London, 2009)
Whittemore, Don and Cecchettini, P. A.: *Passport to Hollywood* (New York, 1976)
Wranovics, John: *Chaplin and Agee* (New York, 2005)

Index

Caught in the Rain (film), 58
The Champion (film), 73–4
Chaplin, Carol Ann (perhaps CC's
daughter), 211
Chaplin, Charles (perhaps CC's
father): background and marriage
to Hannah, 2–3; career, 4–5;
agrees to pay maintenance for CC
and Sydney, 9–10; takes them in,
14–15; possibly helps CC find
first job, 16; decline, 19; death,
20; CC earns partial living by
trading on his death, 21; representations in CC's films, 222
Chaplin, Charles (CC)
GENERAL: accent, 99–100; appearance, 7, 54, 87, 135, 162, 168,
228; artistic representations, 8,
136; attitude to fame, 86, 130,
134; autodidacticism and self-
improvement, 33–4, 42, 139; and
boxing, 74; caricatures, 27–8;
character, 36, 42, 97, 124, 133,
153–6, 169, 180, 190; as conversationalist, 121, 153; and
Dickens, 123–4; and dress, 42;
and economics, 172–3, 179;
favourite films, 78; favourite food,
180; favourite of own films, 171;
favourite reading, 33–4, 122,
212; favourite songs, 14, 94; and
fishing, 107, 238–9; and Hitler,
189–90; imitators, 81; insanity
fears, 30; literacy, 34; as lover,
150, 160–1; and money, 62, 124,
175, 180, 227, 238; and
Napoleon, 158, 187; and patriotism, 175, 216; and politics,
121, 195–6, 199–202, 215–17,
219–20; punctuality

and reliability, 134, 154–5, 174;
relationship with mother, 9, 11,
123, 126; and religion, 231; and
smoking, 87, 135; sociability,
110, 124; songs about, 80; and
tennis, 169–70; unapproacha-
bility, 101; unrecognisability
without makeup, 86–7; and wild-
life, 103; and women, 11, 31,
37–8, 39, 55, 168, 193
LIFE: family background, 2–5;
birth, 2–3; childhood, 5–15;
possible first stage appearance,
6–7; early busking performances.
8; short stay in workhouse, 9–10;
goes to Hanwell Schools, 10–12;
family briefly reunited until
mother goes mad, 12–13; taken
in by putative father, 14–15;
reunited with mother again, 15;
becomes professional dancer,
16–20; asthma attacks, 20; putative father's death, 20; goes back
to live with mother and does odd
jobs, 20–3; mother goes mad
again, 23–4; Sydney takes charge,
24; becomes actor, 25–31; returns
to music hall, 31; joins Karno
Company, 34; rents Brixton flat
with Sydney, 36–7; first love,
37–8; Paris trip, 39; to USA with
Karno troupe, 40–2; finances
mother's move to Peckham
House, 43; second US tour, 43;
hired by Keystone, 43–4; first
films, 49–52; Hollywood
romances, 54; begins to direct at
Keystone, 56–8; films released in
Britain, 60; moves to LA Athletic
Club, 61–2; joins Essanay, 67;

USA, 125–6; death, 166–7

Chaplin, Josephine (CC's daughter), 224, 226–7, 231, 234

Chaplin, Lita (née MacMurray; stage name Lita Grey; CC's second wife): in *The Kid*, 122–3; and *The Gold Rush*, 145, 149–50; affair with CC, 145–6; marriage, 147–9; Charles junior's birth, 150–1; CC ignores, 152; Sydney junior's birth, 157–8; leaves CC, 158; acrimonious divorce, 160–2; CC prevents from putting their sons in films, 179; questioned by FBI about CC, 229; CC forgets her name in old age, 247

Chaplin, Michael (CC's son): birth, 244; trip to London, 226–7, 228; family life in Switzerland, 231; relationship with CC, 234; in *A King in New York*, 235–6; world tour with family, 239; on CC's decline, 247

Chaplin, Mildred (née Harris; CC's first wife), 109–10, 111–13, 115, 118–22

Chaplin, Norman Spencer (CC's son), 115, 116, 117–18

Chaplin, Oona (née O'Neill; CC's fourth wife): meets CC, 204–5; engagement and marriage, 206–8; and CC's immorality trial, 210; on *Monsieur Verdoux*, 215; CC's love for, 222; children, 224; in *Limelight*, 224; CC puts much of his money in her name, 226; trip to London with CC, 226–8; trip to Paris, 228; returns to USA to close down family affairs, 228–9; moves to Switzerland, 230; more

children, 231; family life, 231–2; relationship with CC, 232, 242; favourite child, 234; travels with CC, 236, 238; cancels *New Yorker* subscription, 237; takes ever greater care of CC, 241; drinking, 242–3; publicity trip to USA with CC, 244–5; CC's dependence on, 246, 247–8; CC's death, 248

Chaplin, Sydney (CC's brother): birth, 3; childhood, 5, 8; short stay in workhouse, 9–10; goes to Hanwell Schools, 10; goes to naval training ship, 10; family briefly reunited until mother goes mad, 12–13; taken in by CC's putative father, 14–15; reunited with mother again, 15; shares lodgings with mother and grandfather, 19; job as surgeon's assistant, 21; goes to sea, 20; takes charge of CC, 24; helps CC with lines, 25; helps CC with finances, 25; becomes bartender, 27; acts in show with CC, 27; goes back to sea, 28; joins Wal Pink's Workmen, 31; joins Karno Company, 34, 35; rents Brixton flat with CC, 36–7; marriage, 4–5, 42; finances mother's move to Peckham House, 43; CC writes to from Hollywood, 62, 65–6; comes to Hollywood, 82–3; becomes CC's agent, 83; negotiates with New York film producers, 84, 85, 86, 87; helps CC with ideas, 90; helps CC with investments, 99; holiday with CC, 103; negotiates deal for